EYES ON AMAZONIA

EYES ON AMAZONIA

Transnational Perspectives on the Rubber Boom Frontier

JESSICA CAREY-WEBB

VANDERBILT UNIVERSITY PRESS
Nashville, Tennessee

Copyright 2024 Vanderbilt University Press
All rights reserved
First printing 2024

This book will be made open access within three years of publication thanks to Path to Open, a program developed in partnership between JSTOR, the American Council of Learned Societies (ACLS), University of Michigan Press, and the University of North Carolina Press to bring about equitable access and impact for the entire scholarly community, including authors, researchers, libraries, and university presses around the world. Learn more at https://about.jstor.org/path-to-open.

Library of Congress Cataloging-in-Publication Data

Names: Carey-Webb, Jessica, 1988- author.
Title: Eyes on Amazonia : transnational perspectives on the rubber boom frontier / Jessica Carey-Webb.
Description: Nashville, Tennessee : Vanderbilt University Press, [2024] | Includes bibliographical references and index.
Identifiers: LCCN 2023039664 | ISBN 9780826506474 (paperback) | ISBN 9780826506481 (hardcover) | ISBN 9780826506498 (epub) | ISBN 9780826506504 (pdf)
Subjects: LCSH: Amazon River Region--History. | Amazon River Region--Civilization. | Indigenous peoples--Amazon River Region--History.
Classification: LCC F2546 .C246 2024 | DDC 981/.1--dc23/eng/20231012
LC record available at https://lccn.loc.gov/2023039664

Front cover image: Illustrations of parts of *Hevea brasiliensis*, the rubber tree. *Köhler's Medizinal-Pflanzen*, vol. 3, 1898, Plate 8.

To Dad

Contents

Acknowledgments ix

Introduction. Eyes on Amazonia 1

Chapter 1. Gendered Politics of Empire: The Female *Explorateur* and Visions for the Racial Future of Amazonia 30

Chapter 2. Wandering Wildernesses: Race and Masculinity on the Rio Roosevelt 59

Chapter 3. A Novice Traveler in a Land without History: Nationalizing the Brazilian Amazon 94

Chapter 4. Learning from the Other: Theodor Koch-Grünberg and Richard Evans Schultes 128

Chapter 5. The Reconfigured Travel Narrative: Indigenous Representation and *El abrazo de la serpiente* 161

Conclusion. Transnational Perspectives on the Rubber Boom Frontier 190

Notes 197
Bibliography 223
Index 235

Acknowledgments

As a Fulbright Fellow in 2012, I traveled to Bragança, a small town in the Brazilian state of Pará, where the Caeté River meets the Atlantic Ocean, to immerse myself in the region's rich history, environment, and culture. That year was a clear inspiration for this book and set my path of research and activism. To the community of Bragança, thank you for welcoming and walking with me.

Initial drafts of *Eyes on Amazonia* were written while I was at the University of Texas at Austin's Department of Spanish and Portuguese. The years spent in Austin gave me the confidence and community to pursue this project.

My time in Austin would have been drastically different without my mentor, Dr. Lorraine Leu-Moore. I cannot thank Lorraine enough for her edits and invaluable guidance. She has been an amazing advisor, advocate, and pillar of support, and I am incredibly lucky to have her in my corner. Without her help and input this book would not exist. Her scholarship, intellectual capacity, and abilities as a writer are nothing short of aspirational. I hope this grandbaby book makes you proud!

I am grateful to my colleagues at UT Austin who helped form an initial version of this project, Kelly McDonough, Gabriela Polit, and Seth Garfield, for their availability, willingness to jump on board, and overall support and encouragement. I'm also indebted to their fascinating research and scholarship.

The researchers at the Projeto Nova Cartografia Social in Manaus graciously hosted me for a summer of research early on in this project, and I am continually encouraged by their community-driven work throughout the Amazon region and world.

I am thankful to the faculty and staff in the department of Modern Languages and Literatures at Florida State University. Juan Carlos Galeano helped inspire a new title for this manuscript, and his visions of Amazonia have broadened my own perspective. Celia Campbell became a lifelong friend with whom to reminisce about the swamps of Tallahassee.

My colleagues at the Natural Resources Defense Council—Amanda Maxwell, Carolina Herrera, Andrea Becerra, Sujatha Bergen, Jay Blair, Jennifer Skene, Marilyn Martinez, Susan Keane, Jake Schmidt, and others—allowed me to jump into the world of environmental advocacy and patiently guided me during my two years with the organization. This experience indelibly shaped this manuscript.

Since joining the faculty at the University of New Mexico's Department of Spanish and Portuguese I have been lucky to work with an incredible range of colleagues who have been supportive and welcoming. I could not have tracked down the photographs included in this manuscript—from Germany to Brazil—without the help of Fabiola Parra-Oldham. My students, both graduate and undergraduate, have been a source of energy and enthusiasm that makes it all worth it. I am constantly motivated by their observations, ambition, and critical inquiries.

I am extremely grateful to the reviewers of this volume. Their reviews were discerning, fair, and incredibly encouraging, and they greatly strengthened the manuscript.

Support for this research was provided by the University of New Mexico College of Arts and Sciences Office of Research; a Tinker Field Research Grant from the University of Texas at Austin; and an American Council of Learned Societies and Mellon Public Fellows Award with the Natural Resources Defense Council.

Beyond the support that I have received in the academic world, *Eyes on Amazonia* would not have been possible without my community of friends and family. The Careys have given me a sense of belonging and invaluable memories of dancing and laughing into the night on the shores of Lake Erie. The Webbs have opened their homes and encouraged me. My Kalamazoo family are childhood friends who I would still pick today; truly they are sisters chosen. My Austin community—Catalina Iannone, Patrick Lawrence, Rosalyn Harvey-Torres, Nat Zingg, Daniel Luviano, Stephanie Malak, Megan Coxe, Steph Raddock, Poppy Briggs, Thomas Ostmeyer, Olivia Thayer—continue to make life silly, fun, and exciting. I would not have been able to write this manuscript without Catalina's remote work sessions, occasional edits, constant text distractions, humor, and trips all over the world.

My mom, Jill, has been a source of comfort, safety, and love. My brother, Nate, my best friend, has listened to my bouts of work-related stress with infinite patience and understanding. My dad, Allen, has charted a path for my career and this book. His perspective and feedback made this book what it is today. My little sisters, Ari and Lexi Webb, are the sweetest gifts.

And finally, to my husband Russell Hawkins: thank you for holding me (and for Fredo).

INTRODUCTION

Eyes on Amazonia

In August 2019, images of the Amazon rainforest on fire overtook social media feeds, the front page of every major global newspaper, and online news stories. It seemed that everywhere you looked global anxieties over climate change were perfectly visualized in the image of the world's most famous forest engulfed in flames. Plumes of smoke enveloped the formerly lush greenery and aerial shots revealed literal "hot spots."[1] The contrast between verdant trees and bright orange blazes and the billowing, massive clouds of grey smoke showcased one of the oldest dualities of the rainforest: a green Eden contrasted with a no-longer-so-green hell. The dramatic immediacy of these images created a clear, compelling visual for what was and what remains a long ongoing crisis of resource extraction, deforestation, and an ever-changing climate affecting the largest rainforest in the world.[2]

These fires were not unprecedented; instead, they revealed a culmination of years of development and global warming. The 2019 fires were caused by a prolonged dry season as well as purposefully set blazes to clear land for industrial agriculture. Primarily soy and cattle, the products from these massive industries are exported to grocery stores around the world. Despite forest fires taking place throughout the entire Amazon region, including large swaths of the Bolivian Amazon, the fires in the Brazilian Amazon were met with international anxiety and given close attention. With 60 percent of the rainforest found within Brazilian borders, and the 2018 election of far-right president Jair Bolsonaro, who nicknamed himself "Captain Chainsaw," international policy makers and environmentalists looked on with intense concern at the widespread destruction of the proverbial "lungs of the earth." The power of the image of a forest on fire, its charismatic creatures scorched, sparked action and denunciations

FIGURE 0.1 The Amazon Rainforest wildfires of 2019 burned over 2.25 million acres of forest, leading to international concern about the management and fate of the rainforest. Pedarilhosbr/Shutterstock.com

of Bolsonaro's handling of the crisis from most major governments.[3] This level of catastrophe, ensuing attention, and demand for action demonstrates the continued shift of climate issues into the full mainstream of global consciousness. Local concerns have become international policy issues and wildfires like those in the Amazon are broadly seen as impacting the survival of the entire planet. All eyes turned toward Amazonia.

That global attention made sense. Environmentally, the intact Amazon's capacity as a carbon dioxide sink demonstrates a quantifiable measure of the region's importance. As the world's largest carbon sink, the Amazon rainforest absorbs carbon in its trees and soil and helps regulate temperatures and weather patterns around the world. When the forest burns, it also releases carbon dioxide into the atmosphere. However, the Amazon's capacity as a carbon sink is rapidly diminishing with recent studies showing that it is only land held and managed by Indigenous communities where carbon sink potential is reached.[4] By 2021, a widely publicized study in the journal *Nature* found that parts of the Amazon had indeed become carbon sources rather than absorbent sinks, a result of years of deforestation and climate change.[5]

The rich environment of the Amazon region today stretches across eight independent countries—Brazil, Bolivia, Peru, Ecuador, Colombia, Venezuela, Suriname, and Guyana (and a territory of France, French Guiana), each with their own environmental policies and histories. The complex river system of the Amazon basin forms the environmental and cultural veins of northern South America, spreading and connecting over two million square miles, around one-twentieth of the entire Earth's surface, and containing about 17 percent of the world's freshwater. If the region were itself a country, it would be the ninth largest in the world. Together, the lands that make up the Amazon are now home to over thirty million human inhabitants. "Amazonia" is a catchall term for the basin that makes up over 35 percent of South America and forms the most biodiverse region in the world.

As we consider how to address environmental disasters, particularly in these globally important ecosystems, the humanities can help us critically consider the history, justification, implications, and legacy of extractive projects at the root of climatic events like the 2019 fires. Furthermore, the interdisciplinary field of the environmental humanities can be used to analyze the structures of inequality that have contributed to environmental destruction and consider how those structures can be confronted through teaching, research, and advocacy. Discourses and representations are crucial to the formation of developmental projects, as they construct how we understand and address them. The confluence of nature and culture in the Amazon is one of the most fascinating and, given the critical role of the region, one of the most important areas for scholarly analysis. This book looks at the past to think critically about the present representation of diverse populations and contested land. The ways outsiders have talked about, pictured, and exported images is reflected in the more contemporary outcries to "save the rainforest," or on the other hand, as was the case of Bolsonaro, to raze the forest and reap its profits.

This tension between preservation and development is central to the history of Amazonia. The most intense period of penetration of capital and development projects into the region was the first rubber boom, from approximately 1879 to 1912. Rubber was a critical commodity, crucial to rapidly expanding global industry, and sought after by major international corporations and the most powerful countries. The Amazon basin became central to industrial expansion, as disparate populations were forced into dangerous servitude, transportation and communication were extended, and governmentality stretched over the region. As during the 2019 fires, throughout the rubber boom the forest was cleared to make way for industrial extraction, which in turn brought increased international attention and a scramble to decide the future of the region.

During the rubber boom, information collected and catalogued about the Amazon was of the utmost importance to generate profits for a growing global capitalism. Many of these mechanisms were in place long before the boom at the turn of the twentieth century, and they built on legacies of extractivism, using narrative, mapping, and photography as tools to impose order over nature. Extractivism, as Naomi Klein explains, was a term originally used to explain colonial powers' extraction of raw materials from the earth for export to colonial centers. Extractivism is a relationship of taking from the earth, in turn reducing "life into objects for the use of others, giving them no integrity or value of their own" and reducing nature into "resources."[6] Extractivism works hand in hand with the colonial and imperial project by creating disposable peripheries with the idea that there will always be a new place to exploit once resources are depleted at current sites of extraction.[7] From the times of first colonial contact with the Amazon, the region has been conceptualized and used as a site of unending resources and untapped potential.

Within Amazonia, Brazil, the primary country of focus of this book, is the largest country in Latin America and one of the largest in the world, containing a variety of dramatically different landscapes, cultural contexts, and histories.[8] Divided into five major regions (South, Southeast, Center-West, Northeast, and North), the North region containing the Amazon is by far the largest as it makes up over 42 percent of the national territory.[9] By the early twentieth century, rubber extracted from the North region composed 45 percent of the national economy. In Brazil, as José Murilo de Carvalho argues, there is an overwhelming pride in nature that equates the country itself to an earthly paradise. The sheer size of the country leads into the national myth of *grandeza*, or greatness. As the Amazon River basin is home to the largest forest on earth, and the rainforest so resource rich, Brazil must inevitably become a great empire through development.[10] However, *grandeza* also means that the country seems to always fall short; despite its enormity and natural resources, Brazil has yet to fully achieve its potential, remaining constantly the "country of the future."[11] As a region of potential riches to help fund the future of the country, the Brazilian Amazon became the site of contested territory and resources during the rubber boom, leading a swath of travelers to the region to document it for their various purposes.

This book is about travelers to the Amazon who in different ways documented or reflected on the area during the first rubber boom or in its aftermath. These adventurers, writers, geographers, and filmmakers represented a region in flux, a resource for enterprising individuals, corporations, or national interests. They wrestled with the role that Indigenous and local peoples should play in the region's future. Some advocated a conservation approach toward both the environment and Indigenous cultures, while others argued for domination and assimilation of land and people—and at times these two streams of thought were inseparable. Their fashioning of the region and its people hold conflicting sentiments, ambiguity, and trepidation. These sentiments and conflicts over the future of the region echo today's anxieties about deforestation, climate change, and sovereignty over the rainforest.

Eyes on Amazonia is a study of the complex ways that race, gender, various forms of representation, mobility, empire, modernity, and even the personal identities of the writers have shaped the way the region is seen into the twenty-first century. In the chapters to follow, I offer five comparative case studies of traveler's representations of Amazonia from diverse source materials, in multiple languages, by travelers from different countries of origin and with wide-ranging views of the region and its peoples. While sharing histories of their own experiences, these writers all traverse territories under extreme economic and environmental exploitation at varying moments of emerging national authority. In each case study, the authors find their own cultural identities in flux as they attempt to understand the often-overwhelming present and future of the forest, and the stresses it faces. Throughout the book, I analyze the ways these travelers describe and visualize their surroundings. Their depictions demonstrate the unequal power dynamics within the Amazonian "contact zone," comprising "social spaces where cultures meet, clash, and grapple with each other, often in contexts of highly asymmetrical relations of power, such as colonialism, slavery, or their aftermaths as they are lived out in many parts of the world today."[12] As travelers in the Amazon region, the authors discussed in this volume project futuristic ideas onto a space that is foreign to them, and in turn, they write highly racialized visions of their surroundings. Their travel and interactions with diverse populations and an Amazonian environment cause them to reflect on their own personal and national identities. Ultimately, the chapters of the book come together to create what Michel Foucault has called "a history of the present," a tracing of the power struggles and issues that have shaped how we come to understand current realities—in this case the Amazon region and its crucial role in the present day.[13]

Some of the travelers I examine were closely tied to the rubber boom; others had limited direct engagement in the rubber trade, but their narratives and cultural productions emerge from related historical moments. These travelers' documentations also include intriguing visual depictions through photographs, maps, and film. I begin with the understudied French geographers Octavie and Henri Coudreau, who mapped, photographed, and wrote travel diaries (1893–1906), and at times were employed by the Brazilian government. Next, I turn to Theodore Roosevelt's last highly publicized journey alongside the Brazilian frontiersman Cândido Rondon in 1912 and '13. In these chapters about foreign explorers employed by or collaborating with regional governments, issues of race, gender, and authority loom large. Next, we will look at the writings of the Brazilian vanguards Euclides da Cunha (*À margem da história* [1909], or *The Amazon: Land without History* [2006]) and Mário de Andrade (*O turista aprendiz*, published as a whole in 1976 but written during journeys taken from 1927 to 1929; published in English translation as *The Apprentice Tourist* in 2023), authors who sought to situate the Amazon and its peoples specifically within a Brazilian national culture. The following chapter examines the anthropologic approach of German Theodor Koch-Grünberg and American Richard Evans Schultes—explorers whose research critically investigated the relationship between nature and culture as they sought to open the so-called *world's medicine chest* through scientific inquiry. Their work spans from the heart of the rubber boom (beginning with Koch-Grünberg's travels to the region in 1896) through Schultes's work during the World War II secondary rubber boom and his continued contributions until the time of his death in 2001. Finally, the book finishes with an analysis of *El abrazo de la serpiente*, or *The Embrace of the Serpent*, a 2015 film from Colombian director Ciro Guerra retelling the journeys of Schultes and Koch-Grünberg, which pays homage to the era of exploration and rubber booms while centering an Indigenous protagonist.

The chapters are sequenced semi-chronologically but also move from direct experiences of rubber boom Amazonia toward retrospective reflections and the lasting impact on a collective cultural imaginary. Each case study is comparative in nature; revealing the nuances within different individualized gazes on the region and showing how personal identity informs political projections. While these travelers move through diverse geographic areas within the Amazon basin, they are all preoccupied with the future of the region on both a national and international scale. This transnational analysis of travel, exploration, exploitation, and representation of the

Amazon draws on the workings of colonialism and imperialism to examine the development of Latin American nation-states in an age of emerging global capitalism. At the end of each chapter, there is a brief but necessary addendum that addresses the state of the territory or the result of the ideological imaginings covered in the chapter. These addendums facilitate our understanding of a "history of the present" and demonstrate the ongoing features and impacts of social processes established during the rubber boom. They also allow us to better appreciate the resistance, resilience, and vision of local peoples.

The diverse sources examined in the chapters to follow tell a story by weaving together written word and images to relate an account of events or experiences—the very definition of narrative. Narratives, particularly travel narratives, are linear in nature, as travelers document their movement from one area to the next. This Western chronology is itself emblematic of modernity, where time is structured, managed, and incremental. The broad corpus examined in this book encompasses different contexts and time periods; however, questions of travel, knowledge production, race and identity, and resource extraction thematically connect them. The categorization and collection described within these narratives portray the Amazon as rapidly disappearing and thus in need of conservation, another form of a Western discourse of modernization and development. As such there is a sense of wanting to capture spaces and cultures in maps, photography, and prose. Throughout this book, we will examine reoccurring and relevant themes of racial subordination, resource extraction, and environmental anxiety that accompany nation building in the Americas.

These writers portray the Amazon as a transnational space where competing local and international actors and claims for the land are in conflict. It is a space in flux, featuring movement—national and international, extraction and circulation (rubber and other resources), and peoples migrating both to and from the region. Not all the narratives examined here are explicitly travelogues, yet all of them fall into a category of the travel narrative, a wider expanse of heterogenous material that reflects on or in some way takes part in a journey through a foreign space. These travelers can be read as examples of how Latin American, European, and US intellectuals understood Amazonia during and after the rubber boom, how they rhetorically justified their colonialist projections, and how they fashioned themselves as authorities able to do so in geographies often completely foreign to them. This book thus contributes a discussion of the ways internal and external projects have always interacted and constructed one another in a transnational and global geography. As such, this analysis exposes the inner workings of coloniality and imperialism within diverse forms of travel narrative.

These histories contribute to our understanding of current crises. The climate crisis, epitomized in the 2019 Amazon fires, urges us to re-examine the interrelatedness of nature and culture and question the inequalities of environmental destruction. Rob Nixon argues that "progress" often means environmental degradation with devastating consequences suffered not only immediately but also over time, especially by the poorest and least powerful, in what he deems a "slow violence."[14] Representations of Amazonia set up and continued to open the region to development, furthering a slow violence of environmental extraction and destruction. In the sections to follow, I provide the analytical framework with which I read the wide variety of materials within this book. These sections correspond to the types of material ranging from how the region has been written about and explored, the ways I read these narratives as emblematic of the power imbalances within the contact zone, and finally, the ways photographic and film projects have helped visualize the region. I finish this introduction with a brief contextual history of the Amazonian rubber boom and its legacies on the present day. Each of these aspects contributes to the ways the region is experienced, interpreted, and ultimately managed.

Writing Amazonia

Writing about the Amazon throughout history has captured an assortment of ideas about the forest. Amazonia's narrative archive exposes the vast region as a quintessential "contact zone." Indeed, this book is called *Eyes on Amazonia* for several reasons: to point to the visual and international nature of the narratives I examine, in reference to Mary Louise Pratt's conceptualization of the imperial traveler's gaze that characterizes the contact zone, and finally because of the continual international and national projections onto the region. Travel narratives situated the Amazon in contrast to modernizing urban centers and exoticized it by the supposed Otherness of its Indigenous peoples. These different types of narratives were created through the process of "transculturation," where, in Pratt's definition, the "imperial metropolis tends to understand itself as determining the periphery . . . habitually blinding itself to the ways in which the periphery determines the metropolis."[15] Furthermore, the Amazon region can also be considered a "biocontact zone," to borrow Londa Schiebinger's expansion on Pratt's contact zones, as the epistemological encounters of Europeans who sought to obtain medicinal and plant knowledge from Indigenous peoples and Africans.[16] The Amazon is a particularly rich contact zone, as social clashes have characterized the region since initial colonization and the biodiversity of Amazonia is notoriously unparalleled. As such, the Amazonian contact and biocontact zone provides a compelling backdrop to examine global environmental issues and inequalities.

Despite the diversity of the Amazonian contact zone, the region has been written about, photographed, filmed, and mapped in ways that tend to engage with or propagate the same tropes (an Eden, a green hell, the "world's lungs," a "medicine chest," etc.), particularly when it comes to how the region can fit into a global cultural imaginary. The representations analyzed in this book create the Amazon as a site of possibility and view the region in contrast to colonial centers, created in the process of travel to the region. Most were written either by or with heavy influence from naturalists. In broad strokes, we can separate the writing about the Amazon region by era, with attention to the genres that influence this study. Each era, each genre, each document of travel narrative grapples with defining "the Amazon." Ultimately each also showcases the futility of any simple definition. Instead, they reveal, as Felipe Martínez-Pinzón and Javier Uriarte deem them, "multiple Amazons," intimate frontiers on the delicate relationship between nature and culture.[17]

The first era of international writing about Amazonia is characterized by the colonial chroniclers who wrote about the simultaneous abundance and scarcity (or their inability to harness the abundance) of the region. Initial explorers reported back to the Iberian peninsula about immense riches to be found in the New World, creating an image of the Amazon as a mythical El Dorado. As Charlotte Rogers explains in *Mourning El Dorado*, gold was seen as a living, growing resource that thrived in warmer climates. Gold and other natural resources were considered inexhaustible.[18] This El Dorado was explicitly tied to its New World geography and the promise of unending riches that could contribute to a new global economy. Ultimately, the myth of El Dorado produces a "hollow frontier" where "extractive industries exploit and extract the resources of one area and move to another, often leaving environmental destruction in their wake."[19]

For example, in 1541 Francisco de Orellana, the Spanish conquistador, led the first expedition into the region with the aim, predictably, of finding gold. This trip was chronicled by Gaspar de Carvajal who details full turtle pens and fishing traps along the river, an amazing profusion of food cultivated by flourishing Indigenous populations.[20] The Amazon was portrayed as at once an earthly paradise full of potential and a site of confusion and challenge. He notes the region's monotony of never-ending waterways, and the overall inability of Europeans to survive in a river basin seemingly full to the brim—ideas that would color the region for years to come. Carvajal details villages of "Indians [who] stood waiting ready to fight, like a warlike people,"[21] and notably, women who "were very white and tall . . . with their bows and arrows in their hands, doing as much fighting as ten Indian men."[22] This description was likened by the Spaniards to the Amazons of Greek legend, female warriors known for their beauty and aggressive skill.[23] And so these explorers gave the river and region the name we now know it by, a name with connotations of otherworldliness as well as ferocious and beguiling femininity.

The next narrators of note are the naturalists: the scientists and explorers who sought to understand the collision between nature and culture and worked to categorize and manage what they observed. Toward the end of the eighteenth century and well into the nineteenth and twentieth centuries, documenters of the Amazon moved toward scientific, fact finding, mapping, and collecting missions that sought to implant Western knowledge and complete the "unfinished" Eden of the Amazon or push further to pursue the riches of an imagined El Dorado. For the naturalists, this El Dorado was scientific in nature, where instead of Amazonian warriors and unending gold, the wealth of the region was to be found in its plants, Indigenous peoples, and scientific possibilities.[24] Naturalists had the goal of scientifically documenting their surroundings, but they were also heavily involved in the collection of materials such as samples of flora and fauna to take back to botanical gardens that were flourishing throughout Europe. These botanical gardens were used as tools of colonial expansion to experiment with science but also to better establish trade and commerce of potentially valuable plants. French explorers like Charles Marie de La Condamine noted the scientific wealth to be found throughout Latin America but particularly in the Amazon region. La Condamine was also one of the first naturalists to mention rubber, documenting how Indigenous people in Esmeraldas, Ecuador, produced and used latex.[25]

Inspired by La Condamine, the most famous of the naturalist explorers was likely Alexander von Humboldt, a German geographer who traveled throughout South America (1799–1804) documenting plant, animal, and human life, taking geographical measurements, and bringing back seeds for botanical gardens in Europe. His Spanish American expedition traversed almost the whole of the Western Hemisphere, where he collected specimens and created illustrated volumes that were widely dispersed and enjoyed. Although predating the proliferation of photography, Humboldt wrote and drew the tropics in highly visual terms.[26] The expedition is credited with laying the groundwork for a variety of modern disciplines including physical and plant geography and meteorology. Humboldt, noticing environmental differences during explorations taken throughout his life, even pointed out the possibility of human-induced climate change. His important journeys established a precedent that subsequent naturalists, explorers, and intellectuals (including Charles Darwin) drew on extensively. Humboldt's travels encouraged others to engage in further Amazonian explorations, to find for themselves and their countries the riches of plants, animals, and experiences that he had described.[27] The work of naturalists traveling in Amazonia created knowledge and provided information about the potential economic benefits that could be found in the forest. This information included maps and drawings used in Europe to visualize the geography and people of the region. The work of the naturalists highlights how the Amazon region has been continually represented and used as a site of extractive and scientific potential.

Emerging from the naturalists, whose hold on the Amazon remained for many years, came the *novela de la selva*, or jungle novel, its centerpiece Colombian José Eustacio Rivera's *La vorágine* (1924; *The Vortex*), which follows its protagonist's descent into madness through witnessing the atrocities committed in rubber boom Amazonia. This genre pulled from the well-known works of the naturalists, often describing nature in lush, almost scientific detail, while reclaiming the jungle as a specifically Latin American space.[28] The novela de la selva often follows protagonists as they journey from city centers to forested jungle areas, using similar tropes as the colonial chroniclers and naturalists. Jorge Marcone links the novela de la selva with contemporary ecological issues. He argues that the novelas de la selva offered a political and economic critique where a "return to nature" became a necessary condition to create an alternative modernization in the region and thus to better incorporate it into newly formed nations.[29] Like Marcone, Amanda M. Smith, in *Mapping the Amazon*, offers a nuanced vision of how Amazonian literature, particularly the novela de la selva, can be read as attempts to "record and rescue the textures of a region threatened by the kinds of institutional flattening initiated with the rubber boom."[30] The novela de la selva, one of the most widely read genres of literature about the Amazon, situates the region as a site of extraction while also questioning men's role in that setting.

Another genre that examines nature in relationship to culture is *modernismo*, where, in the Brazilian context, authors used the Amazon to help define Brazil's unique cultural identity in contrast to Europe, while still attempting to create a literature of export. In this genre and movement, Latin American intellectuals sought to rewrite the tropes of travel literature and bring the Amazon into a national cultural history, all the while grappling with the inclusions and exclusions of nation building. *Modernistas* in Brazil looked to the Amazon region as a site of inspiration and pulled from travel and anthropological narratives about Indigenous peoples to create new national patrimony. As Silvia Espelt-Bombin and Mark Harris note on this era, "narratives of place therefore came to inform race and ethnic character in new ways and became tied to nation-building: the Amazon became distinctly Brazilian, a separate but connected entity."[31] The Amazon could become a cornerstone of what made Brazil specifically Brazilian (such as in Mário de Andrade's *Macunaíma*) while also retaining its exoticism.

Each of these eras of writing about the Amazon touch upon the potential bounty, enticing appeal, and perceived danger of the jungle. They also demonstrate the political and environmental contexts of their creation. The travel narratives examined in this book interact with these different genres of writing, rewriting, and reimagining the region for their respective audiences and temporalities. Tropes about the Amazon region, implanted from cultural representations, remain prevalent to this day and have been mobilized in writing about the region to multiple different ends. As I explore in the next section, these ideas demonstrate a racialized hierarchy of knowledge that supports a coloniality of power.

Reading Amazonia

Throughout the corpus just outlined, the Amazon has been conceptualized in a wide variety of ways, almost always by outsiders to the region. These conceptualizations are emblematic of the legacies of colonialism and imperialism. As Aníbal Quijano explains, the colonial project is itself inseparable from modernity. Modernity, in this sense, is an epistemological frame supported by a coloniality of power, which, as described by Quijano, is organized through the implantation during the colonial project of systems of hierarchies, systems of knowledge, and cultural systems. Hierarchies are based on racial classifications that reinforced domination by Europeans, something we will see throughout the travel narratives examined in this book. Systems of knowledge were created using European methods of knowledge production, such as taxonomic classifications created by the naturalists. Cultural systems, as the third element of the coloniality of power, also privilege Eurocentric culture as the only truly modern culture. Coloniality of power as the fundamental element of modernity explains the legacies of colonial contact within the current global order and, more specifically, the Amazonian contact zone.[32]

Within Amazonia, a coloniality of power is enacted through portrayals that privilege Eurocentric knowledge, views, and people. In her analysis on representations of the Amazon region, *Entangled Edens*, Candace Slater explains how the region has been subject to a variety of "giant-making" myths created by outsiders, most prominently those that portray it as either an Eden or a green hell. These visions and stereotypes tend to obfuscate real problems, working to cut the existing population out of political processes and transformational dialogues. At once exotic, enticing, and perversely attractive, a green hell could pull in the outsider, only to swallow them up whole through any series of chaotic events, as happens in *La vorágine*.[33] Marcone argues that the hostility of the jungle in the green hell trope arguably "defends the forest: first, from civilization's violence upon nature and more interestingly, from modernity's desires and fantasies about nature."[34] In the hellish version of Amazonia, the remote and untamed nature of the jungle pushes humanity out, forming a shroud behind which violence and destruction can occur. This appears as a counterpoint to European civilization and values despite their role in administering this violence.

Conversely, as an Eden, the Amazon could offer a refuge from the increasingly modernizing world, while also being seen to have a transformational potential. As an Edenic space—an earthly paradise—the Amazon holds a hope for humanity, a garden before original sin where the modern world can seek respite from an increasingly globalized and complicated reality. An Eden can be an environment that is valued for beauty, for serving human needs, for an abundance of resources, whereas a green hell creates a place where nature is a threat, a source of pain, discomfort, confusion, and lack of order. As Carvalho explains, Brazilian national sentiment, building off the inscriptions by initial explorers, saw the country as an earthly paradise, an Eden that did not need to be built but rather enjoyed, primarily because of its natural abundance.[35] While that designation applied to the entire country, the central garden of this earthly paradise was the Amazon. Initial Western descriptions of the Amazon showcased the impulse to transform and guide a perceived Eden into a utopia, hence the region came to be considered a "demi-Eden," or Eden in need of guided transition toward a utopia.[36]

Eden is a natural paradise that only contains two humans before they spoil it, while a utopia is characterized as a place with an ideal and harmonious society. Based on conversations he claimed to have had with sailors from Amerigo Vespucci's very early visits along the coast of the Amazon region, Sir Thomas More wrote his enormously influential *Utopia* in 1516, coining the term for a place that was both real and "no-where," a world where humans lived in a kind of natural ease and equality. To that end, Quijano discusses the portrayal of the New World as a blank space on which to project utopia and define Europe in contrast. He argues that through the "discovery" of the New World and Latin America in particular, Europe could project a utopia in which the future was "always, not quite," or just out of reach. The Amazon holds the global imagination and continues to attract the hope to someday build a utopian future.[37]

The future-oriented vision of progress is rooted in the idea of utopia, and thus carries the possibility of reclaiming the "dreams and nostalgia of humanity" lost in the Old World and working toward a new, more perfect world.[38] From this perspective, Latin America could be seen in a constant state of development toward modernization, understood as a white, European model. This relies on the production of a static cultural identity and the establishment of an "us" and "them"—or a differentiated Other, as Edward Said argues in *Orientalism* and *Culture and Imperialism*. Thus, utopian modernity is based in contrast with a past-oriented, savage Other, a *barbárie*, with which to define a civilized "center" in contrast.[39] Eurocentric modernity in the Amazon is based on racial and social class distinctions that privilege the subjects over the objects—where the subject is the bearer of reason, rationality, order (and whiteness), over the object—the Other, located outside of imperial centers, in the periphery. In the case of the travelers examined in this volume, they use their writing and documentation of the Other to establish themselves as superior, while at times their interactions in the so-called periphery draw these racialized hierarchies into question. They create scientific knowledge to manage areas and people that are foreign to them.

Part of the coloniality of power, scientific knowledge is a way to dominate and control nature. The claiming, renaming, and controlling of territories and the extraction of flora, fauna, and even people served to establish dominance over space. Plants play a central role in the formation of culture and conversely the formation of empire. Particularly in the Amazon, where rubber (and other extractives like today's boom of beef and soy) spurred literary and cultural representations along with commercial trade for the international market, the collection of plants and information gathered by naturalists formed part of a hierarchy of knowledge, within a biocontact zone where, as Schiebinger explains, "Europe's naturalists not only collected the stuff of nature but lay their own peculiar grid of reason over nature so that nomenclatures and taxonomies often also served as 'tools of empire.'"[40] In collecting and naming nature, the environment is put into Westernized categories that assert control over territory.

The scientific knowledge conveyed by the naturalists documenting their travel and findings in the region is not culturally "neutral" or "objective." Instead, it is embedded in modernity. In the Amazon, as in other parts of the world Europeans invaded, the feminization of land and peoples, the failure to recognize rights of non-Christian peoples, and racism and racial slavery all were part of the ideological justification of domination by European men. The various forms of representation from travel, scientific investigation, extraction, and development examined in this book portray the Amazon as an "unknown" space and thus attempt to move the region from unknowable and un-representable into a groomed, manageable place. A feminization of space was often extended to the bodies within that space and thus used to justify exploitation and control over populations in settings portrayed as wild for specific purposes.

Western thought links masculinity with civilization, mobility, and forward progress.[41] Male exploratory tradition seeks to catalogue "purity" or a virgin, untouched landscape. Portrayals of the land through travel as a feminine frontier create the opportunity for a virile frontiersman to act as an agent of change and establish dominance and industry. As Robert Stam and Ella Shohat discuss about portrayals of the Amazon, "the fact that a densely populated and culturally remolded land was seen as 'virgin' reflects a kind of mental 'ethnic cleansing,' a discourse of imaginary removal. The idea of the 'vanishing Indian' had its own colonial productivity, shaping a widespread impression that Indians had already disappeared or were about to disappear with the next hot breath of conquest."[42] The idea of a "vanishing Indian" therefore connects to discourses of a feminized land and people as well as the push toward "progress." In conceptualizing the land as a virgin, unspoiled wilderness, the potential for "colonial productivity" excludes its inhabitants.

Amazonia has also been regarded as a frontier territory, or a land in processual change.[43] Indeed, as a frontier, the region can be seen as a space of potential conquest, rather than a home, thus justifying extractive practices. Among others, the Brazilian writer Márcio Souza acknowledges the Amazon as a frontier, particularly in terms of historical representation in the twentieth century. Once transformed into a "frontier," a location is available to become conquerable and profitable. The Amazon is portrayed as shrouded in mystery, lacking in "history," thus justifying the developmental processes of modernity and the erasure of the region's inhabitants. The Amazon as frontier is conceptualized by a flexible frontier ideology that takes its shape depending on what is most productive for the time.[44] During the rubber boom, a promise of rubber riches created another Amazonian El Dorado, in its wake producing a "hollow frontier" due to extractive practices, or the left behinds of a boom-and-bust cycle to the detriment of the natural world and its inhabitants.[45] To harness the extractive potential and environmental power of the Amazon, a frontier or wasteland narrative justifies settlement. The Amazon as a "final frontier" upon which to project modern desire is then only useful in its productivity. That productivity is achieved through capital production and its twin preoccupation with creating a modern, idealized utopia. Yet the paradox: by being rendered "productive," its other value—the representation of a nostalgic, innocent past—is destroyed.[46]

The idea of the Amazon as a virgin land and its peoples as rapidly disappearing creates a narrative of justifiable political and cultural dominance, where "progress" is implanted onto others. The state, in the name of progress or development, mobilizes discourses of education and modernization as goals to move a "savage" life into a modern one.[47] As Marisol de la Cadena points out in the Peruvian context, "Letting Indians die was necessary to achieve progress; moreover, it was achieved through cultural technologies, via *alfabetización* and *urbanización*. Presented as literacy and urbanization, the death of Indians was, in fact, their birth as mestizos and, only as such, citizens of the nation. . . . What from an indigenous viewpoint expresses a denial of ontological difference, the state phrases as progress, protection, and cultural improvement."[48] Death in this sense is both literal and cultural. Cultural technologies, or the mapping and making of knowledge, can be destructive of Indigenous ways of life, and very often of Indigenous people themselves. Western thought creates binary categorizations that separate between nature and culture, thus forming systems that exclude other worldviews. De la Cadena describes how Indigenous cosmologies have been explicitly left out of the political sphere, particularly views that resist Western separations such as that between nature and culture.[49] Like characterizations of the Amazon region as a hell, Eden, utopia, or frontier, these representations and subsequent separations serve a political purpose that once again supports a coloniality of power that privileges Eurocentric knowledge and knowledge production.

A central aspect of modernity is the pervasive belief in objective knowledge based in science and reason. Through empire and imperial gaze, this knowledge is used to dominate others. National development in previously colonial contexts also focuses on domination of both peoples and landscapes and is dependent on the social production of space.[50] As Achille Mbembe argues, "Colonial occupation itself was a matter of seizing, delimiting, and asserting control over a physical geographical area—of writing on the ground a new set of social and spatial relations."[51] He deems the writing of new spatial relations territorialization, and within this territorialization, the primary tools are the categorization of different populations, resource extraction, and the manufacturing of a large reservoir of cultural imaginaries.[52] "Savage life" is seen as "another form of animal life" and "savages" are equated with nature in the eyes of the conqueror.[53] Imperial projects in the Amazon depend on the control of product and forces of production (people as labor). This may include the incorporation of Amazonian peoples, land, and ecologies into the heart of national identity (however limited), or control through physical and environmental destruction.

The authors examined in this volume are concerned with collecting information through travel, and some of them are directly involved in the geographical mapping of space. Again, part of the knowledge production pillar of modernity, within the colonial project, European territorial representations became seen as the only legitimate and verifiable models. As Walter Mignolo explains, Western mapping, like naming, "became the paradigmatic model of the true representation of the earth, while Native territorial representations were either destroyed or taken as useful signs to understand their culture, although not as serious alternatives to map-making."[54] Eurocentric approaches to knowledge, in coloniality, are seen as the only accurate depictions of the world. Rather than understanding or dialoging with alternative forms of knowledge, Western knowledge production became conflated with the real. Mapping and re-naming through travel operate to assert control and power over space and the people within that space.

The other side of modernity/coloniality is a decolonial approach, or decoloniality. A first step toward decoloniality is recognizing the ways modernity has shaped knowledge production and systems of power. Decoloniality requires an "epistemic reconstitution," or new ways of thinking, speaking, and engaging with the world.[55] Linda Tuhiwai Smith's seminal *Decolonial*

Methodologies (1999) argues for decentering Western systems of knowledge. She sets out a decolonizing framework by first defining imperialism as the economic expansion and the subjugation of others and explains how it has been embedded in Western ideals of organization and order, or systems of classification that make up the pillars of Western knowledge.[56] In pitting nature against culture in different categories, humanity is put on a higher plane and knowledge is organized via categories that do not necessarily fit local concerns. Due to imperial processes that separated and subjugated based in part on categorizations, a decolonial methodology requires thinking outside of a Western framework and re-examining the West's taken-for-granted separations such as that between nature and culture.

Travel narratives and natural histories produced knowledge supported by a multitude of maps, photographs, and statistics that facilitated the nationalization of territories, ecologies, and peoples while also demonstrating the position of the Amazon in neo-imperial formations. Travel, already an elite activity, is experienced differently across racial, socioeconomic, and gender lines.[57] Through these different materials, a rich and complicated patchwork is revealed; one that shows the evolving relationship between viewers and the viewed, nature and culture. As such, this volume offers a reflection on the ways travelers engaged in various projects of collection for different nations interact with and portray the Amazon region, demonstrating, at each turn, the ambiguities of modernity.

Visualizing Amazonia

Simultaneous with the rubber boom, a technology of observation, knowledge, surveillance, and control—photography—became increasingly available and widely used, and as this study illuminates, photography elicited narratives of Amazonia throughout the world. The photographs reproduced in many of the narratives we will examine become a rich source for understanding the categorization of Amazonian populations, fixing them within a gaze that establishes difference and hierarchy. Deborah Poole describes these processes by identifying how ethnographic photography and film establishes norms of look, dress, behavior, environment, and cultural setting. The images are an important component of narratives and histories, as these visual representations situate Indigenous peoples as static subjects in contrast with the itinerant photographer and their technology from the modernizing and advancing center.[58]

Photography of Indigenous people and exoticized land circulates and reinforces cultural and racial difference, attracts the interest and attention of international audiences, and establishes the Amazon within a popular imaginary. In this sense, the image supports a "centralized model for the control of remote populations."[59] This visually establishes the Amazon as a center of primitive Otherness that in becoming "known" can be defined, organized, and controlled. Furthermore, visuality is part of the process of modernity. Supporting a Western desire to control Latin American territories and peoples, and much like mapping and naming, the photographs of these narratives become "conflated with the known" or assumed to accurately depict reality in modernity.[60] This modernity is based on not just imagining difference but also, and more importantly, on seeing it. All relations of power also demonstrate a possibility of resistance, and particularly for subordinates in relations of power, an oppositional gaze that asserts agency and awareness of being viewed.[61] Visuality can reveal an ambiguity between both subjects and photographers, a reversed gaze that we will examine in Chapters 1, 2, and 4.

The photograph in Figure 0.2 showcases a central theme of this book: the destruction and extraction of natural resources from the Amazon. This image was created as part of the Brazilian government's efforts to map and manage Amazonia, led by colonel Cândido Rondon, one of the explorers of Chapter 2. The forest and landscape loom large and the centered men are small in comparison. Yet their stances tell a different story: they have felled the jungle, taming nature. They have cut the trees to set up telegraph poles, which will later turn into settlements and roads. The trees are tall, thin, and dense, yet also susceptible and defeated. They have been cut down and rearranged to incrementally build. The men, appearing defiant and self-assured, have parted the sea of trees, clearing a new Amazonian landscape, one where the sky is visible and clear. They have done the work of moving wilderness into landscape, thus engaging in "landscape creation."[62]

This photograph was produced as part of the Rondon Commission's charge to open the region to small settlements on the Amazonian frontier. The Commission used photography as a tool of nation building, showcasing Indigenous peoples in various stages of acculturation and the landscape in various stages of management. The Rondon Commission widely publicized their photography that showed Indigenous peoples and Amazonian land in stages of development to "display the state's power to represent the hidden interior."[63] In the wealth of images created by the commission

FIGURE 0.2 The construction of a bridge and road by the Rondon Commission in 1911. Courtesy of Acervo do Museu do Índio/FUNAI – Brasil, CRNV0288

(some of which are examined in Chapter 2), we can see the fashioning of the Amazonian frontier into a knowable, and as such, conquerable, space through photography.

European powers have used the so-called tropics to play out fantasies of "self-realization, projects of cultural imperialism, or the politics of human or environmental salvage," as Felix Driver and Luciana Martins examine in *Tropical Visions in an Age of Empire*.[64] In visually creating tropical spaces, travelers could fashion a region suited to their aims, as we will see in the chapters to follow. Driver and Martins distinguish between view and vision, where vision engages the viewer and creates an active participant, in contrast to the view as a product of enlightened reason. Again, the question of who holds the gaze is central. In this sense, the view is like an imperial gaze where the observed is defined in terms of the observer's set of value preferences. The imperial gaze can assert its control through hierarchically categorizing what or whom it falls on, again privileging Eurocentric knowledge production.[65]

Photography also became a means to create political change. By the end of the nineteenth and beginning of the twentieth centuries, photography was used to influence and alter public opinion. By visualizing issues such as poverty, political and social injustices, war, or crime, documentary photography could change policy and mobilize the public for social causes.[66] At times, photography was a means of representing the suffering of the Other. Thus, this Othered subject could be seen as representative of an entire group's experience.[67] Carolina Sá Carvalho argues that when photographers had themselves experienced violence or repression, they were uniquely able to capture and see violence in ways that others do not, such as in the case of Irish nationalist and diplomat Roger Casement. In Casement's travels throughout Amazonia, he was tasked with documenting the rubber industry in the Putumayo region, where he photographed and wrote about the culture of terror being implemented by rubber plantation owners against Indigenous peoples. An Irish citizen, and as such a subject of the British colonial enterprise himself, Casement could notice and visualize abuses that may not have been readily apparent to others.[68] Thus we can see how photography not only demonstrates the relationships between subject and object but also the tenuous and political lines of personal identity.

Photography of the tropics, or more specifically of the Amazon region and its inhabitants, showcases varying levels of engagement with the Other. As we will see in the chapters to follow, at the surface level, some explorers used photography as a tool to communicate the potential workforce of Indigenous people in the Amazon, classifying racial difference. Others used it to document people and land they feared were in the process of disappearing. All the photography examined in this volume demonstrates the relationship between photographer and subject, and the strategic choices made in their compositions. In some instances, as with images of the 2019 Amazon fires with which this introduction begins, the image can provoke outrage and ensuing action. In political and historical contexts of rapid change visuals are a key aspect of analyzing the unequal processes of modernity.

Rubber Boom Amazonia

During the first rubber boom (ca. 1879–1912), international powers were intent on harvesting rubber wealth, and a system of globalized extraction was firmly established, ultimately setting the groundwork for the future of the region. From the outset of European contact, Amazonia served as a space marked in contrast with Europe and inscribed with a renewed hope for reinvention via extraction. In the colonial period, Portuguese, Spanish, French, Dutch, and the British fought for control of the lands of northern South America to set up plantation and extractivist economies. However, the region was settled by Europeans in a less dense manner than more central regions with immediate economic returns to the colony (such as sugar from the Caribbean islands and Northeast Brazil or gold and silver from Andean mines). Portuguese and Spanish missionaries spread out along the basin, creating missions aimed at converting, colonizing, and forcing Indigenous peoples into their service. Nonetheless, the environment was considered uninhabitable because of the threat of disease, tropical heat, and lack of transportation. Extractive industries in the Amazon were often preceded by "collecting expeditions," on which plants and other natural resources found in the region were collected, documented, and taken back to Europe.

Brazil was named by the Portuguese for its abundance of pau-brasil, or brazilwood, and during the colonial era, brazilwood eventually made way for sugarcane, coffee, minerals, rubber, beef, and soy. Creating the circumstances to export these goods required the imposition of science over nature and an abundant labor force to move raw resources back and forth to colonial centers. Europeans extracted a wide variety of goods from the Amazon—called *drogas do sertão*, or backcountry/wilderness drugs, including plants, animals, food stuffs such as Brazil nuts, wood, etc.,—and utilized existing Indigenous trade networks to navigate the river system and increase extraction. These extractivist operations set up systems that transformed the environment and "displaced, deracinated and enslaved native and non-native peoples of color."[69] Historical patterns of social inequality, ethnic discrimination, and environmental conflicts in Latin America are a product of the conditions produced by colonizing powers inserting the region into the international economy as a site of extraction.[70]

Hierarchies based on racial classifications were implanted onto the Amazon region, as mixed-race populations (in the case of Brazil in particular) were used by the state as a steppingstone toward a future racial harmony based in eventual white homogeneity. As lines were drawn to demarcate borders, and an extractivist economy flourished, the population of the Amazon region shifted. By the nineteenth century, Indigenous peoples who had culturally assimilated and mixed Brazilian and Indigenous peoples made up a large swath of the Amazonian population and most often formed part of the peasant class. There were also African people who were forced into slavery and brought to the coastal Amazon. Some of these enslaved Africans escaped into the jungle and founded independent settlements. In Brazil, the smallest of these communities are called *mocambos*; larger settlements are *quilombos*, or *palenques* in the Spanish-speaking Amazon, many of which still stand today despite having confronted violent attacks since their initiation.

At the turn of the twentieth century, the Amazon basin transformed both ecologically and demographically. While an extractivist economy was already in place, the extraction, exploitation, and international competition over rubber increased it by an order of magnitude. New technologies, including the vulcanization of rubber (by American Charles Goodyear in 1844) and the development of machinery and transportation made rubber a commodity essential to the Second Industrial Revolution (1870–1914). Indeed, British naturalist Richard Spruce, in his travel narrative published in 1908, noticed how the rubber trade had impacted the region, writing about the plumes of smoke from new Amazonian cities spurred on by the booming rubber business. He notes how other industries were quickly abandoned as the prices of rubber soared and people flocked to the industry.[71] Neither in boom nor bust did rubber involve extensive interference from the public sector. This lack of state attention to the Amazon facilitated exploitation by outside powers. The perception of the Amazon as an impenetrable world of dense and extravagant vegetation, a "green hell," diminished the likelihood of the transformation of the region's economy to benefit Indigenous and local peoples.[72]

The first rubber boom was simultaneous with the modernizing of nation states and led to the delineation of national boundaries and definition of territorial interests. Exploration, mapping, border creation, and contestation emerged from the international demand for rubber. While outsiders had been exploring Amazonia since initial colonial contact, the interest in rubber inspired a flurry of naturalists and cartographers from across the globe to be the "first" to define regions, locate the complex systems of rivers and tributaries, identify plant and animal species, and situate Indigenous groups on the map. While some geographical mapping projects formally staked claims to Amazonian territory, the work of other naturalists and foreign explorers (such as Henry Walter Bates, Richard Spruce, or Alfred Russell Wallace) provided information that could be used to extend imperial control over the region. In Amazonian travel narratives, exploration was a tool of both science and imperialism. However, amid other global scrambles for power, the region was often overlooked because countries with a colonial outpost (like French Guiana) maintained control over their territory in the region or lost land to Brazil.[73]

During the rubber boom, the Amazon was an internationally contested area despite most countries with a stake maintaining control over their land. The "scramble for the Amazon" takes place in the context of other imperial competitions for land and resources, in particular the scramble for Africa and the subsequent division of the continent among West European colonizers at the Berlin Conference (1884–1885).[74] These scrambles in the name of the "three Cs," or commerce, civilization, and Christianity, had devastating consequences for local peoples and the environment. The period also included the 1898 Spanish-American War, which established the United States as the preeminent imperial power in Latin America, to some measure in parallel with European exploration and exploitation of various countries in Africa.[75]

The rubber boom occurred not only during the Second Industrial Revolution but also during the era of new imperialism, a period of colonial expansion by Europe and the United States, primarily in Africa and Asia. Different from the era of direct imperial control, new imperialism refers to the period of economic and political expansion in foreign countries during the nineteenth and twentieth centuries by Europe and the United States.[76] The scramble for Africa, new imperialism, the Second Industrial Revolution, and impulses in the Global North of civilizing missions throughout the world formed a global backdrop for cultural representations that reflected and dialogued with political projects. The rise of the United States as a world power, particularly in relation to Latin America at the beginning of the twentieth century, marked a shift where US intervention in the region was seen as justifiable because of racist and ethnocentric ideas.[77]

During the Second Industrial Revolution, new industries based on inventions such as the telegraph, automobile, and modern chemicals transformed daily lives and created widespread change. These new innovations were based on scientific reasoning and approaches that reorganized existing industries toward increased efficiency.[78] Steel, electricity, and railroads helped propel the United States to the role of dominant manufacturer in the New World, while Latin America continued to export natural resources. As Latin American nations established independence and consolidated, social and economic inequality increased. Theories of the "scientific" racial superiority of people of European ancestry were used to justify the subordination of non-Europeans. Newly formed Latin American nations, established within former colonial boundaries, became oligarchic republics built on social structures of exclusion.[79] In Brazil, regional conflicts led to the eventual overthrow of monarchy and the formation of a new republic.[80]

The narratives in this book trace the social transformations of the period as they move from direct colonialism (the process of a country taking physical control of another) into an ideological imperialism (political and monetary dominance, with an expansionist bent). The production and transmission of knowledge of the Other, of land, resources, and people is a crucial tool of domination and part of modernity. The documentations, categorizations, and representations examined in this volume set forward, reiterate, and establish hierarchical power relations across race, class, linguistic, cultural, educational, and national lines. Writing about the Amazon that touches on the rubber boom era can thus help us to better understand the history and peoples of the region.

As the international demand for rubber increased, attention turned to the Amazon region and how to best harvest this commodity and render it as profitable as possible. Rubber plantation owners, or rubber barons, rounded up Indigenous people, forcibly removing them from their homes to tap rubber trees, in some areas wiping out more than 90 percent of the Indigenous population and asserting power through violence.[81] The obfuscated history and remote jungle environment, Michael Taussig argues, was used as a screen behind which violent acts could be hidden. The constructed image of Amazonian Indians was never in focus; shrouded in the jungle, Indigenous peoples could be portrayed in whatever ways best justified abuse and domination.[82] The supposed lack of knowledge about this space, the purposeful denial of history, and the representational darkness surrounding Indigenous peoples made their subjugation more easily justifiable and contributed toward creating a "space of death" and a "culture of terror." This is the proverbial "heart of darkness" where violence is perpetrated without consequences, out of sight of Western consumers reaping the benefits.

During the rubber boom, in Brazil and the broader Amazon, rubber barons' wealth skyrocketed and inequality deepened. A shortage of labor needed to support the demand for rubber caused rural peasants destabilized by droughts in the Brazilian Northeast to migrate in large numbers to the region (some pictured in Figure 0.2), while Indigenous people were almost always coerced under a regime of slavery.[83] Due to the dispersed growth of rubber trees, these deterritorialized rubber gatherers, scattered throughout the jungle, were less likely to engage in collective organization.[84] Belém became the first Brazilian city with electricity, and the barons built massive mansions as well as opera houses in emerging cities like Iquitos in Peru and Manaus in the center of the Brazilian Amazon. In the 1870s Henry Wickham, a relatively unsuccessful British entrepreneur, stole seventy thousand rubber tree seeds from the central Brazilian Amazon near Santarém. These seeds were eventually taken to British, Dutch, and French colonies in Asia. As the rubber trees began to grow in Asia, prices for Amazonian rubber dropped and the rubber boom had effectively busted by 1913.[85] The scrambles for power, control, and territory that occurred during the rubber boom and its subsequent bust solidified the region as a site of violence, extraction, and, ultimately, unrealized potential. These legacies are analyzed in the chapters to follow.

Overview of Chapters

Chapter 1 examines Octavie and Henri Coudreau, French geographers and explorers contracted by the French and later the Brazilian government to map rivers in the Amazon basin. Henri, already an explorer of the region, was joined by his wife, Octavie, in 1899 to map the Trombetas River in the state of Pará. Midway through their trip Henri died of malaria, but Octavie continued writing, photographing, and mapping the region under contract for the Brazilian state. Her collected texts showcase the gender dynamics in imperial exploration as Octavie positions herself as a masculinized authority based on her racialized perceptions of her surroundings.

As another incursion in a foreign land, and the basis of Chapter 2, Theodore Roosevelt, former United States president and renowned big game hunter / adventurer, journeyed to the Amazon in 1912 after his failed bid for a third term in office. With intense media coverage, Roosevelt was joined on this expedition by Cândido Rondon, the Brazilian military officer and explorer of the Amazon region. The juxtaposition of these two leaders demonstrates the sometimes-conflicted vision of modernity in an Amazonian context from North American and Brazilian perspectives. Roosevelt views the Amazon as an arena to showcase his level of rugged masculinity and a space to develop for transnational resource extraction. Rondon, however, seeks to bring modernization to the Amazon through technology and the gradual incorporation of Indigenous peoples into the new Brazilian nation.

In another well-publicized journey, which is the basis of Chapter 3, Euclides da Cunha, a Brazilian author, journalist, sociologist, and engineer, traveled to the Amazon as part of a geographical commission to demarcate a border between the Brazilian and Peruvian Amazon. He wrote a collection of essays and notes about the trip compiled and published posthumously in 1909 as *À margem da historia*. A primary preoccupation of intellectual elites in Brazil at this period was how to create a "civilized nation," which appears in Euclides's essays that highlight the potential of Brazilian mixed-race workers and his vision for the settlement of the region.[86] As such, he positioned internal migration as the path toward creating small settlements in Amazonia. In comparison, Mário de Andrade, a Brazilian modernist, author, musicologist, and art historian, traveled to the Amazon in 1927 to take photographs and write a travel diary that mixes ethnography with songs, poems, and photographs. By comparing Euclides and Mário's works, I examine the two authors' views of how the Amazon region fits into an emerging Brazilian nation.

Chapter 4 moves us into a broader geographic focus than just the Brazilian Amazon with explorers who work throughout the region including in Brazil, Colombia, and Venezuela. The explorer/anthropologists Theodor Koch-Grünberg and Richard Evans Schultes were prolific in their writings about the region and their work to incorporate Indigenous practices, languages, and plant knowledge into the global mainstream. Chapter 4 looks at how both anthropologists took a pedagogical approach in their interactions with Indigenous peoples and the land while still falling back on a paternalistic power dynamic of extraction.

Following the analysis of Koch-Grünberg and Schultes, Chapter 5 examines Colombian director Ciro Guerra's film *El abrazo de la serpiente* (2015) as a travel narrative that rewrites the journeys of Chapter 4's explorers and depicts thematic issues of exploration, extraction, and culture during and after the rubber boom. This film uses an Indigenous protagonist as well as a fictional plant to raise questions about knowledge production, preservation, and indigeneity. While this more contemporary film breaks from the traveler's documentations of past chapters, it thematically reconfigures the travel narrative form and focuses on issues of knowledge production, Indigenous voice, and visuality, thus fitting in with the corpus analyzed in previous chapters.

Each of these comparative case studies demonstrates a novel approach toward travel and the creation and proliferation of travel narratives about the Amazon. By taking a comparative approach between explorers, it becomes apparent how the authors' particular contexts and personal identities shaped their visions, as well as the intertextuality involved in exploratory endeavors. As previously mentioned, the chapters are accompanied by brief addendums that connect geographically or thematically to the issues written about by the corresponding chapters' travelers. As such, we can see the lasting impact, the "history of the present," of cultural and biological contact within these zones.

Reverberations into the Present

As we will see throughout the case studies examined in this book, the ways outsiders have imagined the Amazon region have been used to justify various developmental projects. These outsider visions have left lasting traces on this globally important region. The impacts of climate change in the Amazon, a slow violence that has seemed to massively speed up, is spurred on by extractivism, industry, global capitalism, environmental pollution, and degradation that threatens the extinction of plants, animals, and humans. Perhaps because of these consequences, the Amazon is often seen as global patrimony, an area so important that it is an international duty to protect it.

As the 2019 Amazon wildfires raged, countries argued about the best way to exert international measures to control a world resource that lies primarily within Brazilian borders.[87] After a bloc of European nations pulled out of funding Amazon conservation as a response to Brazil's systematic loosening of protections on the region, Bolsonaro reiterated the pervasive idea of *cobiça internacional*—that foreigners covet the Amazon—not so subtly stating that "Brazil is like a virgin that every pervert from the outside lusts for" in response to attempts at outside intervention in the aftermath of the fires.[88] And certainly, international eyes have been set on Amazonia since initial colonization. Echoing centuries of international discourse about the forest and its peoples, recent rhetoric, visions, and developmental plans for Amazonia can be traced back to the "discovery" of the new world and the apex of international attention toward the region—the first rubber boom. Indeed, over a century earlier, Euclides da Cunha emphasized Brazil's unique position and ability to lead the Amazon to a future of prosperity.

Not only are cultural representations of the utmost importance for actual political action, but because of the current reality of climate change, the fate of the Amazon is of even greater consequence. Increasing temperatures in the coming years will lead to more drought, the loss of ecologies and species, and threats to human health. Most Amazonian countries are falling behind on goals to curb deforestation, despite efforts such as the tripling of protected territory in Colombia and the reelection of the more environmentally friendly Luiz Inácio "Lula" da Silva over Bolsonaro in the 2022 Brazilian election.[89] Even with these necessary strides, it is with urgency that, as scholars, students, and environmentally conscious citizens, we must look at the history of extraction, development, and representation of the Amazon region. In so doing, we can begin to understand the immense importance of the forest and its historic role in the global imaginary, and most importantly, we can more responsibly interact with Amazonia.

CHAPTER 1

Gendered Politics of Empire

*The Female Explorateur
and Visions for the Racial Future of Amazonia*

> My wife is amazing, voilà, she has become an Indian! She is
> barefoot along the river, under the sun and fishing! I feel
> as if I should send for her, I'm afraid she'll get sunstroke.
>
> —HENRI COUDREAU,
> on his wife Octavie, *Voyage au Trombetas*, 1899

In 1899, Octavie Coudreau, a twenty-eight-year-old Frenchwoman, came to the Trombetas River to join her husband on what was to be his last voyage. The Coudreaus and their crew traveled through a particularly rich contact zone as the Trombetas, a northern Amazon tributary in the Brazilian state of Pará, was home to a multitude of small escaped-slave communities, or *mocambos*, along with a variety of Indigenous groups.[1] Octavie's husband, Henri, a geography and history professor, had moved to French Guiana years earlier, where he explored and mapped the region, working for both the French and Brazilian governments at the height of rubber boom border disputes.[2] Octavie, trained in France as a geographer, initially came to help her husband and serve as his cartographic assistant for their exploration of the Trombetas River.[3] Within this context of contention, cultural contact, and most importantly geographical production, a female explorer appeared as an anomaly. In contrast to Henri, little is known about Octavie's past or about her life after her seven years of service in Amazonia. Toward the end of the Coudreaus' journey and mapping project, Henri died at forty years old from malarial fever. After Henri's death, Octavie picked up the pen, continued on to finish the Trombetas journey, and travel narrative *Voyage au Trombetas* (1899). Henri's death launched a substantial career for Octavie in her own right, as she went on further explorations contracted by the Brazilian government, completed six publications, and gained official recognition by the French Geographical Society.

While traveling in Amazonia, Octavie Coudreau's gender limits her, yet her race and nationality offer her a separate set of privileges. The ways that she represented and traveled through the Amazon, particularly through small Black communities, offer a point of departure to discuss wider implications of race, gender, and imperialism in this transnational space. Octavie's geographical training sets her apart; however, her contributions and narratives are almost unreported on. As Avril Maddrell addresses in *Complex Locations*, women have largely been ignored in the writing of geographical history and their contributions unacknowledged in the field, particularly before 1970. As suggested by Maddrell's book's title, she seeks to establish a more inclusionary historiography of geography by acknowledging the complex relationship of female geographers to the discipline.

Beyond the general lack of acknowledgment of the role of women in geographical projects, there are several reasons why Octavie may have been largely ignored by the canon. For one, Octavie chose to write the bulk of her narratives and correspondence as simply O. Coudreau, leaving her gender and identity ambiguous and causing some archival confusion. Secondly, the Coudreaus were quite radical for their time, as Henri had been a foundational member of the failed anarchist colony of Counani and sympathized more with Brazil than France in several border disputes. Finally, Octavie held extreme racial positions on Black populations—so extreme that they were deemed too racist for turn-of-the-century thought that leaned heavily on phrenology and a sense of the white man's burden.[4] Through a critical examination of Octavie Coudreau's geographical fieldwork as detailed in her travel and geographical narratives, this chapter analyzes Octavie's contributions while unpacking her role in imperial power structures. Here, within the period of new imperialism, Octavie enacts measures to exert forms of physical, cultural, and institutional control over a foreign territory. I look at her self-identification, photography, and descriptions of Indigenous and Black people in the jungle in their restrictions and implications toward identity and place. I argue that movement—in the sense of travel as well as between social categories—creates Octavie's coloniality of power. This chapter thus contributes a gendered analysis of travel, particularly how personal identity impacts projections of empire on racialized bodies as well as the environment, ultimately demonstrating the confluence and conflict between travel, gender, and race.

Henri's description of Octavie in the epigraph to this chapter from his portion of *Voyage au Trombetas* portrays Madame Coudreau as comfortable, yet still out of place in the physically demanding Amazon region. Apparently Octavie waded barefoot in Amazonian waters, much like the Indigenous peoples that her husband Henri admired. This brief passage both indigenizes Octavie and points to her (European) feminine fragility in the tropical sun. Octavie must still be "sent for," or managed under her husband's authority. However, this comment also points to Henri's own difficulty exerting control over her in this environment, where Octavie could move at least somewhat freely. As a female explorer in the jungle, Octavie Coudreau's narratives and geographical work illuminate a woman taking on authority and leadership and demonstrating significant skills in map-making, photographic documentation, and travel and ethnographic writing. Indeed, Octavie becomes perhaps the first female photographer in the Amazon basin.[5]

This chapter engages in a gendered analysis of Octavie's unique perspective while examining her role in the exercise of imperial power through territorial conquest and the project of knowledge production. Octavie's identity shifts as she becomes a grieving widow, thrust into a position of power abroad while still dealing with the limitations of her gender during this time. Furthermore, she travels through the Amazon, a rapidly changing region where multiple races and imperial powers interact in a contested contact zone. This chapter thus examines the unfixing of gender identity as it relates to movement within a liminal space. The Coudreaus' interactions with their crew and the varying Indigenous communities and *quilombos* they came across shape their narratives and reflect race relations in an increasingly modernizing Amazon. Not only outsiders to the region, but outsiders to Brazil itself, the Coudreaus attempt to offer guidance for the state from their perspective as subjects of a colonial center. Their advice privileges and pushes for the increased migration of white Europeans to Amazonia. Furthermore, while Henri promotes land conservation, Octavie is primarily concerned with eliminating Black people in the region. The asymmetrical relationship that the Coudreaus' have with their crew and the Black and Indigenous populations they come across displays the highly racialized conflict within this contact zone.

Octavie Coudreau (1870–1938) was an author, explorer, cartographer, photographer, and adventurer who produced six captivating narratives detailing subjugation, categorization, and collection in the Amazon region at the turn of the twentieth century. Female geographers' historiographies have been the subject of study; however, as Mona Domosh notes in her analysis of Victorian journeyers, women are often examined as "travelers" rather than as institutionally recognized and supported geographers.[6] In *Travel, Gender and Imperialism* (1994), Alison Blunt examines the intersection of race, class, and gender, and emphasizes the need to move beyond dichotomies of male and female travelers, finding her point of analysis in the ambiguity and ambivalence of racial constructions. She argues that analyses of difference should avoid "artificial binary oppositions" through contextualization and complication.[7] Beyond gender binaries of male/female travelers, the way the Coudreaus experience race and portray their surroundings demonstrates an ambiguity of experience. As a site in which new possibilities unfold for the grieving widow, the Amazon at the turn of the century was in a state of flux due to the rubber boom and increased efforts to incorporate the area into the Brazilian nation. This multiracial context forms the backdrop that Octavie moves through where there is a marginality to the identities she prescribes to both Indigenous and Black people. Impelled by personal events along with a contested zone as context, Octavie's landscape and cultural descriptions, narratives of exotic adventure, photographic images, and hand-drawn graphic maps point to revealing intersections of race and gender in colonial territorialization.

Natural histories of the Amazon written by white male explorers around the turn of the twentieth century are not uncommon.[8] Conversely, female explorers during the same period are less common and their accounts of independent voyages even more so.[9] This chapter examines the workings of coloniality through the gaze and actions of a female explorer (a self-described "explorateur") whose narratives and material production offer insight into women as protagonists within an imperialist adventure narrative. As Maddrell addresses, female travel writers of the nineteenth and early twentieth centuries were overlooked as legitimate geographers (generally based on whether they took geographical measurements). Octavie, however, was producing geographical measurements and census information of local populations. Accompanying this production, Octavie's prose is sentimental and self-reflective. In some ways, this style could be used to soften the harder scientific findings that Octavie exposes, demonstrating a sliding gender/power scale where Octavie includes sentimental prose next to geographical measurements and census data to work from a position of (relative) power. Through a negotiation of gender, she both self-identifies and negates her position as a geographer-explorer, moving within limitations. This gender negotiation also depends on a sense of racial superiority, particularly over the Black people she encounters. For example, she often writes about Black populations in contrast to Indigenous peoples and in relation to women: "We see everywhere the runaway slave that has the same moral characteristics: meanness, deceit, and treachery vis-à-vis the white if it arises, and insolence and tyranny toward the Indian . . . in their mocambos they unite to rob women [from neighboring Indigenous groups]."[10] By declaring that Black people have targeted women and children, Octavie uses her position as a woman to project racial superiority and as such, control, framing herself as the patriarchal protector of Indigenous peoples.

A perceived racial superiority gives female travelers a sense of authority in a foreign land. In an imperial power structure, anything outside of a white male subject formed part of the complex of the primitive, where other subjectivities were immediately considered more primal.[11] As a woman, then, Octavie was already an Other, particularly while her husband was alive. However, in his death, she begins to bend the rules by positioning herself as a scientific and racially superior authority, moving upward in the imperial hierarchy. Thus, when categories become un-fixed, there is not only instability, but there are also new possibilities. This un-fixing depends on movement and travel as that is what bolsters Octavie's authority and is the tradition with which she identifies. Octavie, despite taking geographical measurements and producing detailed maps of Amazonian tributaries, rationalizes her authority by identifying with a male exploratory tradition, a perceived racial superiority, and by justifying her reasons for exploration as wifely duty.

When the Coudreaus set off for the Trombetas River in 1899, the Brazilian Amazon was experiencing a moment of heightened national and international interest and attention. Rapidly expanding global capitalism during this period included the development of steam power, railways, machinery, chemistry, automobiles, and the vulcanization of rubber, which fueled a frenzy of exploitative development in colonies and former colonies in Asia, Africa, and South America. In Europe, geographical societies were formed to sponsor and train geographers for expeditions. The Société de Géographie de Paris, established in 1821, was the first of its kind and one of the first such societies to admit women. As a female leader of expeditions, Octavie's narratives indicate a longing for dominance through racial superiority, unfettered movement, travel and access, and the production of scientific knowledge—all elements of modernity.

Framing Imperial Practices

In producing cultural and geographical knowledge for the command and control of capital production, Octavie Coudreau is complicit in the domination of colonized subjects, even as she experiences domination herself within the gendered power structure of early twentieth century Europe. In *Imperial Leather*, Anne McClintock examines what she deems the three themes of Western imperialism: "Transmission of white, male power through control of colonized women; emergence of a new global order of cultural knowledge; and the imperial command of commodity and capital."[12] While McClintock's study primarily addresses the ways gender forms a crucial point of subjugation within an imperial hierarchy, she acknowledges that "white women were not the hapless onlookers of empire but were ambiguously complicit both in colonizers and colonized, privileged and restricted, acted upon and acting."[13] While recognizing the agency of women in the creation of empire, McClintock argues that no matter their race or class, women reaped far fewer benefits of imperialism than men.[14] Initially offered the chance to travel and explore due to her position as Henri's wife and later widow, Octavie is not of the most elite—she must continue to work since Henri left her with few financial resources. Yet due to her force of character, commitment, and ultimate enjoyment of exploration and cartography, she took on four more substantial expeditions. Although the Coudreaus are emblematic of imperial explorers, in some respects they are resistive and indeterminate in their relationship to this both imperial and commercial project. Octavie's material productions complicate her position as a liaison of modernity, development, and subjugation.

To briefly analyze the direct narrative switch between Octavie and Henri, I primarily examine *Voyage au Trombetas* (1900), a fascinating 134-page travel diary started by Henri and finished by Octavie. I also discuss Octavie's next publication after *Voyage au Trombetas*, entitled *Voyage au Cuminá* (1900), which provides a wide range of photographic and cartographic material produced exclusively by Octavie after her husband's death. There is little analysis of Octavie Coudreaus' work; however, there are several sources that reference Henri Coudreau, including a biography, and some mention in Susanna Hecht's excellent *The Scramble for the Amazon*.[15]

The Coudreau's journals include, in addition to narration, their own maps and Octavie's photography. In imperial projects, maps and photographs provide modern representations authorized as scientific "truth" that serve as tools in the naming, describing, and controlling of subject territories and peoples. Map making precedes and helps to legitimize territorial conquest.[16] The Coudreaus' production also demonstrates a modality of visuality as set forth by Nicholas Mirzoeff in "The Right to Look." Mirzoeff argues that through classifying (naming and mapping), separating, and aestheticizing, imperial visualities created a "centralized model for the control of remote populations."[17] The Coudreaus' maps, photographs, and accompanying documents attempt to organize the social behavior of Black and Indigenous people, establish control over resource extraction, and facilitate industrial development, while simultaneously tracking the movements of their trip. By identifying the Other, ethnographic photography and film establish norms of look, dress, behavior, environment, and cultural setting. These tools establish and fix cultural, racial, and gendered hierarchies.[18] Photography works within narrative histories to increase international attention and visually describe and establish the Amazon as a peripheral wilderness within the international popular imaginary.

Transition from —trice to —teur

As shown in the photograph in Figure 1.1, taken before their first joint expedition, Henri sits in the middle, looking straight at the camera with his arms commandingly crossed, dressed entirely in black. Nonetheless, the distinguishing element in this photograph is Octavie, at once out of place yet at ease in the left center of the photograph. Her arms rest passively on her lap, her face seemingly scowling not quite directly at the camera, making her appear impatient, ready for action, yet still constricted, confined, and static. Her clothes are bulky and impractical for a jungle environment, in contrast with the pants and loose hanging shirts of the men. Here Octavie's attire suggests an adherence to sartorial conventions of female dress despite her foreign environment. With Henri as the focal point, it is immediately clear who the expedition leader is, and where the authority lies. The crew appears in sailor outfits, their matching hats distinguishing their secondary role on the expedition. The crew was made up of local guides, most of whom were from nearby mocambos. Like many other explorers of the region, Henri and Octavie employed some of the same crewmembers on a regular basis and had favorites among the crew. This photograph is taken in a studio, where the curtains and manicured backdrop capture the moment before departure. This voyage in the Trombetas River basin included nine men (and one woman), in two large canoes.

FIGURE 1.1 Octavie and Henri Coudreau and their crew before their expedition on the Trombetas River (1899). Courtesy of the Bibliotheque de Geneve, BGE V 3368

The Trombetas basin is considered particularly tricky territory to navigate. Located in the heart of the Amazon region, there are multiple waterfalls and rapids that made voyages such as these almost impossible without the expertise of local guides. Around 1800, a number of enslaved people escaped and used these difficult waters to their advantage, eventually settling along the Trombetas and Cuminá basins.[19] Maroon communities established themselves on the land, harvesting Brazil nuts, occasionally bartering with Indigenous groups, or serving as guides for foreign explorers in the region. These local experts offered new paths to navigate the difficult riverscape that included waterfalls that had been previously impassable. The *mocambeiro's* knowledge of the landscape through which the Coudreaus traveled made them invaluable yet still exploitable resources for the explorers.

Several months after this photograph was taken, Octavie Coudreau became a widow, bringing her to identify as a masculinized *explorateur*, rather than *exploratrice* as might have been expected. As the sole European and expedition leader on subsequent journeys, Octavie immediately took on a dominating role, a shift upward in the imperial hierarchy, however, one that still required careful navigation. Octavie begins her part, the last chapter of *Voyage au Trombetas*, by detailing Henri's death from malaria. She worked as a nurse on the trip and at Henri's side on his deathbed. Henri often describes how she pulls crew member's teeth and mends wounds along the journey. The last chapter of *Voyage au Trombetas* begins like previous sections with an overview of where the chapter will take the travelers (and the reader): "Descent of Porteira—the Death of Henri Coudreau—Painful separation—Dark funeral." This spatial trajectory outlines the story of the chapter, a sort of tour before the map. Octavie describes in anguishing detail her frantic search for help along the river. In the immense darkness of remote Amazonia, she held her lantern high, cutting the night, with Henri dying in the back of their canoe as she finally pulled ashore to the mocambo Cachoeira Porteira. In the style of other travel narratives, she adds a touch of literary flare by chronicling the sky on the night of her husband's death, "It was a sad spectacle—a funereally terrible yet beautifully illuminated and star-studded sky above the black water and our heads."[20] By the time the crew arrived ashore, it was already too late.

After pages of laments and mourning for her husband, Octavie begins to document her surroundings in a somewhat similar style to Henri. However, the subject is immediately less about the particular geography of the region and more about the inhabitants and her own feelings of isolation: "I have longed for this departure and now that I am in the middle of this vast Amazonian forest, I feel alone, sorry, and almost desperate."[21] Octavie's sense of isolation is amplified as the only European on her journey and within the vast forest, and she longs to continue moving. As Susan Morgan notes in her analysis of Victorian women's travel books about Southeast Asia, "The feminine rhetoric of imperial domination is understood to repeat, copy, imitate, mimic the masculine rhetoric its function is to serve. Their cultural aims are similar—in fact, his defines hers—but their specific positions and content are different."[22] Morgan finds that there is an emphasis on the domestic sphere by women versus an emphasis on the city and outside world by men. While traveling, white female writers could use their position abroad to express a sense of power based on nationality and racial superiority. Despite moving outside of the domestic sphere, Octavie feels a sense of isolation because of her racial position, gender, and the loss of her husband. For Octavie, in the middle of the jungle, the domestic disappears, although an emphasis on a sense of racial and national superiority does not.

Octavie's narratives and geographical endeavors in *Voyage au Cuminá* differ from most other female travel writing as she was entirely outside of the urban centers, in a multiracial context far from a traditionally conceived "domestic sphere," and she worked to create maps along with narrative.

While identifying as an *explorateur* is not necessarily unique to Octavie—many female travelers almost inevitably chose to identify with male exploratory traditions—she continually comes back to this designation that helps to define and bolster her mobility and authority.[23] Octavie's explicit choice to identify as a female *explorateur* situates her in a role that is not fully masculine, yet decidedly not feminine:

> If I am an *explorateur*—this word cannot stand to be feminized—it is not for love of glory, which is far too fickle a goddess, and blinder than Fortune. It is not for the love of Geography, I think I will like Geography enormously once I am done with it. If I explore it is to allow me to bring the remains of my husband to his elderly parents so that Henri Coudreau does not forever remain in a foreign yet friendly land, it is to finish work begun five years ago, because all useful work is primarily to raise awareness of countries still ignored by the masses.[24]

Here Octavie hesitatingly refers to herself as an explorer ("if"), calling attention to her femininity as out of place in this role. Indeed, for her, the word itself cannot even be feminized. Octavie is a reluctant geographer; however, through geographic production her gender can be ignored or more importantly, shifted. This shift means that she can move forward within an ambiguous gender construction. Rather than explicitly contributing to a geographical canon of knowledge, Octavie positions her knowledge production as obligation to Henri and in the wider, universal frame of enlightening the masses. Octavie explains her objective as above all dutiful to her husband by finishing his work on the Trombetas, and secondarily practical and scientific, moving from traditional female to male roles. However, even this secondary objective carries a sense of duty not only to Henri but to the production of scientific material, another manner of expressing a desire for control over place.[25] This position as a reluctant geographer allows her, like her male counterparts, to create an adventure travel narrative and photographic legacy that transmits knowledge of unknown lands to imperial powers and audiences despite her gender. The death of Henri in fact gives Octavie the opportunity to continue traveling and to receive official contractual appointments as a lead geographer. Indeed, it is only after Henri dies that Octavie finds a voice in writing and begins publishing her travel journals.

Figure 1.2 demonstrates an Octavie significantly changed from the woman who set off down the Trombetas by her husband's side, by this point

Figure 1.2 Octavie the *explorateur*. Courtesy of the Société de Géographie, National Library of France, 4-SG BON H-3302

a genuine *explorateur*.²⁶ Octavie here appears alone, in trousers, her clothing and glasses (as seen in Figure 1.1) no longer limiting her or restraining her movement. She has seemingly taken on a separate social and gender identity, rearranging her sense of self for the world to see. Octavie was often mistaken for a man while traveling and left this misconception uncorrected to legitimate her position as expedition leader and avoid potential questions to her authority.²⁷ However, with Indigenous communities who were distrustful of encounters with white men, Octavie would reveal herself as a woman, receiving a warmer reception as a result. Gender is a tool that Octavie purposefully and artfully wields to her advantage while traveling. In this photograph, Octavie nonchalantly places her hand in her pocket, staring off into the distant West, with her left leg positioned dominatingly atop the studio landscape in the background. On her breast is a watch chain, presumably with a watch tucked inside a pocket, evidence of her ability to manage the activities of others and an emblem of the modernization and the forward progress of her exploratory work. Octavie presents herself as a heroic *explorateur*, figured alone and taking an authoritative and visionary command over her manicured surroundings. This photograph shows a more active, virile, masculine persona than the Octavie of Figure 1.1. There is a certain sense of Octavie's agency transmitted through both her dress and stance—although the role of *explorateur* came about due to her husband's death, Octavie has *chosen* to continue, commit, and fully inhabit this new role.

Documenting the Other

Octavie's gender does, however, shift the gaze of the imperial explorer, evident in a comparison between Octavie and Henri's material productions, both narrative and photographic. Narratively, there is a similarity between Henri and Octavie of both theme—enjoyment of the landscape and Indigenous peoples—and style—a travel diary that records the day-to-day actions of the adventurers. However, Henri's narratives leave out the personal impressions and much of the descriptive language that Octavie uses. Gerry Kearns differentiates between three categories of writing that imperial explorers implemented: objectivity, sentimentalism, and anti-historicism.[28] Octavie's writings demonstrate a sentimentalism that renders the writer "impotent" by feeling lost in nature, or, in Octavie's case, in lamenting her husband's death. In this imperial sentimentalism, writers express feeling together with fact. Conversely, Henri's writing falls into the realm of the objective, where the geographer stands apart as a seemingly unbiased observer of the imperialist scene through classifications of flora and fauna, land, and peoples. A sense of self-discovery rather than just a discovery of the unknown was more apparent with female travelers. While Octavie's narratives repeat her husband's chronological style, there is the disappearance of the invasive masculine gaze on Indigenous women, a sense of immediate perceived threat from mocambos, and a varying sense of self in relation to both populations and the landscape not seen in her husband's work.

Henri Coudreau was a well-known cartographer and explorer. Having worked in the Brazilian Amazon since 1895, and the French Amazon since 1884, he was a seasoned veteran of the geography, landscape, and ethnic makeup of the region. In 1895, Henri began service explorations of the northern Brazilian state of Pará, contracted by the state government of

Brazil. This was highly contested territory, particularly during the rubber boom. After each voyage he published a natural history complete with maps, drawings, and detailed observations of his surroundings. Different from other naturalists with similar projects, Henri's political belief was in anarchy, supporting "colonization for the people" rather than a "colonization of exploration."[29] On a geographical expedition in 1883, Henri pinpointed the small region of Counani between French Guiana and Brazil. Together with a group of other Frenchmen, he worked to establish an independent colony that would serve as a utopian refuge for Europeans sick of the rules and regulations of modern society. Counani, however, was short-lived and received recognition from neither France nor Brazil. By 1888 it was essentially defunct. Later, gold was found in the territory, and it became hotly contested, eventually leading to the French and Brazilian government's decision to bring in Switzerland as an arbiter. The Swiss ultimately decided in favor of the Brazilians and the land remains in Brazilian possession until today.

The anarchist leanings of Henri meant he had a sense of solidarity with struggles for national independence that would lead to further social revolutions. This sense was revealed as Henri consistently sided with the emerging Brazilian nation against French territorial interests. Henri also lent his services as a geographer during the Questão do Amapá (or Contesté Franco-Brasilien), an 1895 border dispute between French and Brazilian governments over a territory division at the Oiapoque river (also eventually settled in favor of the Brazilians).[30] Along with being an anarchist-naturalist, Henri spoke multiple Indigenous languages and fluent Portuguese, at times serving as an interlocutor between Indigenous groups of the region. Having proven his skill in cartography and language during the Questão do Amapá, Henri Coudreau was commissioned by the Brazilian government in the same year to map three rivers in Pará state, causing rumors in France of a possible role as a double agent for Brazil.[31]

As apparent in their writing, Henri and Octavie idealized what they deemed to be the primitive nature of Indigenous peoples. Henri tends to favor the "wild" Indians he encountered on his journeys. For Henri, the "untouched" Native peoples are attractive due to their supposed ease and ability to travel freely within their environment. Indigenous women have a particular allure:

> The Arara Indians are the most excellently mysterious of the Xingu region. Those that I saw had a clear complexion and elegant comportment. They seem to be the most mobile indigenous group of the region: now on the

Iriri, now on the Curuá de Ituqui, today on the banks of the Xingu, tomorrow on the right edge of the forest—they don't seem to stay in any fixed place. The tribe is famous, especially for their beautiful women.³²

For Henri, the Arara Indians, always in motion, form the ideal Indigenous group: they have an "elegant" comportment that lets them move easily in a jungle environment. The fact that this community is always out of reach despite Henri's efforts to locate them adds to their "mystery." For Henri, the Arara are seen as particularly attractive because of their "clear" complexion in contrast to other, darker, populations in the jungle, once again demonstrating a racialized hierarchy. Furthermore, Indigenous women, semi-nude and mobile, in Henri's telling, create an appealing contrast with European women, covered and confined.³³ Indeed, Henri was rumored to have had multiple relationships with Indigenous women before Octavie's arrival in the area, which perhaps motivated her to join his adventures in the first place. Attraction coupled with mobility harkens back to the epigraph of this chapter, in which Henri refers to his wife as an Indian wading in the waters of the Amazon.

Like her husband, Octavie admires the seemingly unrestricted Indigenous people, whom she documents extensively. Once Octavie becomes the leader of her own crew of men, she comes to consider herself a defender of Indigenous people. In a moment of relative ennui on the Cuminá River, Octavie references a frequent argument between the crewmembers and herself: "To make me change my mind they continually try to impress me. They repeat their eternal phrase—'Indians aren't people, they are bugs of the forest'—to which I reply: 'You [crew members] are brutes, there is no doubt that the Indians are better and superior both morally and intellectually.'"³⁴ Here Octavie exhibits high praise for the mental and moral capacity of Indigenous peoples—in contrast to the Brazilian crewmen who, in her telling, see Indians as undesirable parts of the forest. She thus positions the Brazilian crewmembers as brutish and savage, in contrast to Indigenous people whom she praises for what she deems as their natural superiority, by being uncorrupted by civilization. Unlike Henri, Octavie references the intelligence rather than physicality of Indigenous peoples. Ultimately, Octavie asserts her own superiority through telling the crewmembers they are wrong. As an educated, white European, Octavie's interpretation of the nobility of Indigenous peoples bolsters her own position of authority over her crewmembers. Whenever Octavie addresses her crewmen, she highlights her own sense of authority by infantilizing and scolding. Beyond a

FIGURE 1.3 Pianocotô Indigenous people interacting with their surroundings. Courtesy of the Bibliotheque de Geneve, BGE Fb 1469

rhetorical authority, Octavie often beat her crewmembers into obedience, establishing a dominance based on violence and fear.

Further demonstrative of the ways Octavie views Amazonians are the photographs she produces. In Figures 1.1 and 1.2 Octavie is a subject, but in *Voyage au Cuminá* and following narratives Octavie is the photographer. This shift is especially important as Octavie can represent her surroundings from her perspective, while Henri included detailed sketches, but few photographs.

Octavie's photographs of various Indigenous people exhibit her perception of their mobility, and their alignment with the landscape, like Henri's narrative descriptions. Octavie's photographs often display Indigenous peoples actively engaged in various pursuits such as building canoes, eating, or moving through the forest. Figure 1.3 shows three Pianocotô people squatted near brush and branches, almost blending into the forested background. These Pianocotô are obviously not in a settled area, and they appear barely clothed. The photograph seems candid, as some of the subjects look at Octavie while others continue about their routine, demonstrating a certain comfortable, or at least accepting relationship. Through Octavie's lens, Indigenous people outside of settlements are viewed as in sync with

FIGURE 1.4 A Pianocotô man in his dugout canoe. Courtesy of the Bibliotheque de Geneve, BGE V 3368

their environment—worthy of preservation and protection yet not quite fitting in with ideals of order and modernization. Indeed, settlement and modernization would seem to diminish the mental and moral superiority that Octavie attributes to Indigenous peoples.

In Figure 1.4, a Pianocotô man sits in his dugout canoe. This man sits waiting, rather than crouching like the Pianocotô in Figure 1.3. The placement of the canoe is ready to launch, another indication that there is freedom in motion. This vessel is different than what Octavie and her crew members travel in, partitioned off wooden boats that are wider than this crafted canoe. Here the separation between nature and culture is blurred as the man is cocooned within a tree that he has transformed into a canoe. Movement and motion through the landscape creates the appearance of a harmonious relationship between him and his surroundings. The trees together with the riverscape determine how the man has chosen to use them. While seated and posed, motion is a current in this photograph that demonstrates wider implications about Indigenous people in the jungle, who here can be read as mobile and unhindered. There is a freedom of movement and interaction with the environment that disappears in Octavie's photographs of mocambeiros and her crewmembers.

FIGURE 1.5 Octavie's guide from a local *mocambo*, Guilhermo.
Courtesy of the Bibliotheque de Geneve, BGE V 3368

This photograph of Octavie's guide Guilhermo is the only close-up portrait of a man included in *Voyage au Cuminá*, likely taken in a studio. Guilhermo looks directly at the camera, his brow furrowed, and his gaze somewhat concerned. His tilted head seems to indicate a kind of pleading with Octavie, the photographer. His expression reveals at once an intimacy and barrier. Guilhermo plays a central role as Octavie's guide and informant throughout her trip. As McClintock notes, in these manicured, immobile portraits there is a certain violence: "The immobility of the sitter conceals behind the surface of the photography the violence of the colonial encounter."[35] Motion or the possibility of it disappears in this photograph. The camera, wielded by Octavie, freezes her subjects, while the blank backdrop takes Guilhermo out of context. Furthermore, Guillermo's striped and buttoned shirt indicate a certain Westernization, in contrast to the shirtless Pianocotô people. While Guilhermo serves as Octavie's "guide," indicating a superior sense of surrounding and adaptability to the environment, he remains her subordinate. Octavie's photography demonstrates her usage of the imperial gaze, which reflects her own definitions and value-preferences about those that she observes. As

E. Anne Kaplan puts forward, the imperial gaze assumes the centrality of the white, Western subject.³⁶

In contrast to Octavie's progressive and almost reverent view of Indigenous peoples, her sentiments and documentation of Black people in the jungle are racially marked and numerous in comparison to Henri's. Octavie's vision for development of the Amazon region revolved around white migrants coming to the area to "civilize" Black settlements: "If this European colonization and national colonization in the settlement of Pará does not begin soon on a large scale, I wonder if the Pará region will not fall prey to negro races of the Caribbean, whose rapid swarm may well threaten to transform the Amazon not into a Wild West, but a sort of Sudan."³⁷ Octavie situates her mission on a global scale, warning of the perceived threat to white settlers through reference to Sudan (most likely a nod to the Mahdist War of 1881–1899). Here Octavie describes Black people as insects; they "swarm," presumably taking over a place, moving together in large number. In contrast, in her opinion, Europeans should move to immigrate and settle Pará, ending the frenzied swarm and demonstrating a different type of voluntary, controlled movement. As Domosh notes on female explorers, "their authority in the field was derived from their role as outsiders—as representatives of the white race—yet the basis of that authority is what made them insiders in a culture in which they had no authority."³⁸ This struggle to define and prove her authority can be seen as Octavie situated herself as morally superior to her crewmembers through her acceptance of Indigenous populations, while conversely locating Black people in the jungle as out of place and in need of control.

Figure 1.6 appears toward the beginning of Octavie's travel on the Cuminá River. In her journal, Octavie describes Black settlements on the Cuminá as small and abject, like those on the Trombetas, yet in this section of the narrative she focuses much less on them than on Indigenous communities. The only photograph capturing a *mocambeira* (female resident of a mocambo) is shown in Figure 1.6, of a woman named Figêna.³⁹ Figêna sits looking away from the camera, in contrast to photographs of Indigenous peoples looking directly or candidly at the lens. This woman seems to be waiting passively, almost patiently. She is wearing Western attire, and in the background a cleared settlement and a self-sustaining economy are apparent. This is the only photograph from *Voyage au Cuminá* in which a woman is shown alone, and notably it is a Black woman. There seems to be a certain refusal to engage with the camera, yet Figêna is seated and clearly posed, perhaps, in a manner like Octavie in Figure 1.1. This representation fixes

FIGURE 1.6 Figêna, a *mocambeira* woman. Courtesy of the Bibliotheque de Geneve, BGE V 3368

Figêna in a primitive domestic sphere and in some culturally intermediate yet clearly hierarchized space between Indigenous and European. While Octavie has control over the creation of the image, and its selection and publication, questions still arise: is Figêna looking away from the camera at the request of the photographer or is it an act of resistance to the photographer? The photograph silences its subject, but is the angle of Figêna's chin and the set of her jaw also a refusal to speak?

In comparison with the photographs of Indigenous people (often demonstrating a sense of movement or an active involvement with their environment) that make up the bulk of Octavie's photography, this image strays. This construction of racial difference shows a feminization of the gaze where Figêna, while seated passively, is not overtly or immediately sexualized. However, the photographs produced by Octavie show her racial categorization and hierarchy of Amazonian populations, where Black Amazonians are distinctly out of place, and static. Poole suggests that photographs shot in a studio took on an increased appeal as the subjects could be pictured alone, and could appear rare, thus putting forward an argument that their large number (in Poole's case, Native American Indians) was rapidly dwindling into disappearance. Octavie's photographs show Indigenous peoples in action shots or in groups, while pictures of mocambeiros show them alone, isolated, and clearly posed for a shot. This supports several arguments. One is that in their isolation, Black people can perhaps be swept out of the jungle. Secondly, Indigenous peoples, who are busily in motion and part of a larger network, should be left alone or employed for their various skills.

Henri pays less attention to his crewmembers in his narratives, fleetingly commenting on their origin and mocambos in general. Henri begins *Voyage au Trombetas* with the journey setting off from Cachoeira Porteira as they take four men from this community on the trip as regional guides and oarsmen. This mocambo was formed, according to Henri, when enslaved people ran away in an attempt to escape a draft for the Paraguayan War (1864–1870). Throughout Henri's portion of *Voyage au Trombetas*, mocambos are often described in passing or as a source for potential crewmen to guide them on their voyage. Often, the racial characteristics not just of the mocambeiros but also of their interactions with Indigenous groups are described: "Fifty of these mocambeiros and their descendants live there today, peaceful but quite miserable citizens, in the part of Trombetas immediately downstream of the first waterfalls."[40] In this passage, Henri refers to the mocambeiros' life in peace, albeit "miserable" in terms of poverty; they are seen to live in harmony with both the environment and Indigenous groups, which is in stark contrast to Octavie's descriptions of the same communities. All of the communities that the Coudreaus encounter were formed around the geography of the region—especially in the case of mocambos, where enslaved people were able to find some refuge in the forest and subsist off of the land. The large waterfalls of Cachoeira Porteira, the mocambo to which Henri refers here, blocked slavecatchers from capturing escapees.

In contrast to Henri's passing and neutral descriptions, when Octavie picks up the pen later in *Voyage au Trombetas*, she writes extensively about the Black settlements she encounters. Octavie gives her own history of how mocambos formed, describing mocambeiros as "negres marrons du Brésil," or "Black maroons of Brazil," who have settled throughout the Amazon. Octavie finds these mocambeiros offensive, because, by her telling, they have captured and enslaved Indians (especially women and children) living outside of their settlements, "In their mocambos they unite on issues of mutual insubordination to rob women. They tried to turn to the practice of slavery, searching for captives from neighboring Indian groups where they attempt to remove the women and children."[41] This paints a picture of a violent contact zone where white outsiders are needed to manage these conflicts. It comes in contrast to Henri's "peaceful" designation toward the same mocambo. Her description of mocambeiro settlements demonstrates Octavie's perception of attempts by mocambeiros to take Indigenous women and children, which may have alerted her to her own vulnerable position as a white woman in the jungle. Regarding Indigenous people, Octavie is as paternalistic as her husband, though with more attention to the experience of women. Regarding Black inhabitants, her position moves from her husbands' paternalism toward an assertive control and management, perhaps in a racialized perception of personal risk. Octavie's vision for an ideal future of the Amazon region centers on white settlement to protect Indigenous people and to keep Black people more closely monitored. While she views the groups differently, both require increased social discipline modeled and organized by white people of European ancestry.

As shown in Octavie's photographs and narratives in the Amazon, there are at least three modes of mobility in the jungle: the ability to travel and document through identifying as an *explorateur*, the freedom of mobility within the jungle for Indigenous peoples, and the forced migration of Black people. For Octavie, movement becomes how she interprets her environment and copes with the loss of her husband and perceived isolation. The moments when Octavie remains sedentary and inactive are the ones she deems the most dull and tiresome. "The most boring moments of the trip are those where we're not moving forward. These forced stops are always of a great sadness. Any force that stops us fills me with sadness."[42] Octavie's stated need for action and movement contrasts with Figures 1.1 and 1.6, where activity is the realm of a European *explorateur*—the privilege of mobility, of whiteness and masculinity—steamrolling forward toward modernity and industrialization while Black bodies sit waiting or are forced to migrate.

Mapping Virgin Landscapes

Where Octavie's ideals for Amazonian development revolve around white migration, in terms of natural resources she is more directed than Henri in reporting on areas for settlement and industrialization. Octavie as *explorateur* offers guidance for potential locations for coffee and nut plantations ("In Rio Cachorro timbers abound, the land is excellent for growing and there is the *castanha*"[43]). In *Voyage au Cuminá*, Octavie expresses a longing to go back to France; however, she again emphasizes her dedication to her mission, as working, movement, and a forward trajectory help her grieve and justify her identity as *explorateur*: "But here it is truly about the dreams of my imagination. I have other things to do than literature or feeling. I am here to draw an accurate survey as comprehensive as possible of the Cuminá River, a sub-tributary of the Amazon."⁴⁴ The challenging environment and circumstances of Octavie's exploration offer her stimulation and excitement. Although she argues that she has other things to do than "literature and feeling" her prose is demonstrative of the effect that her travels had on her sentimentalist style. Ultimately, however, a sense of dedication to geographical accuracy and an exploratory mission is used to at once justify and masculinize her position and assert control.

While Octavie offers suggestions and justifications, Henri stresses a care and guardianship of the land—part of his perceived duty as a patriarch: "and as the supporters of progress and Brazilian civilization decide to try [to develop the Amazon], beware of falling into the error that ruined many countries, a mistake of deforestation, therefore depriving a country of the freshness essential to equatorial climates."⁴⁵ Henri's warning against deforestation demonstrates a tension between conservation and development. This tension is like the contradictory desire to at once "civilize" Indigenous peoples while maintaining "uncivilized" qualities, as tokens of an unspoiled, unsullied past that does not quite fit within the imperial project. He also situates himself as an authority for the developing Brazilian nation. With both conservation and Indigenous peoples, Henri exhibits an intense attraction and awareness of their importance, never explicitly pushing for assimilation or destructive industrial projects. As he fashions it, ideally, Henri or someone like him could remain a patriarchal keeper of both the forest and Indigenous groups.

The cataloguing, mapping, and classification of the landscape and peoples in this region form part of a larger colonial project, of which Henri serves as a somewhat bizarre negotiator. Within his narratives he is highly critical of extractive industries and other adventurers out to make a quick profit and return to their easy lives in Europe. According to Henri, "within colonized settlements, one can come to distrust those adventurers who come to rob one of a virgin land full of natural resources and, after having made their fortune, leave a broken and bruised earth, returning to enjoy peace in Europe, living off of the fruit of their thefts."⁴⁶ Somewhat settled Indigenous communities as well as mocambos must have been distrustful of Henri and his mission, making his work more difficult. Not to mention the earth itself, perhaps given more consideration than the people living there, is being threatened, as he says, left broken and bruised. As an anarchist-colonist (itself an oxymoron), Henri recommends migration to Amazonia to settle the land and begin to harvest its wealth. This is a vision he elaborates in depth in his publication *La France Équinoxiale* (1886), in which he details Counani as an anarchist utopia. As Hecht explains, "Ahead of his time, Coudreau viewed the region as especially important for extractive goods of rubber, cacao, and Brazil nuts; in short, he viewed Cunani as an economic powerhouse, not even counting the gold in the alluvium."[47] Thus, in pointing out the errors of previous colonizers, Henri can help to justify the benefits of long-term settlement for economic growth.

In a hand-drawn map from *Voyage au Trombetas* of "Indigenous Tribes of the Trombetas River Basin," names of different Indigenous groups appear throughout the basin, at times overlapping. The ethnographic project undertaken by Henri during *Voyage au Trombetas* experienced multiple setbacks, due to geographical difficulties where the crew was blocked by large rapids from going further into Indigenous territory. "We are powerless before this natural beauty, we welcome it and we bow down; then continue, sadly forced to give up the project to go to the Indians where I had intended to have a great geographical, ethnographic, photographic and linguistic harvest, all because I cannot pass these rapids!"[48] Henri's regard for the natural environment of the Amazon is apparent and even humbling, despite being blocked from a natural historian's ideal "harvest," a crop of linguistic and ethnographic knowledge. In the case of the map in Figure 1.7, these fluctuating territorial borders become colonized in their documentation. This ethnographic map asserts knowledge of both bodies and place, or bodies in place—a combination of ethnographic and cartographic production. Both landscape and ethnographic descriptions are anchored in natural history with the difference being that "one produces land as landscape and territory, scanning for prospects; the other [ethnographic] produces the indigenous inhabitants as bodyscapes, scanned also for prospects."[49] This map demonstrates a production of both ethnography and cartography, or bodyscapes within landscapes, part of the project of territorialization.[50]

In contrast to Henri's ethnographical map, *Voyage au Cuminá* ends with twenty of Octavie's cartographical productions, a visual showcase of the movements of the trip in full color and exhibiting different scales of detail on areas of the river basin. These maps, like descriptions, photographs, and stories, serve to organize and "know" the region. Henri's previous narratives include black and white ink-drawn maps of different Indigenous territories (as in Figure 1.7), making Octavie's cartographical production appear especially aesthetically appealing in contrast (Figure 1.8).

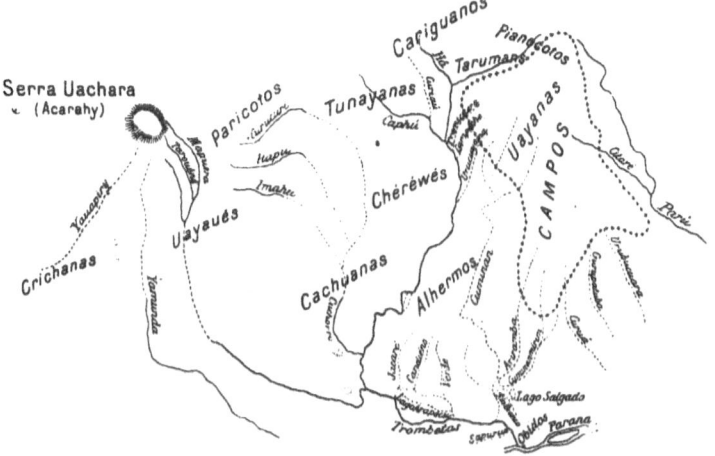

FIGURE 1.7 Indigenous groups of the Trombetas Basin. This area is now a designated natural reserve, still housing some of the same Indigenous groups and multiple recognized *quilombo* communities.
Courtesy of the Bibliotheque de Geneve, BGE V 3368

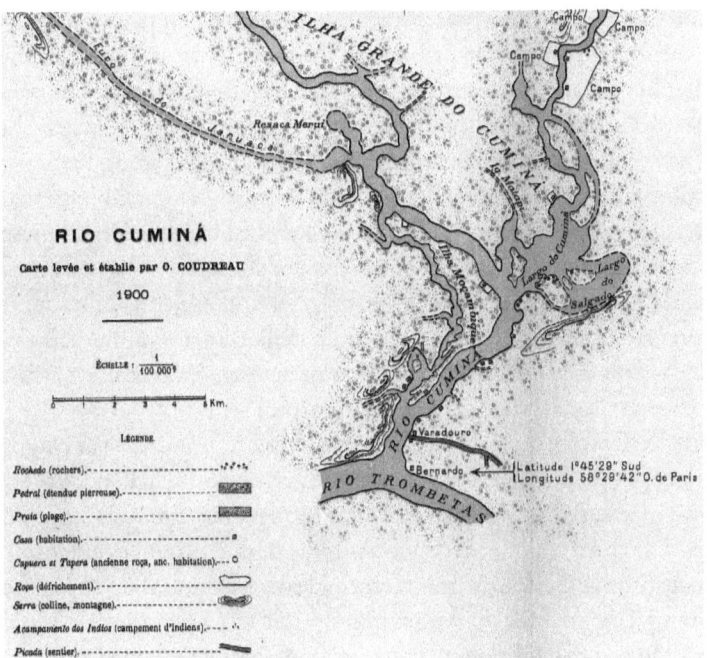

Figure 1.8 Octavie's hand-drawn map of the Cuminá River.
Courtesy of the Bibliotheque de Geneve, Fb 1469

Maps, as part of the body of natural history materials created by Octavie, function as scientific knowledge, providing a "truth" that can legitimize and aid in the construction and reinforcement of empire.[51] The map provided here is hand-drawn and scaled, a representation of Octavie's journey. The act of tangibly graphing these places serves in some ways to "devirginize" the landscape—mapping onto the grid a previous unknown. Furthermore, these maps, narratives, and photographs are then used as representational tools that, as Felix Driver explains, "serve to sustain more directly colonial and imperial projects ... to explore unknown country was in this sense also to subdue it."[52] As a woman involved in "subduing," the constant justification of actions through racist diatribe and movement between gender norms justify Octavie's own perceived role in the imperial project.

Conclusion

Octavie's writings, photographs, and maps transmit a frank intimacy with the reader as we textually bear witness to the loss of her husband and her transformation into an *explorateur*. In a telling moment from *Voyage au Cuminá*, Octavie becomes overwhelmed upon arriving at one of the waterfalls that her crew passed during *Voyage au Trombetas*. Next to the waterfall she sees the same table and tablecloth from months before when she was there with her husband. Her reaction to this familiar scene demonstrates a certain sense of survival, self-preservation, authority, and perseverance: "I gave the order to immediately remove the table and relieved myself by smoking a cigarette."[53] Octavie is a complex character—a grieving wife, a bold and determined explorer, a geographer and expedition leader, a racist appreciative of Indigenous peoples, a skilled cartographer, an ethnographer, and an adventure-writer who can be seen wading in the waters of Amazonian tributaries or smoking a cigarette.

Octavie Coudreaus' interactions with her crew and the varying Indigenous peoples and mocambos they came across both challenge and reflect imperial ideologies of race, gender, and modernization in an especially resource-rich contact zone. Octavie's photographic productions complicate her position as a liaison of modernity, development, and subjugation by feminizing the gaze yet masculinizing herself to gain authority. However, her trajectory, both literally as she goes forward on her expedition and theoretically as she moves between different identities, shows the ways gender and identity become unfixed through travel and movement. As seen in the photograph of Figêna (Figure 1.6), there is a challenge to the sexualized male gaze while an imperial racial hierarchy remains intact. Octavie's subjectivity is that of an imperialist abroad, and her constructions of racial difference, emblematic of her time, demonstrate the tenuous place of Black people in the Amazon region. In many ways, Octavie perhaps relied on a more explicit racism than her husband to give herself a more masculine authority. White women were complicit (or in this case explicit) in upholding racial hierarchies if, or indeed because, they had some access to masculine privilege abroad through their race. Ultimately, Octavie's photography showcases her personal evolution, the progress of her trip, and the imbricated racialized and gendered position of herself and her photographic subjects in motion toward modernization.

Octavie Coudreau died in 1938 at sixty-eight years old, seemingly disappearing from the archives after her last publication, *Voyage au Rio Curuá* (1903) and return to France in 1906.[54] Although Octavie's role as a female geographer and *explorateur* in this region at this time is exceptional, her vision of race and power fits within other imperialist projects. Her identification as an *explorateur* demonstrates a struggle to assert dominance over her surroundings through a particularly masculine gender identification. While Octavie's self-identification as an *explorateur* feeds into the overt masculinity of exploration, she also demonstrates the constant negotiation that this role entails. Her legitimacy is tied to a masculinized identity founded upon both a racial hierarchy and the ability of mobility, which she inhabits but never fully. To end as she begins *Voyage au Cuminá*, "Now is the time to shake off the torpor that overwhelms me, the active life begins."[55]

Poetic Justice for the Residents of Cachoeira Porteira

As discussed in this chapter, Octavie's narrative, photography, and maps detail her thoughts on Black and Indigenous groups in relation to the future of Amazonia. In her books *Voyage au Trombetas* (1899) and *Voyage au Cuminá* (1901), Octavie explored the Trombetas River basin. This basin housed (and continues to be home to) many Black *quilombo* communities. In the case of Cachoeira Porteira, a *quilombo* on the Trombetas River, Octavie included detailed census information, maps, and photographs in her travel narrative published in 1901.

In my research on Octavie, I worked with an Amazonian NGO called Projeto Nova Cartografia Social da Amazônia (PNCSA), or the Amazonian

New Social Cartography Project, associated with public universities in the Amazon region and headquartered in Manaus. The PNCSA is a collaborative organization of geographers, ethnographers, and other researchers who teach mapping and cartography techniques to local communities.[56] They use social mapping (a visual method where participants draw relative locations and tell spatial or symbolic stories) to help people think about their personal histories in a place-based tangible manner. Through this work they support communities in developing critical knowledge, skills, and historical understanding to gain legal land and resource rights. The PNCSA, drawing on a partnership between researchers and community members in a reciprocal and horizontal manner, develops and publishes pamphlets, articles, and books about the history and geography of villages, created by the communities themselves.

Once a community decides to do a mapping project, the PNCSA sends a group of researchers to help give workshops, teach geographic information system (GIS) mapping technology, and record the history of the community. Given these types of real-world interactions that involve marginalized communities, outsider advice or intervention is often problematic due to historical precedent, lack of transparency, and a tendency to privilege Western knowledge and approaches. However, the PNCSA's model of a space-based approach to reinforce ongoing community initiatives is meant to counter this imbalance. This is intended to create a reciprocal relationship and sustain projects. PNCSA researchers work to foster development by and for the community, rather than implementing a model of change where it is not necessarily wanted. The PNCSA thus uses social and cultural mapping to help establish and defend the rights of marginalized communities.

The small community of Cachoeira Porteira offers an example of the intersection of social and imperial mapping projects, as well as intercultural initiatives and the lasting impact of cultural contact. As discussed briefly in the chapter, Cachoeira Porteira was formed when enslaved peoples sought to escape the Paraguayan war draft at the end of the nineteenth century. When white men came after escaped enslaved people who had found their way to the waters surrounding the community, they were unable to pass because of the large waterfalls, and thus considered the falls a *porteira*, or a door that only Black people could pass through.[57] The ethnic makeup of this part of the Trombetas basin is primarily of African descent, although the surrounding areas are heavily populated by Indigenous groups and mixed-race rubber tappers. These different ethnic groups have a long history of interaction—at times peaceful and at times violent (as mentioned by Henri Coudreau's descriptions included in this chapter).

Several descendants of the crewmembers who accompanied Octavie and Henri on their journey still live in Cachoeira Porteira today. During one summer spent in Manaus, I learned more about Cachoeira Porteira from a young woman who was from the community and busy doing research for her thesis about social mapping projects. She told me a story that still circulates among the people of Cachoeira Porteira about the fateful night of Henri's death on the river, as also told in Octavie's narrative. She described how the story of Octavie in distress, holding up a lantern, its yellow glow cutting the immense darkness, has been passed down orally through generations.

In Manaus, the PNCSA informed me that they use Octavie's maps in workshops with local *quilombos*. These historical, cultural texts, created as part of the initial process of Amazonian exploitation, are now being re-read (in Octavie's case in community-based workshops) to better define and defend Indigenous and minority culture, land, and rights. Ironically, Octavie's work is now being used as a tool of political advocacy by the descendants of the very same Afro-Brazilian people disparaged in her writings.

In initial workshops with Cachoeira Porteira, the PNCSA presented the maps and census information made by Octavie as examples of how the community had been historically represented by outsiders. After visual and GIS workshops, activists are given the tools to self-represent and delineate their own territory. Researchers also share final products (pamphlets/maps/oral histories) with the community and online once they are finished. The maps and other publications that the PNCSA helps produce include markers of culturally important locations such as churches, schools, or places that carry a certain historical significance. They can include symbols for where different groups have historically lived, or other ethnic markers. In the case of Cachoeira Porteira, the PNCSA helped communities to identify areas of import.

The effort has been successful. On February 27, 2018, Cachoeira Porteira was historically given *dominio coletivo*, or collective domain, from the state government, effectively granting the community title to their land. Through years of collective action and advocacy, more than 220,000 hectares of highly contested Amazon territory was granted to the descendants of formerly enslaved peoples.[58] The small community where Octavie Coudreau first landed after the death of her husband in 1901 is now the largest titled *quilombo* land in Brazil. While there are around three thousand officially recognized *quilombos* in Brazil, many do not possess title to their land. The success of Cachoeira Porteira is thus even more impressive. Today home to 145 families, around 500 people, the residents of Cachoeira Porteira primarily live off small, self-sustaining farms and from collecting and selling Brazil nuts.

The document used to present Cachoeira Porteira's case of having historical domain over the land to the government of Pará included collective history, census data from Octavie Coudreau, and community-made maps, among other proofs of territorial occupation. With the help of the PNCSA, this community collected the documents needed to make their case and went through the process of mapping and then re-mapping their land. After years of fighting off first slave catchers and then developmental projects such as a highway and a hydroelectric dam, as well as conservation initiatives that sought to block the community's ability to hunt and farm the land, this was a huge and important victory. Indeed, this land title is a sort of poetic justice for the people of Cachoeira Porteira, who through the decades have demonstrated remarkable and inspiring resilience.[59]

CHAPTER 2

Wandering Wildernesses
Race and Masculinity on the Rio Roosevelt

After a presidential bid for a potential third term to lead the United States in 1912, Theodore Roosevelt, the indomitable lover of nature and adventure, was defeated. At the age of fifty-five, Roosevelt received an offer from the Museo Nacional de Buenos Aires to take a speaking tour in South America, after which he planned to join his son Kermit, who was working on the railroad in Brazil, for a leisurely Amazonian trip. As the planning for this journey gathered speed, the itinerary changed from a simple trek through known areas of South America into a geographical and scientific exploration of previously unknown territory in the Amazon. Approached by the Brazilian government to accompany Roosevelt and offer expert guidance of the region, Colonel Cândido Rondon, the foremost Brazilian explorer of the Amazon, who had been working for years establishing telegraph lines and opening the Brazilian interior, agreed to help lead the renamed and rerouted Expedição Scientífica Roosevelt-Rondon. This trip called Rondon away from his Telegraphic Commission project, yet the explorer recognized the publicity and big-name opportunity that a joint expedition could give his other work. Rondon suggested exploring the Rio da Dúvida, the River of Doubt, the headwaters of which he had encountered during one of his telegraph missions and whose route was yet unmapped.

In this chapter, I address transnational masculinities and race within the Amazon basin by examining documents and photographs from the Roosevelt and Rondon Scientific Expedition undertaken in 1913 and 1914. Exploration within the Amazon is a highly gendered enterprise, as was seen with the *explorateur* Octavie Coudreau of Chapter 1. It is a familiar trope that male exploratory traditions typically feminize or infantilize land and people in transforming supposed "wilderness" areas from the unknowable and unrepresentable into manageable, known places.[1] Like the Coudreaus, Roosevelt and Rondon perform their own forms of gendered and racial superiority as they implant technologies and project empire over the Amazon territory and its inhabitants. While Roosevelt's journey in Brazil has been widely commented on, this chapter contributes a comparative analysis of the racialized projections from the journey's two vastly different leading explorers, as such demonstrating distinctly Brazilian and American visions of race, wilderness, and the future of Amazonia.

This chapter thus explores the relationship between landscape and power—the external imperial influence of Roosevelt and the coloniality of power represented by Rondon's civilizing mission. Like the projects of Octavie and Henri Coudreau, this expedition was concerned with mapping territory and plotting the future of the Amazon region. Through travel in this exoticized space, the two expedition leaders' differing personal and national identities reveal contrasting expansionist visions. Roosevelt and Rondon were both prominent figures in their respective countries, and both shared the vision that their countries should participate in the global economy as superpowers through resource extraction and industrialization. They were also notorious outdoorsmen. Roosevelt, the twenty-sixth American president and member of a wealthy family descended from mid-seventeenth-century Dutch immigrants, and Rondon, a Brazilian military officer of mixed Portuguese and Indigenous descent, envisioned empire and modernity differently.

Documentation of the expedition was extensive and includes a silent film, photographs, news articles, and travel diaries of all major participants (excluding Rondon). Roosevelt's *Through the Brazilian Wilderness* is a 360-page travelogue that he wrote during the journey. *Rondon conta sua vida* is Rondon's life memoir, published in 1958, which includes his reflections on the trip years later. *Through the Brazilian Wilderness* was originally published as a series of essays for a North American audience in *Scribner's* arts and culture magazine, before appearing in its entirety as a separate publication in 1914. Following in the tradition of other travel narratives that Roosevelt studied (and quotes extensively), he presents himself as the ideal scientific and geographical male authority figure—what he deems a "wilderness wanderer." Rondon's memoirs were recorded by Esther de Viveiros, who transcribed his detailed life story as dictated in his own words. Despite the international fame that the journey with Roosevelt brought him, Rondon dedicates just three brief chapters of the 626-page account of his life to the trip. The photographs analyzed in this chapter are found in *Through the Brazilian Wilderness*, and from the Rondon Commission's work around the same time. The photography of this trip provides a venue for examining perspectives on the Amazonian frontier, Indigenous peoples, and the geographical mapping of space.

From the earliest periods of exploration, textual and photographic representations of the Amazon have established the region as a global final frontier of rugged, uninhabited wilderness. As mentioned in the introduction, and as scholars such as Pedro Maligo, Nancy Stepan, Candace Slater, Stephan Nugent, Patrícia Viera, and others have addressed, the Amazon is often represented as either a "green hell" replete with hostile flora and fauna, or a worldly Eden, beautiful and untouched.[2] Roosevelt tends to exaggerate a sense of perceived danger that establishes the Amazon as a final frontier against which his masculinity can be tested. In this chapter, I argue that Roosevelt's portrayal of the Amazon as a hostile wilderness stands in contrast to Rondon who thinks of the Amazon as a utopia that remains to be built, where civilization can expand and flourish. For Rondon, the Amazon offers the possibility of realizing the new Brazilian nation's dream of modernization through territorial domination and technological innovation. Roosevelt values precisely this lack of technology that makes the wilderness an exotic, premodern space for the staging of his masculinity. Desperate to experience an "authentic" wilderness, Roosevelt actively seeks adventure; Rondon, however, travels with the explicit purpose of introducing technology and establishing settlements of acculturated Indigenous peoples to build his Amazonian utopia.

These visions also demonstrate the difference between a United States and Latin American perspective on wilderness. In the US, as William Cronon and others have examined, by the nineteenth century, wilderness carried the connotation of a pristine, untouched area worthy of preservation. This vision, as Jennifer French notes, provided the "justification for preserving vast territories as national parks in the western US, and a cultural trope that intentionally or not erased the historical genocide of Native Americans from the cultural landscape by representing places like Yosemite National Park as pristine, uncontaminated, sacred space."[3] In Latin America, on the other hand, wilderness, translated as *desierto* or *sertão*, rather than a sacred space, was characterized by its relationship with the civilizing process. That relationship was fraught with anxiety according to leading intellectuals such as Domingo Faustino Sarmiento and Euclides da Cunha (one of the subjects of Chapter 3), who saw taming the wilderness—setting up small farms for immigrants to cultivate—as part of the civilizing project and an essential element for the future ascension of "wild" regions and, as such, emerging Latin American nations. Wilderness was thus thought of as a space where Europeans or creoles "may themselves be agents of chaos and confusion in a space that is either neutral or benevolent: not the absence of civilization so much as its perversion by corrupt individuals."[4] Thus, the question, when examining Latin American visions of wilderness, hinges on how and by whom the wilderness can be civilized.

Rubber Boom Frontiers

At the turn of the twentieth century, Brazil was attempting to incorporate its lesser-known regions of the interior, particularly Amazonia. The rising popularity of the bicycle and, later, Henry Ford's Model T, unveiled in 1908, led to a demand for rubber that helped propel the first Amazon rubber boom. With the support of the Brazilian government, the Rondon Commission was founded in 1907 and Rondon began establishing telegraph outposts in the Amazon Basin. Setting up these harbingers of modernity, the Commission also surveyed and mapped the land, encouraging settlement of the interior and the gradual incorporation of Indigenous people into the Brazilian nation, based on a positivist model. In 1910 Rondon helped found the Serviço de Proteção ao Índio (SPI, later FUNAI) based on his principles of gradual integration and "nonviolence" toward Indigenous peoples. Born in Mato Grosso in 1865, Rondon was a descendent on his mother's side of Terne and Bororo peoples (his mother died when he was two years old) and his heritage informed his policy.[5] As Todd Diacon notes, Rondon was proud of his Indigenous ancestry despite frequent attacks by other government officials and the press who thought that his heritage made him uncomfortable in "civilization."[6] While Rondon acknowledged his Indigenous descent he never openly self-identified as a *caboclo*, a rural figure with mixed Portuguese and Indigenous heritage, the term a sometimes-pejorative marker of racial difference.[7]

At the turn of the century, Brazilian nationalism and social thinking became increasingly intertwined with public health concerns.[8] The concern with sanitation that so preoccupied nation builders also implied a racial "cleansing," a gradual move toward whiteness, and the modernity associated with white civilization.[9] However, even as Brazil was, in accordance

FIGURE 2.1 "Colonel Roosevelt and Colonel Rondon looking over the vast landscape, ... From a photograph by Kermit Roosevelt." Plate following page 174 in *Through the Brazilian Wilderness* (New York: C. Scribner's Sons, 1914). Courtesy of the Library of Congress, The United States and Brazil: Expanding Frontiers, Comparing Cultures, https://lccn.loc.gov/14019126

with contemporary racial "science," attempting to establish a national, pure, racial identity, the caboclo came to be seen as "redeemable" because of their preponderance of white blood.[10] The caboclo became the focus of national debate over Brazil's racial future, in some cases even the basis of a future Brazilian race in formation. As a caboclo, Rondon could serve as a sort of cultural ambassador and face of Indigenous protection in Brazil, a stepping stone toward modernity and an ideal civilizer of the wilderness. Following the ideology of the time, Rondon could be considered a "backward" caboclo yet redeemable because he lacked Black heritage and because of his leadership position. Drawing on his positivist ideals, his Indigenous background, and his military education, Rondon saw cultural integration of Indigenous peoples and infrastructure development as equally important in the establishment of a modern Brazil.

Brazilian positivism at the turn of the twentieth century shaped the national approach toward the Amazon and played a large role in the ideology of Cândido Rondon. Beginning with the French philosopher Auguste Comte, positivism is a philosophical belief system based on scientific verification and logical or mathematical proofs. This dismisses many religious practices (in the Brazilian case, a staunch rejection of Catholicism), while creating hierarchies of branches of knowledge, with technology and science at the very top. Put simply, positivism is a belief in science and facts over religion. In Brazil, where the elite were educated in European and particularly French philosophy and language, positivism took hold midway through the nineteenth century, before Brazilian independence.[11] By the turn of the century, positivism's motto played out on the republic's flag as *ordem e progresso*, order and progress, and as an approach toward peripheral regions like the Amazon of strategic and gradual incorporation through technological integration.

To the north, as westward expansion in the United States came to an end and with the Spanish-American War of 1898 erasing Spain as a world power, ideals of Manifest Destiny turned outward. Roosevelt set up the United States as an imperial power, with the Roosevelt Corollary (1904) to the Monroe Doctrine (1823) that allowed the US to intervene in Latin America in the case of "wrong-doing by a Latin American nation," essentially paving the way for future intervention in the region.[12] With the perceived closure of the US western frontier, Roosevelt turned an imperial eye south.

Roosevelt's exploits abroad included a well-documented Smithsonian-sponsored safari-hunting tour in Africa in 1904, solidifying the reputation of the former president as an international big game hunter and explorer of the wild. Roosevelt's brand of masculinity reflected an ideology of imperial domination over the Other where adventure was meant to tame or defeat. While Roosevelt's domestic concerns turned to wilderness conservation, abroad, his environmental interests tended more toward expansionist missions, in which the goal was to obtain knowledge (and thus potential control) of so-called virgin territories. During the export boom of the late nineteenth and early twentieth century, exploratory trips of South America became well-funded missions of academic institutions, geographers, adventurers, and even ex-presidents who employed various new technologies of documentation and cataloguing in their endeavors. The former president considered himself a naturalist due to his initiative to record, measure, document, and eventually bring back specimens of flora and fauna. Following previous naturalist explorations, Roosevelt intended his trip as a fact-finding geographical mission; as he stated, "Our trip was not intended as a hunting-trip but as a scientific expedition."[13] This idea of scientific exploration helps to legitimize Roosevelt's role as a naturalist, giving him authority to collect, observe, and record. For Roosevelt, people had become products of over-civilization, and the jungle was a place where man could face a challenge and ultimately emerge triumphant over the wilderness.

The literal putting-on-the-map accomplished by Roosevelt and Rondon during this trip is representative of the larger process of gradual incorporation of the Amazon region and peoples into the Brazilian state and the global economic system. The twenty-sixth US president, famous for embodying a rugged masculinity through westward expansion and imperialism, had long been preoccupied with definitions of manhood (white, heterosexual, and American) as he sought to create a nation and purvey a global ideology that rejected effeminacy and degeneracy through physical challenge, violence, and exclusion.[14] Roosevelt's motivation for participating in this project involved a need to reclaim masculinity post election defeat through domination of the wild and of the Other. Rondon, in many ways perhaps an embodiment of the masculine explorer Roosevelt sought to be, worked to implement modernity and assimilate the Indigenous peoples of the Amazon into the Brazilian state, exerting a paternalistic control. Technological superiority and surveillance forms part of the masculine identity of both explorers in the Amazon and informs their perception and representation of Othered peoples in the jungle.

To analyze and compare these two men within this journey I first turn to their self-described identities and a few photographs that encapsulate the ways they embody imperial control. Next, I look at their observations on race and their staging of racial Otherness. I finish by examining their mapping endeavor—how they express a superior knowledge over the landscape that feeds into a racial superiority. Thus, I move from the self, to the Other, to the land, all aspects that make up the contrasting visions of Rondon and Roosevelt's Amazon. I argue that for Roosevelt, the region could be a global repository for potential development while Rondon imagines the region as an area to be incorporated within a specifically Brazilian context.

A Wilderness Wanderer and an Accomplished Frontiersman

With support from the Brazilian government and plenty of international press, the Roosevelt-Rondon expedition took off in 1913, reaching the mouth of the Rio da Dúvida in February 1914. In the short film *River of Doubt: Roosevelt/Rondon Expedition*, Roosevelt and his men are initially shown in Rio de Janeiro, hobnobbing with Brazilian elites and receiving the royal treatment, riding in carriages over cobbled city streets. This opening is a stark contrast to the rest of the film and narrative that increasingly descends into the geographical space of the Amazon as "the unknown." This contrast, however, provides vital information to the audience: there is potential for European-style cities and civilization in the tropics. As the crew moves to less "civilized" zones, encountering a jungle of naked Indigenous peoples and wild animals, footage shows Roosevelt handling a dead jaguar, reminiscent of his big game hunting trips in Africa. At one point a still robust Roosevelt appears leaning gingerly over the side of a riverboat steamer, pointing, and shooting his rifle at stray alligators, yet continually missing his mark. The film culminates in a shot of the Brazilian map and an announcement of the accomplishments of the journey. Edited after the trip, the film splices a before and after that bookends the journey. According to Roosevelt and Rondon's narratives, as the travelers went down the uncharted river, they confronted obstacle and adventure, including run-ins with Indigenous groups, hostile animals and insects, multiple diseases and injuries, and the death of three men in their party. At one point, Roosevelt, suffering from malarial fever, ultimately told the expedition to go ahead without him, nobly giving himself up to an almost certain death. Rondon, a true leader, stepped in and the crew carried Roosevelt on, until, after months of travel, the expedition finally re-encountered "civilization"—a small settlement of rubber tappers—having mapped more than one thousand miles of river. In this section I examine Roosevelt and Rondon's self-described personas through their narratives and photographs. Their self-perceptions form a crucial point of entry for understanding the ways their raced, classed, and national identities inform their goals and visions of the Amazonian wilderness.

On this journey, as told in *Through the Brazilian Wilderness*, Roosevelt is a commanding traveler, maverick, pioneer, and leader. Amid descriptions of flora and fauna and the thrill of observation and hunting, Roosevelt creates a set of definitions that center around the "true wilderness wanderer" who never travels the "beaten path." This wilderness wanderer exemplifies the masculine identity that Roosevelt seeks to reclaim post election defeat as his legacy and image. A wilderness wanderer, says Roosevelt, is someone with the capacity to confront any unanticipated danger and the wherewithal to document it: "The man does little; he merely records what he sees. He is only the man of the beaten routes. The true wilderness wanderer, on the contrary, must be a man of action as well as of observation. He must have the heart and the body to do and to endure, no less than the eye to see and the brain to note and record."[15] By Roosevelt's definition a wilderness wanderer is transformed into something beyond just an ordinary man, he can act *and* actively observe. Thus it is this agency and individualism, along with the danger of his destination, that establish him as superior. By writing *Through the Brazilian Wilderness*, Roosevelt is enacting the wilderness wanderer, demonstrating the brawn and the brains required to fulfill this definition. The act of categorization and collection, half the definition of the wilderness wanderer, is one of the key strategies of imperialism; through incorporating Otherness into a Western model of knowledge, imperial powers can visualize and then justify their conquest. The wilderness wanderer must be physically strong, while also managerially inclined, able to record and manage the actions of others.[16] A wilderness wanderer—a frontier surveying, masculine explorer—could reject technologies that stripped a sense of active masculinity while also employing it to map, civilize, and manage. There is a technical superiority implied in the act of recording; a true wilderness wanderer must be able to wield the tools of imperial surveillance while moving through difficult terrain. This involves repeatedly emphasizing the danger and hostility of the Amazon that requires taming though knowledge and observation. Here, Roosevelt seemingly imagines the wilderness as a backdrop against which to prove his virility. As such, the wilderness he describes is at once untouched and hostile.

Roosevelt, as a wealthy, powerful outsider in the Brazilian interior, pushes toward adventure that contributes to his masculine identity; yet by putting this territory on the map—shifting the very wilderness that defines his manliness into the known—he self-defeatingly destroys the manliness he is trying to define. As Cronon observes, wilderness itself is a construction of modernity dependent on the illusion of a dying frontier and the necessity of a dominating male to rediscover it:

> In the myth of the vanishing frontier lay the seeds of wilderness preservation in the United States, for if wild land had been so crucial in the making of the nation, then surely one must save its last remnants as monuments to the American past and as an insurance policy to protect its future. . . . To

protect wilderness was in a very real sense to protect the nation's most sacred myth of origin.[17]

The supposed vanishing North American frontier serves to promote ideals of a wilderness abroad, while domestic protection preserves the "myth of origin" of the nation, or the undisturbed, Edenic, virginal, value of nature. For Roosevelt, who had spent years exploring the American West and writing books about his exploits, this perceived lack of virgin territory presented a crisis of manhood. Where could a wilderness wanderer wander if the wilderness did not exist? As Slater writes about *Through the Brazilian Wilderness*, Roosevelt considered the Amazon a wilderness "because it was not known or mapped, nor in existence among books and scholars whose lives were far from the place itself. Adventure was the clear and only avenue to knowledge."[18] Adventure here becomes a means to collect knowledge, to strip the River of Doubt of doubt itself. Danger feeds into an idea of adventure fueled by travel and movement that make up the landscape of Roosevelt's perception of the wilderness.

Figure 2.2, from the inside cover of *Through the Brazilian Wilderness*, shows Rondon and Roosevelt together, captioned as equal-ranking colonels. Throughout this trip Roosevelt chooses to go by his army title rather than "former president," portraying a sense of identity based in combat. The explorers stand as though on a pedestal above their surroundings, which they survey with authority, while also glancing down toward the photographer, Lieutenant Cherrie, another North American on the journey. This situates the two men on an equal plane (even their outfits match), but above the rest of the crewmembers of the trip and the landscape itself. From this elevated viewpoint, the intrepid explorers can presumably see and do all. Rondon here carries the big stick, ready to lead down the unknown river. Their stances with arms akimbo appear robust, confident, and authoritative. This photograph demonstrates a masculine power that Roosevelt seeks to project along with the colonialist mindset of domination. Elevated above the landscape, their surveying gaze and explorers' garb invoke the image of the imperial explorer. Roosevelt's white American masculinity is in some ways troubled by the very presence of Rondon as a partly Indigenous man who is a joint leader of this expedition and the expert on the trip. As Poole explains, the Indigenous person was constituted as an object, while conversely the ethnographer could be a reasoned, thinking subject.[19] Rondon is both Indigenous and non-Indigenous, somewhere between subject and object. Rondon, in his role as an explorer on behalf

FIGURE 2.2 Photograph (originally captioned "Colonel Roosevelt and Colonel Rondon at Navaïte on the River of Doubt from a photograph by Cherrie") used as a frontispiece in *Through the Brazilian Wilderness* (New York: C. Scribner's Sons, 1914). Courtesy of the Library of Congress, The United States and Brazil: Expanding Frontiers, Comparing Cultures, https://lccn.loc.gov/14019126

of the Brazilian military, has adapted and thrived in the Amazon, and thus embodies the hope that the Brazilian nation had in miscegenation and incorporation of the wilderness. This demonstrates a position of tension in Rondon's identity, as he is a bearer of civilization while at the same time an outlier of the very nation he represents.

In setting up telegraph poles throughout the north and northwest of Brazil, Rondon believed that technology and exchange would lead to the nationalization of Indigenous peoples living in the region.[20] In establishing these outposts, he also worked to further resource exportation. Nonviolence was mandatory for Rondon and his troops. He believed that Indigenous peoples were simply at a lower developmental state that required gradual, paternal guidance toward civilization. As such, Rondon rejected the idea of religiously converting Indigenous peoples, instead expecting that they would eventually adopt the technology-driven ideology of positivism. However, in this approach the goal is still the destruction of indigeneity.[21] For the Brazilian state, the implementation of technology and development in the Amazon region, of clear economic interest due to the rubber boom and other potential development projects, would lead to the gradual acculturation of Indigenous peoples. While Rondon's policies paved the way for future development and ultimately destruction of the way of life for many Indigenous civilizations, his policy of nonviolence is often lauded as ahead of his time. As Diacon acknowledges, "General Cândido da Silva Rondon firmly believed that he could both protect Indians living in the Brazilian northwest and at the same time develop the region through infrastructural expansion, colonization and support for the rubber industry."[22] A coupling of development and paternalistic protection formed the basis of Rondon's mission in the Amazon.

Rondon's use of technology toward that end is two-fold: First, his missions revolve around the idea of opening communication with the frontier by establishing telegraph outposts. Second, he made sure that everything was extensively documented both on film and in photographs. The establishment of telegraphs conquers distance and opens communication with the interior, while photography visualizes this process and those involved. The films and photographs Rondon helped produce in his missions create a vision not just of the Amazonian landscape, but of peoples in the process of becoming Brazilians—the process of nationalizing (and modernizing) the Amazon.[23] Through photography and film produced in his explorations, Rondon helps to create an image of the Amazon as part of a new, emerging, modern nation. In so doing, as Fernando de Tacca notes, Rondon created a vision of Indigenous peoples ready and willing to be pacified: "Images show docile Indians subject to changes thanks to civilizing progress. Thus, an image of subjection is constructed, rather than an impediment to the territorial occupation of the nation."[24] An image of subjugation could serve Rondon's nonviolence and incorporation message while of course this "civilizing progress" ultimately leads to the elimination of the Other. As the "civilizer," Rondon is emblematic of the hope that the Brazilian nation at this time placed in the redemption of caboclo. On this journey and in Rondon's previous and subsequent missions in the Amazon, the camera emerges as a form of surveillance over land and populations, a tool of imperial gaze. The camera works as a device of documentation and preservation while also

Wandering Wildernesses 71

FIGURE 2.3 Rondon interacting in a staged-for-the-camera exchange with Paresi people on behalf of the Rondon Commission's telegraphic outpost work in 1913. Courtesy of the Acervo do Museu do Índio/FUNAI – Brasil, CRNV0837

demonstrating a technological superiority that categorizes, collects, and generates knowledge. Photography and exploration together, therefore, open frontiers and respond to a desire to visualize and to know, one step further toward civilizing the imagined wilderness.

In Figure 2.3 there is a clear message of gradual incorporation that draws on the sexualized exotic, moves to the semi-civilized, and focuses back in on Rondon as the guiding light of (social and racial) progress. We see Rondon with a group of Paresi people, involved in a staged-for-the-camera exchange. Centered are naked women, while those with clothing frame the image. Rondon, again in exploratory garb, hands a naked woman a gift, enacting a key trope of empire, the exchange of goods. The interaction appears convivial, yet a clear message is portrayed: in exchange there will be a gradual move toward so-called civilization. The Paresi men are clothed in shirts and trousers, while the women are naked other than the two dressed in full gowns framing the photograph, demonstrating both the sexualization of Indigenous women and the capacity of incorporation (and thus economic usefulness) of the men. As McClintock explains, there is a long history of fetishizing of foreign lands by imperial powers who looked at land and women in Asia, the Americas, and Africa as part of a "porno-tropics." This fetishizing is coupled with a desire to "know" a female interior and thus convert it into a mapped, known, male exterior. This conversion requires a male, paternal figure as the bearer of knowledge and reason. The focal point of the image, Rondon, actively reaching over and staging exchange, shows us a caboclo who has whitened himself through territorial conquest and his work in civilizing other Indigenous populations. While there is another explorer next to Rondon, it is important that he is the one handing over the gift, passing the baton of progress, suggesting that he has attained a level of civilization that the Paresi can perhaps achieve.

The Paresi interact with the camera's gaze in a variety of ways. In particular, the woman to the far right of the photograph gazes at the camera, at once playful and questioning. She smiles back directly at the camera, uninterested in the exchange, demonstrating her own "right to look." Mirzoeff describes the ways Othered subjects return or resist the gaze as countervisuality. This ability to exercise control over visual representation is used to maintain Western hegemony; however, as Mirzoeff explains, historically oppressed populations have claimed a "right to look," a countervisuality, and thus some autonomy. This playfulness suggests a subtle subversion of the seriousness of the civilizing moment and an unwillingness to participate in the staged encounter of the rest of the image. Her mocking countergaze echoes the gaze of the woman seated in the middle of the photograph who also stares back at the camera. She appears somewhat disdainful, and uninterested in the exchange going on behind her. As with Octavie Coudreau's photographs of Black and Indigenous people in the region, there is an assumed fixing of racial hierarchies in the visuality of the photograph itself, with the white explorer as the default standard of civilization; followed by the redeemed caboclo, now an agent of civilizing history; then the assimilated Indians; and the still-savage Natives at the bottom of the pecking order.

Images such as these work as a part of Rondon's agenda of gradually encouraging Indigenous peoples to become Brazilians, showcasing potential and at the same time creating an archive of a way of life that is being pushed toward an end. Photographs showcase a racial categorization of Amazonian populations, meant to demonstrate a hierarchy based on comparative difference.[25] Together with racial categorization, many of these photographs establish the landscape as a conquerable frontier where Rondon has begun to lay the groundwork for future development. Indeed, he is working to set up small settlements. Taken at face value for their authenticity, these images created an idea of on the one hand an exotic Other, and on the other, a population that was receptive, known, and ready for modernization.

Like Rondon's photographic project, Roosevelt's travel carries a very specific purpose—not to just hunt but to map and catalogue in the spirit of travel and adventure—partaking in his own brand of tourism. Roosevelt's invented wilderness wanderer uses Indigenous people to build a case for exotic adventure. In contrast, Rondon spent decades of his life *working* in the Amazon. Rondon in many ways embodies the wilderness wanderer of Roosevelt's fantasy, and Roosevelt dedicates a good deal of *Through the Brazilian Wilderness* to outlining his respect for Rondon: "Three times he penetrated into this absolutely unknown, Indian-haunted wilderness, being absent for a year or two at a time, and suffering every imaginable hardship, before he made his way through to the Madeira and completed the telegraph-line across."[26] Rondon's "penetration" into the unknown landscape and the danger of these foundational journeys earn him respect from Roosevelt, a respect of which Rondon is rather wary. Again, the sexual element of conquest is explicit, and penetration is shown to maintain the heroism of male explorers while also demonstrating the abundance and fertility of land and peoples.[27]

At a pivotal moment in the expedition, after the loss of a *camarada* (a local assistant to the trip) named Simplicio in the rapids, Roosevelt and Rondon convene, and Roosevelt airs his concerns about the safety of the journey. Rondon, in the practical and pragmatic leadership style he was known for, informs the former president of the impossibility of turning back, but instead compromises in shortening the journey as much as he can.

> And thus, we both came to an agreement, as Mr. Roosevelt concluded: "I knew two great colonels in my life: the one that resolved the Panama problem and . . . Rondon . . ."
> Reminding myself that he was a *verista*, I said nothing. . . .
> Continuing the topographic survey without the necessity of moving rapidly would allow us to fully take advantage of our technical resources.[28]

There is perhaps a tone of resigned annoyance whenever Rondon talks about Roosevelt in his memoirs, whereas Roosevelt repeatedly goes out of his way to compliment and praise Rondon, even dedicating *Through the Brazilian Wilderness* to him as a "gallant officer, high-minded gentleman, and intrepid explorer."[29] This passage demonstrates a theme of the expedition where Rondon attempts to talk Roosevelt down, somewhat allowing for

Roosevelt's demands to be met in the creation of his adventure. However, Rondon is always sure to press the importance of "technical resources" and the mapping of the river above all else. As the journey moves forward, and the North Americans continually fall ill, Roosevelt and Cherrie push to shorten the route and take less time to survey the land, much to the dissatisfaction of Rondon, for whom the mapping of the river is the goal, rather than the novelty of adventure. The admiring tone with which Roosevelt writes about Rondon demonstrates a patronizing attitude, where Roosevelt has nothing to lose as a symbol of white "civilization" and Rondon must work toward whiteness through his success as an explorer.[30] The relationship between the two men was characterized by Roosevelt's unabashed adulation and Rondon's more resigned acceptance of Roosevelt as the leading name on the expedition. The tension evident in Rondon's body language and facial expressions and in his writings about his dealings with Roosevelt reflect the position that he occupies between subject and object of the civilizing project.

The two explorers' self-fashioned identities demonstrate their national concerns as well as racialized positions within this contact zone. This once again fits with competing ideas of wilderness; Rondon works toward increased settlement while Roosevelt is consumed with adventure—adventure that could be used to prove his capacity and potential to manage Amazonian territory. Rondon, as a redeemed caboclo and bearer of order and progress, gives us some insight into an internal coloniality that works toward assimilation. Conversely, we see with Roosevelt's wilderness wanderer a character whose purpose is engaging in adventure, enjoying a position of privilege, and ultimately signifying a civilizing, external force.

Encountering and Staging Otherness

Moving from Roosevelt's wilderness wanderer and Rondon's embodiment as such, the two men's representations of Indigenous peoples demonstrate their ideas about technology, masculinity, and imperialism. An inextricable part of the idea of the wilderness depends on the Indigenous peoples populating the area, whom both Rondon and Roosevelt believe must be gradually incorporated into the nation, although in varying ways. Rondon, as a caboclo-civilizing force, represents Indigenous peoples as malleable, able to be brought into the fold. Rondon's views on the *camaradas* highlight their grit and ability to survive under duress—a point of pride in contrast to the supposedly racially superior North Americans. Rondon's memoirs emphasize the importance of the Amazonian caboclo, suggesting their role as settlers:

> The eminent head of the American Commission never again enjoyed the health with which he began the expedition; his son Kermit was also very frail because of fever. Lira and Cherrie with gastric infections; our men, attacked by fever, overwhelmed with fatigue, weakened, would have literally been defeated if they did not have the temperament of our admirable caboclos.[31]

While Roosevelt and the other important leaders from North America never fully recuperate from the journey, the camaradas, "our men," although beat down and overworked, show a resilience presumably unique to their racial makeup. While we are not privy to the identity politics playing out in Rondon's head, the figure of the caboclo represents (and Rondon embodies) the possibility of racial progress. Rondon observes the caboclos' ability to not only survive but thrive, as such encapsulating racialized hopes for the ultimate progress of Brazil as a nation. As Richard Pace notes, "in a sense an evolutionary sequence is introduced where civilization (superior) and semi-savagery (inferior) are distanced (the Native American Amazonians would be the true savages). Ideologically, this aids in the unquestioned continued political-economic domination of the urban over the rural."[32] Thus, caboclos could be seen as a higher step on the evolutionary ladder toward civilization or whiteness, at least partially because they were portrayed as able to survive an Amazonian environment. In keeping with his vision of wilderness, Rondon's goal in settlement and acculturation was to gradually turn Indigenous groups into small-scale farmers.[33] Indigenous peoples could become productive workers, like caboclos, and thus could be seen as valuable for the growing nation.

In Roosevelt's account, there are varying degrees of perceived Indigenous civilization—ranging from the camaradas to the "semi-civilized" Paresi and the completely "wild savages," or Nhambiquara. In film footage from *River of Doubt: Roosevelt/Rondon Scientific Mission*, one shot shows the camaradas lined up next to each other as the camera pans from man to man. The men are of Indigenous and African descent, wearing clothing that at the beginning of the expedition is already dirty and falling apart. Charged with most of the heavy lifting on a journey that lasted more than six months and faced constant setbacks and challenges, the camaradas at the lowest level of the trip's hierarchy had the most difficult tasks. In Roosevelt's descriptions of camaradas, they are skilled, experienced, and hardworking: "The paddlers were a strapping set. They were expert rivermen and men of the forest, skilled veterans in wilderness work. They were lithe as panthers and brawny as bears. They swam like waterdogs . . . one or two of them were pirates, and one worse than a pirate; but most of them were hard-working, willing and cheerful."[34] Roosevelt's description of the camaradas is based entirely on their expertise of the forest, and what he describes as their bodily abilities and experience in the wilderness. In Roosevelt's telling, the camaradas are not men, but animals. As the journey continued, one of the camaradas, after months of arduous travel, even murdered another porter and was left behind in the jungle. Rondon had previously faced issues of recruitment for his telegraphic missions as no one wanted to brave the jungle for such little pay. These camaradas are not voluntary wilderness wanderers seeking adventure—they are either army recruits who have been assigned or rubber tappers in need of money, risking their lives for the sake of Roosevelt's adventure. Roosevelt seems to want to refute possible stereotypes of "laziness," as the work ethic of the camaradas elevates them to a higher level of humanity, citizenship, or whiteness: "one could not but wonder at the ignorance of those who do not realize the energy and the power that are so often possessed by, and that may be so readily developed in, the men of the tropics."[35] Thus, in Roosevelt's hierarchy, the bodies of the camaradas are worthy of praise and further development or civilization in order to harness their "easily developed" raw power. As such, Roosevelt perceives their skill in the wilderness, like that of Rondon, as a marker of civilizing potential. In making these observations Roosevelt also sets himself apart as an observer with the superior capacity to manage based on his race, gender, and nationality.

For Roosevelt, while the camaradas are already an established workforce, in descriptions of the Paresis people, a certain attraction based on future potential is apparent: "The Paresis Indians, whom we met here, were exceedingly interesting. They were to all appearance an unusually cheerful, good-humoured, pleasant-natured people. Their teeth were bad; otherwise they appeared strong and vigorous, and there were plenty of children."[36] Here, Roosevelt emphasizes the Paresis' possibility as future workers, which to him form the basis of their value. In his telling, the Paresis have begun the process of incorporation by living in settlements around Rondon's telegraph stations, engaging in small-scale farming, and dressing in "shirts and trousers."[37] Roosevelt chooses to explain the Paresis as an interesting but childish people who have begun the "civilizing" process with success. In processes of national incorporation there is a general paternalism wherein Indigenous peoples become children of the land that require a strong, masculine leader to take an interest and fashion them into children of the nation, an impulse directly articulated by Roosevelt.

According to Roosevelt, in contrast to the relatively "domesticated" camaradas and the somewhat agreeable Paresis, the Nhambiquara remain unsettled and considered dangerous—yet still appealing. As Roosevelt writes about Rondon's fair treatment of Indigenous peoples, he remains wary of the Nhambiquaras' chances of incorporation into the nation: "In spite of their good nature and laughter, their fearlessness and familiarity showed how necessary it was not to let them get the upper hand. They are always required to leave all their arms a mile or two away before they come into the encampment. They are much wilder and more savage, and at a much lower cultural level, than the Paresis."[38] Roosevelt seems to almost respect the insubordination of the Nhambiquara, while also wishing to assert his dominance and make them bend to his will. Adding to his argument of the Nhambiquara as part of the construction of a hostile wilderness, despite a good nature and future potential, they are still not to be trusted, as in coming to camp the travelers must leave their weapons behind. As such, Indigenous people like the Nhambiquara can add to the Roosevelt's adventure narrative. Furthermore, the former president's attraction to Brazilian "savages" elevates them above the Africans of his previous experience, "Nowhere in Africa did we come across wilder or more absolutely primitive savages, although these Indians were pleasanter and better-featured than any of the African tribes at the same stage of culture."[39] These "stages of culture" categorize local people in the different contact zones that Roosevelt enters. In his fashioning, in Africa, perhaps local peoples are more developed or closer to US ideals of civilization, yet the Brazilian Indigenous person is more appealing because of their racial makeup and role in wilderness creation and expertise.

Roosevelt often details Nhambiquara beauty at length, especially focusing on unabashed nudity and good-looking women: "They did not have on so much as a string, or a bead, or even an ornament in their hair.... The women and girls often stood holding one another's hands, or with their arms over one another's shoulders or around one another's waists, offering an attractive picture."[40] The imperial male gaze sexualizes and transforms this otherwise quotidian scene into "an attractive picture." This attraction is linked to the idea of the Amazon as distinctly feminine, unknown, and ripe for conquest, and the inseparability of the forest from its peoples. There is also of course the sexual element to conquest, and an attraction to the conviviality of the Nhambiquara as they are comfortable not only in their nudity, but with each other (as seen in their physical intimacy with the same sex).

In an article published in *The Outlook* in February 1914, just after his Brazilian adventure, Roosevelt delves into his observations on racial issues in Brazil. He begins by stating diplomatically that he is not condemning the Brazilian or North American attitude toward Black people but rather setting forth and stating, "what the Brazilian attitude is in fact."[41] He compares Brazil to the United States in terms of how they have dealt with what he deems the Indigenous and "negro problem." He expresses surprise at how Brazil has created an environment of miscegenation to gradually work toward whiteness but is concerned that this will lead to the contamination of the country, "In Brazil . . . the idea looked forward to is the disappearance of the Negro question through the disappearance of the Negro himself—that is, through his gradual absorption into the white race."[42] According to the former president, the United States, on the other hand, treats other races with the respect that each man deserves, yet prefers to keep the races separate. Roosevelt's view on Indigenous populations as expressed in this essay is a point of comparison and illustrates, perhaps, how Roosevelt views Rondon as someone of Indigenous heritage. "If I were asked to name the one point in which there is complete difference between the Brazilians and ourselves, I should say that it was in the attitude toward the black man. As the Indian becomes civilized he is absorbed into the population, as is the case with us in Oklahoma, and whoever has Indian blood in him is proud of the fact. The president of Brazil is one of these men, and there are a number of others among the leaders whom I met."[43] There is a certain pride that comes with Indigenous heritage despite the continual insistences Roosevelt makes that most leaders he met in Brazil were as white as any elite class in North America or Europe. As he says, "the evident Indian admixture has added a good, and not a bad element."[44] This can be seen in the ways that Roosevelt talks about Indigenous people on his trip and in his admiration of Rondon. This attraction comes from what Roosevelt perceives as a certain ability to survive in the wilderness and at the same time a possibility of future assimilation. Roosevelt's written perceptions of race in the Amazon and Brazil at large stand in contrast to to the photograph in Figure 2.4, which stages an encounter between Roosevelt, Rondon, and the Nhambiquara.

Wandering Wildernesses 79

FIGURE 2.4 Roosevelt and Rondon meeting a "party of Nhambiquaras, very friendly and sociable and very glad to see Colonel Rondon. From a photograph by Kermit Roosevelt." Plate following page 216 in *Through the Brazilian Wilderness* (New York: C. Scribner's Sons, 1914). Courtesy of the Library of Congress, The United States and Brazil: Expanding Frontiers, Comparing Cultures, https://lccn.loc.gov/14019126

Here, the colonels are shown seated on horseback, noticeably above the Nhambiquara who circle around, unclothed and looking at the camera. Rather than staring up at Roosevelt or Rondon, those to the right of the photograph are all covering their mouths, staring, seemingly concerned or intrigued by the camera and photographer. Meanwhile, Roosevelt and Rondon pose their arms back in the same dominant manner as Figure 2.3. The Nhambiquara include men and women and one small baby. The caption lets us know that the Nhambiquara were "very glad" to see Rondon, despite looking with concern or curiosity toward the camera. Again, elevated above the landscape and people next to them, Roosevelt and Rondon carry guns on their laps; perhaps this is the big stick with which to ensure a happy greeting. The background shows what appears to be a clearing, as the forest has been felled in one of Rondon's telegraph settlements. This sparse background stands in contrast to Octavie Coudreau's photographs of Indigenous people who appear amid a stereotypical jungle environment with visible lush flora. This photograph can perhaps demonstrate that the Nhambiquara could be settled. The photograph stages an imperial encounter that is once again challenged by the gaze back at the camera. Rather than engaging in a "very friendly and sociable" manner as the caption dictates, there is a posed, even tense aspect to this meeting. There is a dynamic of countervisuality like in Figure 2.4, where in gazing toward the camera there is perhaps a refusal to interact and happily greet these explorers. This image visually frames difference in dress, stature, class, and race, while suggesting a possibility of integration through the landscape and caption. This photograph demonstrates a key manifestation of both racial and technological superiority. As Roosevelt and Rondon sit mounted, guns on display and in full explorer garb, there is a factor of violence and intimidation that the caption glibly ignores.

Throughout his memoirs, Rondon asserts his dedication to the cause of Indigenous pacification and incorporation into the Brazilian nation, embodied in the motto his troops knew by heart: "Die if you must . . . never kill!"[45] Rondon was dedicated to his notion of nonviolence that involved gradual assimilation (Roosevelt notes with shock, "He never killed one!"[46]), and after setting up camp during his telegraph expeditions, he would spend time teaching Indigenous people the national hymn of Brazil, along with raising the Brazilian flag every morning, working toward incorporation through building a national culture.[47] Rondon also acknowledged Roosevelt's agreement to his rules and deferment on treatment of Indigenous people: "Our understanding was perfect. Mr. Roosevelt understood my incentive, what pushed me beyond all else—political-social work, the pacification of Indians through goodwill, through justice and understanding, and to bring them toward civilization gradually, with the guidance that the light of positivism gave to me, concerned in bettering the human experience, in educating in the broad sense of the word."[48] As he states, Rondon sought to "pacify" Indigenous people through good will, bringing Native peoples from the perceived darkness of a remote past into the light of present-day advances through degrees of citizenship, order, technology, and education. Rondon's vision of education meant gradually pacifying Indigenous people through an exchange of gifts (Figure 2.3) such as clothing and a show of technological superiority with tools like the camera, firearm, and gramophone. These three technologies represent a trifecta of imperial rule—the camera serves to survey and document, categorizing Indigenous populations; the firearm carries the big stick symbolism as a threat of violent dominance; and the gramophone projects the sounds of cultured civilization through the jungle. After establishing peaceful contact with Indigenous groups along telegraph lines, the Rondon Commission would sometimes employ more settled peoples to help in the construction, maintenance, and operation of the lines. This became another way to technologically integrate Indigenous communities into the modernizing Brazilian nation and demonstrates the degrees of civilization represented by

Rondon as a caboclo.[49] Photography functions as a technology of change, as pictures of new technologies and the process of their creation helped create a visual narrative of development, expansion, and ultimately a new civilization in the tropics.[50] Not only a new civilization—for Rondon, this could be a better civilization, an Amazonian utopia.

Wielding these tools of empire on his previous expeditions, on this journey Rondon has the task of appeasing Roosevelt's thirst for adventure while maintaining his policies toward Indigenous peoples and checking in on his advances in the interior. For Rondon and his positivist ideals, humanity and universal fraternity are the only course toward incorporation: "The incorporation of Indians, savages, aborigines—not at all *bugres*, this unreasonable insult of French origin—as well as the proletarian masses, still camped on the margins of civilization, constitute particular cases of the utmost importance and urgency of the general problem, a religious problem imposed with ever-increasing vehemence."[51] Rondon rejects and heavily criticizes attempts at conversion of Indigenous peoples and the "proletariats," or those on the margins of civilization. Demonstrating his ideals of progress, the only truth lies in scientific exploration and humanism, tools that help to create a nation. To accomplish this, following Rondon's model, Indigenous people must be turned into Brazilians, with the first step being mapping their land and establishing contact. Rondon believes this transition should be gradual as he sees Indigenous people as simply at a lower level of development, needing to be brought into the national fold through exchange and acculturation.[52] Despite policies that were sympathetic for his time, this absorption—the forceful assimilation of Indigenous peoples into the Brazilian nation—was highly destructive.

Justifying his approach, and offering his view of history, Rondon expresses remorse for the way that Indigenous peoples were treated by Portuguese colonizers, "Thrown off the land, of which they were the legitimate owners, by the invader who came with shows of peace only to bring blood, ruin, destruction, all the while he [the Indian] is the most worthy of goodwill. It is about the redemption of the most sacred debt of honor, the reparation of the most painful faults and social errors of our ancestors."[53] As Rondon describes, the conquest of the Americas led to the destruction and blood of Indigenous people—the original owners of the land. Rondon's mission is then to repair the social mistakes of his predecessors. There is a hint of the idea of the noble savage here—that Indigenous populations are innately good, closer to nature, and as such, uncorrupted by civilization. These sentiments are reflective of Rondon's positivist ideals yet are complicated by his goal of settling the forest. These same technologies and placement on the grid lead to a reconquest of space and people, paving the way for future development and the destruction of Indigenous ways of life.

Rondon's projects involve the documentation of geographical space, as well as the physical characteristics and census data of Indigenous populations, a manner of surveillance and control based on a Western model yet with more attention to the role of Indigenous peoples and the individuality of different groups. As Rondon notes in his memoirs, "We break with the tradition of those who previously penetrated the jungles who, as part of industrial adventures or scientific studies, trampled the land, trespassing without recognition the land of the Paresi, Nhambiquaras, Queri-queri-uates, Orumis, Jarus, Urupás, Ariquêmes, Caritianas, and Caripumos, without causing them the least bother or violence."[54] In his telling, Rondon's telegraphic missions move away from the previous norm, and instead of trespassing into territory where they are unwanted, the commission recognizes, respects, and distinguishes between land and group. In calling out groups by name, Rondon acknowledges the heterogeneity of each community. Rondon's work means nation building based on a positivist model, which essentially saw Indigenous groups at a different and much earlier stage of social evolution, rather than as racially inferior.[55] Despite acknowledging Indigenous territories, the goal was to create Brazilian territory out of Indigenous lands and Brazilians out of Indigenous peoples, again, nationalizing the Amazon. This directly connects infrastructure development with racialized ideologies of domination. Social evolution, for Rondon, would lead to progress based on a positivist model of technology and development—a gradual acculturation.

Wilderness Mapping, Development, and Masculine Environments

Along with masculine authority over the Other, a vision of progress and potential helps make up part of both Roosevelt and Rondon's visions of the Amazon. In a North American context, with industrialization came a desire for supposedly uncorrupted land, and a sense of nostalgia toward the wilderness became a prominent theme to help define masculinity.[56] The nostalgia provokes a return, while in a Latin American context the wilderness remains to be developed. In this section I examine how Roosevelt and Rondon's imagined Amazons represent the land and environment. Their cultural representations shape narrative tropes about the Amazon that remain prominent until today, as noted in the addendum to this chapter.

Roosevelt's Amazon is a space described as delicate and beautiful but also violent and unforgiving: "In the deep valleys were magnificent woods, in which giant rubber-trees towered.... Great azure butterflies flitted through the open, sunny glades, and the bell-birds, sitting motionless, uttered their ringing calls from the dark stillness of the columned groves."[57] Here, deep valleys hold the key to further industrialization (rubber trees), while innocent butterflies flit forward from a "dark stillness," meaning that there is developmental potential in what Roosevelt characterizes as an unenlightened emptiness, another popular trope about the Amazon, that of an empty wasteland. This vision of wilderness is a made up of beauty behind which lurks danger, a part of its seduction. Roosevelt's descriptions of the flora and fauna of the Amazon create a sort of femme fatale of the jungle. While, in his fashioning, the female nature contains the power of the unknown, it is waiting for the masculine conquering power to tame it. The takeover of this imagined wilderness involves a sexual element where Indigenous peoples and lands are initially represented as ripe for the taking.

In many cases, landscape domination is a violent process spurred on by (masculine) technologies of conquest, perhaps the most important of which is the firearm. As previously mentioned, both Rondon and Roosevelt are almost always pictured with rifle in tow, ready to shoot at any menace. Throughout his narrative, Roosevelt complains about the lack of big game in Amazonia in comparison to his previous trips in Africa. At the same time, he makes sure to emphasize the number of smaller pests including blood-sucking bats, vicious piranhas, gnats, and mosquitoes that contribute to a hostile wilderness.[58] The ability to hunt and dominate game in this pre-animal-conservation era is quite obviously associated with masculinity. In Figure 2.5, Roosevelt, in his exploratory garb, holds up his prey's face, demonstrating mastery over the already dead jaguar. The background is dense in foliage, hinting toward the difficulty in acquiring the animal and standing in contrast to photographs featuring Indigenous peoples with a background demonstrative of potential progress (Figures 2.3 and 2.4). "But the jaguar was a formidable beast, which occasionally turned man-eater, and often charged savagely when brought to bay. He [Rondon] had known a hunter to be killed by a jaguar he was following in thick grass to cover."[59] As an occasional man-eater and apex predator, the jaguar becomes even more of a prize to subdue and thus legitimizes its killing while fortifying Roosevelt's sense of masculinity. This is one of the very few big-game

FIGURE 2.5 "Colonel Roosevelt with his first jaguar," photographed by his son Kermit. Plate following page 80 in *Through the Brazilian Wilderness* (New York: C. Scribner's Sons, 1914). Courtesy of the Library of Congress, The United States and Brazil: Expanding Frontiers, Comparing Cultures, https://lccn.loc.gov/14019126

animals that Roosevelt was able to snag on his journey. Hunting is another arena in which Roosevelt fails to demonstrate the masculinity he seeks. Due to the nature of the jungle, Roosevelt cannot kill enough big game to prove his dominance; instead he is continually bitten by smaller pests, and nature, it seems, dominates him.[60] There is the tension between conservation and preservation, where a sense of wild danger or a place to participate in the sport of big-game hunting must remain sustainable to be dominated in the first place. The wilderness becomes a commodity, where wilderness wandering is something that cannot be sustained because of the very consumption of space.

Throughout the journey, Rondon, sanctioned by the Brazilian government, gives names to freshly discovered rivers, rapids, and plains as they come across them. One tributary becomes the Rio Kermit (after Roosevelt's son), another Rio Cherrie (after the North American naturalist George Cherrie), a group of rapids is renamed Simplicio after the death of the eponymous *camarada* on them, and eventually the Rio da Dúvida is renamed the Rio

Wandering Wildernesses 85

FIGURE 2.6 The Rondon-Roosevelt Scientific Commission photographed at the end of their journey, renaming the Rio da Dúvida as the Rio Roosevelt with a signpost. Courtesy of the Acervo do Museu do Índio/FUNAI – Brasil, CRNV0896

Roosevelt, moving from doubt into the known. As Mignolo explains on the colonial politics of naming, like mapping it serves a political and economic agenda of increased control.[61] In one of the more famous photographs from the expedition, Figure 2.6, a significantly less hefty Roosevelt stands next to a large wooden signpost with the Rio Roosevelt carved into it, while the other leaders of the trip stand around him, hats off as a sign of respect, with Rondon staring brazenly into the camera. Roosevelt appears reverent (and tired), with his hand over his heart, seemingly moved to have this river bear his name. In contrast, Rondon's hands are relaxed nonchalantly in his pockets with his gaze suggesting the confidence and remove of a self-possessed leader. The signpost has been thrust into the forest ground, claiming the area for the expedition and changing the Brazilian map and landscape until today. One of the few physical records of the expedition, this signpost is what verifies their trek years later. Not only physically disrupting the natural setting, this signpost also becomes a declaration of territory for modernity, geography, "civilized" man, and it suggests the importance the Brazilian nation

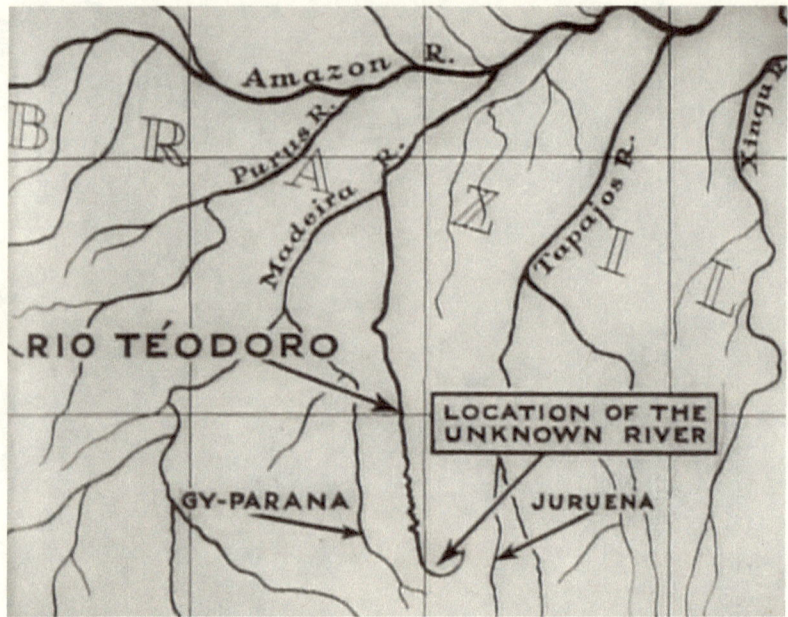

FIGURE 2.7 The Rio Téodoro replaces the River of Doubt in a still from the film made about the journey, *River of Doubt*. Courtesy of the Library of Congress and the Theodore Roosevelt Association, Oyster Bay, New York

at this stage of development gives to the United States. Furthermore, there is the monumentality and phallocentric nature of the signpost itself, as a left-behind monument that claims and disrupts the territory. Naming serves to organize the wild, entering the landscape into a new degree of civilization through being placed on the grid. In this case the social is inextricable from the spatial order as supposed virgin territories contain Indigenous inhabitants. As McClintock explains, the desire to name demonstrates a longing for a uniform, single origin, "alongside a desire to control the issue of that origin."[62] In mapping and re-naming, an idea of superior control is enacted and the wilderness stops being a place of wandering, becoming fixed. This organization links Roosevelt not only to Rondon but to Brazil for as long as the river is contained within the Brazilian map.

As the film *River of Doubt: Roosevelt/Rondon Expedition* announces toward the end in a still, "For the first time this great river has been explored from its source, and geographers are busy tracing upon maps, what looks like an elongated fishhook."[63] The camera focuses on a map of the area of exploration, showing the Madeira, Tapajos, Gy-Parana and Juruena rivers until the River of Doubt is (re)mapped in bold, the contours of the river traced over the existing map. Next, RIO TÉODORO in bolded capitals covers the other rivers, naming and claiming the waterway. The Rio Téodoro thus takes on a dominating importance over the other, previously mapped rivers. While the official name of the river is the Rio Roosevelt, as Rondon describes, "And so, as ordered by the Brazilian Government, this river, the largest tributary of the Madeira River, with its source at 13 degrees and its mouth at 5 degrees Southern latitude, entirely unknown to cartographers and, in large part, from its own local tribes, has received the name Roosevelt. Modestly, he [Roosevelt] suggested that it should be named Theodore." [64] Here, Rondon emphasizes the previously unknown origin and route of the river that by his telling even local groups did not know. In contrast, through scientific measurements, the Brazilian government has obtained direct coordinates, demonstrating their technological superiority and thus, in a sense, justifying their conquest of space. It is through their journey, then, that the river officially becomes a part of Brazil. Roosevelt "modestly" proposes naming the river Theodore over the Brazilian government's suggestion of Roosevelt. While the river is successfully named Roosevelt, his recommendation of Theodore is put into the film and some initial maps of the journey. Presumably, this show of modesty seeks to separate Roosevelt's name at least partially from the river since Teodoro would be less immediately recognizable as belonging to Roosevelt. However, the Brazilian government actively seeks this explicit connection, suggesting that they had planned the renaming of the river since the beginning of the voyage, and demonstrating a certain ideal of progress through name recognition with the United States. This naming and mapping can be seen as representative of the larger project of incorporation and documentation, bringing the Amazon from wilderness into landscape, developing the frontier, and attempting to transform Indigenous peoples into Brazilians.

Throughout *Through the Brazilian Wilderness*, Roosevelt sets forward suggestions for how the Amazon can harness its natural potential and immense landscape for future development. As others have discussed, Roosevelt viewed the Amazon with a frontier ideology, in that it was valuable not only as a playground for this grand adventure, but also as a place to develop and settle in a similar manner to the western United States.[65] Furthermore, ever with an imperial eye, rumors abounded that Roosevelt was intent on staking claim in the Amazon for the US, and some of his appearances were met with harsh criticism from Brazilians wary of outside control.[66] As Roosevelt observes, "there is much fertile soil in the neighborhood of the streams, and the teeming lowlands of the Amazon and the Paraguay could readily—and with immense advantage to both sides—be made tributary to an industrial civilization seated on these highlands. A telegraph-line has been built to and across them. A railroad should follow."[67] Paying homage to the technological advancements led by Rondon, Roosevelt notes the potential of the river-scape, and in the areas where he perceives the most possible development, begins to downplay the harshness of the environment, remarking that the area could be relatively pleasant for settlers. Here he engages with a Latin American vision of wilderness and the perceived need for settlement—preferably by white North Americans. Both sides of the river or perhaps both civilization and wilderness could benefit from industrialization. Through development the area can be transformed from a green hell (constructed to showcase Roosevelt's manliness) into an industrial Eden.

Rondon envisions the Amazon as a place for technological advancement, Brazilian nation building, and scientific exploration, all of which work together to form a more settled wilderness. In putting up telegraph lines, the Rondon Commission was mapping and delineating previously murky territory between countries, initiating contact with Indigenous groups, and working toward further colonization of the area. Ultimately, gradual acculturation of Indigenous peoples and a general taming of the wilderness was the goal. In their telegraphic and exploratory missions, the Rondon Commission was laying the foundation for future settlement: first comes the telegraph, then the railroad, and then true order and progress. The telegraph would lead the way to technological and territorial advancement, much as Roosevelt also predicts. Technology would lead to social development and a modernized Brazil. The creation of telegraph posts of course alters the surroundings, once dense forest is felled and outposts like those pictured in the background of Figures 2.3 and 2.4 become small settlements that gradually grow. As Rondon describes, "science transforms the world, and the paradise dreamed by people of bygone eras begins to take shape in the eyes of the modern generation, with possibilities that the past could not have even dreamed. Central heating and air conditioning resolved the problem of 'vital space,' because it was possible to obtain, for pretty much anyone, an agreeable climate with the desired temperature."[68] Remarking on climate control, we can see the faith and dedication that Rondon has in technology and technological advancement. As Rondon describes, technologies previous generations could only dream of are now possible for the modern generation, and these tools serve to make the Amazon increasingly livable and settleable. The best way to work toward incorporation begins with the mapping, photographing, or knowing process and continues with the implementation of new technologies until, at last, the wildest areas become managed and conditioned.

Conclusion

After the end of the voyage and Roosevelt's return to the United States, the Rio da Dúvida, renamed the Rio Roosevelt, officially became part of the Brazilian (and world) map. In 1919 Roosevelt died of cardiovascular disease, the roots of which some attribute to malaria he contracted during the trip. Rondon, on the other hand, carried on his telegraphing mission and died of natural causes at age ninety-two in 1958, with the northwestern Brazilian state of Rondônia bearing his name. In their self-descriptions, Rondon and Roosevelt spout an explorer ideology where Rondon seeks technology and Roosevelt seeks adventure, however both within the sphere of the perceived unknown. Rondon, as a caboclo, serves as the ideal force behind gradual conquest, embodying the racial progress of the Brazilian nation. Their descriptions and photographic representations of Indigenous peoples demonstrate Rondon's belief in assimilation and racialized progress along with Roosevelt's imagined wilderness. While wanting to patronizingly bring Indigenous peoples into positivism, Rondon embodies a similar contradiction to the wilderness wanderer—the impulse toward preservation and protection together with the perceived need for development that can only truly occur with destruction. Roosevelt's imagined Amazon is based in ideas of movement and travel, and in contrast, Rondon's Amazon seeks fixity as a settled space. In "penetrating" the jungle, or mapping, recording, and renaming throughout their journey, there is a sense of enlightenment, bringing the feminized backlands into the world of the known, and the transformation of the River of Doubt into a mapped and knowable space.

Both Rondon and Roosevelt grapple with the place of the Amazonian wilderness within a world geography and increasingly globalized culture. For Rondon, the Amazon is not so much a wilderness as his home. His vision of the future revolves around the gradual incorporation of the people and land that depends on technological integration. Roosevelt, on the other hand, fashions the Brazilian wilderness as a place to go *through*; an arena to stage his masculinity while peppering his text with imperial visions that hinge on white (preferably North American) management of the people and land. This chapter contributes a reading of these narratives as emblematic of the relationship between nature and culture embodied in the two explorer's visions of wilderness. These visions are dependent upon the positionality of the explorers and their projections of empire onto the Amazon. In the next chapter, we move from the transnational imperialism of actors such as Henri and Octavie Coudreau and Theodore Roosevelt into internal colonialities created in cultural representations by Brazilians about the Amazon region. These colonialities build on Rondon's views of gradual incorporation of Indigenous peoples and dialogue with a distinctly Brazilian idea of wilderness. In this shift, we see some intertextuality, where the narrative and visual culture put forward from trips such as these lends itself to the imaginary of different travelers grappling with the potential futures of the Amazon.

Continuing Conflicts and Extractive Reserves on the Rio Roosevelt

In 1914, after almost five months of remote wilderness travel, Theodore Roosevelt was seriously ailing. Suffering from malaria and a leg injury, he told the rest of his party to leave him behind to die. In just the nick of time, the depleted American ex-president and his Brazilian counterpart, Rondon, encountered rubber tappers along the recently renamed Rio Roosevelt in a dramatic and lifesaving stroke of fate. Those desperate moments were chronicled in *Through the Brazilian Wilderness*, and they also left a deep and lasting impression on the people the party encountered and the land they traveled through.

In a 2019 *National Geographic* interview with a rubber tapper and farmer named Raimunda Rodrigues da Silva, who lives in what is now the Guariba-Roosevelt extractive reserve, she recounts how her grandfather once knew the river as Castanho, then later as the Rio da Dúvida, and finally as the Rio Roosevelt. Da Silva also remembers how community leaders would tell the story of the ex-president's frantic arrival, as crew members knocked on doors for help and food, echoing the story told to me about Octavie Coudreau in Cachoeira Porteira and underscoring the lasting impact of these moments of cultural contact.[69] Elders who live in the area also remember Cândido Rondon as a well-mannered man who photographed and filmed everything.

The story of the descendants of the people the Roosevelt-Rondon expedition encountered and the land where they washed ashore exemplifies the conflicts that now characterize the Amazon region: the struggle over territory and land rights, a fight for sustainable economic initiatives, and the resilience of local peoples.

Near where the Roosevelt-Rondon expedition first re-encountered so-called civilization, or a dispersed group of rubber tappers along the Rio Roosevelt, stands what is today called the Guariba-Roosevelt extractive reserve. The Guariba-Roosevelt reserve lies between the Roosevelt and Guariba rivers in the northeast of Mato Grosso state and is composed of a series of protected lands including two state parks (Guariba and Tucumã), two ecological stations (Madeirinha River and Roosevelt), and two Indigenous demarcated lands—the Kawahiva and Piripukura.[70] The extractive reserve was initially set up in 1996 with financing from the Interamerican Development Bank (IDB).[71]

The reserve covers 405,806 acres of Amazon forest and is located 745 miles from the state capital Cuiabá. Around eighty families, who participate in rubber tapping and nut collecting as well as tending their own plots of land, currently live within the reserve.[72] According to an analysis with data from the Brazilian Satellite Forest Monitoring Service (PRODES), 43,404 acres of the Guariba-Roosevelt (11 percent of the total area) had been deforested by 2019.[73] Of this total, only 17 percent (7,203 acres) were already deforested at the time of the creation of the reserve, in 1996. The remainder (36,200 acres) has since been deforested, mainly by squatters who stay on the land and harvest wood. In 2019, the reserve had the third highest number of deforestation hot spots in the entire nation.

Extractive reserves, broadly speaking, are state-owned, designated areas where land usage, access, and rights are given to locals. The establishment of extractive reserves was led by rubber tappers (most prominently Chico Mendes) in the Amazonian state of Acre beginning in the 1970s, before their establishment throughout the Brazilian Amazon. Fighting against the longstanding exploitation of workers by large landowners, Mendes and other activists unionized and protested, famously drawing international attention and subsequent pressure, at great risk to their personal well-being.[74] On an extractive reserve, land is communally managed, and communities can practice subsistence farming as well as some small-scale extractive practices such as fishing, rubber harvesting, or nut collecting. Within reserves, residents practice a type of sustainable forest-based livelihood.[75] Mendes championed extractive reserves to give agency and land rights to rubber tappers, and to disrupt a system of debt peonage, a legacy of the rubber boom. He engaged communities who already participated in sustainable environmental practices and presented reserves to stave off deforestation and environmental degradation as large landholders continued to turn to profitable monoculture plantations.

Over the last forty years, extractive reserves have been established throughout Brazil, primarily in strategic areas to ward off the so-called arc of deforestation—a curve on the southeastern edge of the forest where deforestation due to cattle ranching, logging, and soybean production is occurring most rapidly.[76]

Today, the residents of the Guariba-Roosevelt extractive reserve, the only extractive reserve in Mato Grosso state, continuously fight off forest fires, illegal mining, and unsanctioned cattle raising. Hydroelectric dams have also sprung up throughout the region, beckoned in by highways like the BR-364. In fact, the BR-364 was built along Rondon's telegraph lines. Highways are one of the greatest harbingers of deforestation in the Amazon as they facilitate further extractive industry. Indeed, the reserve is in one of the most dangerous areas for small-scale extractors, Indigenous peoples, and environmental protectors in Brazil because of these constant threats.

The reserve is home to not only small-scale extractivists, but also several Indigenous groups including the Nhambiquara and Cinta Larga, both of whom are mentioned in *Through the Brazilian Wilderness*. The dispute for land between the years 1950 and 1970 resulted in state-sponsored massacres of the Cinta Larga, some with the participation of members of the Indian Protection Service (SPI), conceived by Rondon in 1952 precisely to protect Indigenous people. Federal government documents, such as the 1967 Figueiredo Report, indicate that around three thousand Cinta Larga may have been killed in this period.[77] The Cinta Larga have also been plagued by decades of conflict and today must continually combat diamond mining. The discovery of diamonds in the Guariba-Roosevelt Reserve by mining companies such as Sopemi, in 1970, linked to the South African group DeBeers, led a rush of miners to the Roosevelt River, aggravating the conflicts. With around two thousand Cinta Larga living between Rondônia and Mato Grosso, diamond mining has been occurring on their land since at least the year 2000.

In this remote corner of the Amazon, residents of the Guariba-Roosevelt reserve struggle to organize and improve contact with outsiders and find fair prices for their products like Brazil nuts and rubber. In 2010, they created an Associação de Moradores, a community organization, to collectively make decisions about conservation initiatives or other projects with which to get involved. The president of the community organization, Ailton Pereira dos

Santos, recalls that despite the difficulties that the community confronts with squatters and illegal logging, once they began collectively organizing, life significantly improved.[78] Despite the consistent threats and difficulties faced by extractive reserves throughout Brazil, the model is still widely considered to be one of the most "important tools to simultaneously decrease deforestation rates in the region, while also responding to social justice demands."[79]

It's not hard to see the Roosevelt-Rondon expedition as just one instance of interlopers intent on changing the region, and whose legacy of imperial thought and actions laid the groundwork for these continued and future threats. Yet, despite this, communities like those living in the Guariba-Roosevelt extractive reserve continue to fight for their collective territorial sovereignty and ability to live off their land.

CHAPTER 3

A Novice Traveler in a Land without History

Nationalizing the Brazilian Amazon

> And the Amazon, in constructing its actual delta in such remote areas as another hemisphere, bespeaks the unrecognized voyage of earth in motion, changing with the passage of time, never stopping even for a second, and shrinking, in an uninterrupted process of deterioration, the great land surfaces over which it travels.
>
> —EUCLIDES DA CUNHA,
> *The Amazon: Land without History*[1]

In the above epigraph, Euclides da Cunha uses nature to describe the universe, and throughout his writing on the region, the Amazon appears central to his understanding of Brazil's emerging national identity. Described as awe-inspiring, all-encompassing territory, Amazonia is a site of contradiction and change. In Euclides's essays *À margem da história* (literally "At the Margins of History"), published in 1909, the river and landscape form a malleable backdrop that a burgeoning Brazilian nation can develop, encompass, and contain with the right migrations. Euclides writes the Amazon as a spectacular natural phenomenon, involved in a constant process of change. He critiques previous depictions of the region to instead situate a Brazilian vision for the future of the region.

In Mário de Andrade's *O turista aprendiz* (*The Apprentice Tourist*), written between 1927 and 1929 and published as a whole in 1976, he too situates Amazonia as part of Brazil's natural, cultural exceptionality. For example, an alligator's movement transforms into a divine experience: "The forward thrust of the alligator left me in a very serious religious state. I swear that I felt God in the thrust of the alligator. What speed! What vast eternity in that gesture!"[2] Euclides da Cunha and Mário de Andrade spent much of their time in the Amazon remarking on active and impressive forces of nature, and the interaction between nature and culture. Both authors see nature and the national territory of the Amazon as a land in motion, ripe with potential and representative of the greatness contained within the nation. Building on the visions of settlement put forth by Cândido Rondon and the international interest in the region represented by Theodore Roosevelt in the previous chapter, in this chapter I analyze how Euclides's and Mario's depictions of the natural environment and Amazonian peoples demonstrate their attitudes toward the collectivity or individuality of the region, respectively, and, as such, its specific place within the Brazilian nation.[3] I argue that these visions, written by two of the most important Brazilian literary figures of all time, create the Amazon as a fundamental part of the nation. Where Euclides describes the Amazon as Brazilian territory, Mário establishes the region as cultural patrimony.

This chapter examines the Amazonian journeys of these two prominent Brazilian intellectuals. Euclides, writing about the Amazon during his 1904 trip at the height of the rubber boom, describes the region as a land brimming with possibility because of the unique and plentiful natural features and Brazilian settlers found therein. Mário, traveling to the Amazon post rubber boom in 1927, portrays a diversity of flora, fauna, and most importantly, people as central to Brazilian national identity. Their writings illustrate that Amazonia can be used for differing agendas, though both emphasize travel, movement, migration, and a new national identity. Euclides believes that through migration the Amazon can transform and develop into an integrated part of the Brazilian nation, while Mário seeks to make sense of a modern Brazil made up of groups moving from one place to another.[4] Because both authors experience the region through travel, like the writers from the two previous chapters, they present a touristic snapshot of the Amazon.

Euclides da Cunha and Mário de Andrade led personal lives fraught with rumor and intrigue. They both wrote foundational fictions of Brazil, and, for their time, held progressive and complicated views on race, culture, and national identity. In their most famous works, these authors focused on two prominent yet peripheral regions of Brazil—the Northeast and the North (Amazon). Euclides, in *Os sertões* (1902), his most famous work, writes an epic narrative of the Canudos rebellion in the backlands of the Northeast, while Mário in both *Macunaíma* (1928) and in *O turista aprendiz*, moves trans-regionally, from the Amazon to the Northeast, and in the case of *Macunaíma* on to the Southeast. Mário and Euclides travel to the Amazon from the more urban South of Brazil with the intention of describing their experiences to a wide audience, having established national reputations before their respective journeys. They demonstrate a fascination with the "primitive," and in their travels to the Northeast and Amazon they find a land and culture that resists or even defies modernity. Through their narratives, Euclides and Mário attempt to bring Amazonian land and peoples from periphery to center and establish them at the heart of Brazilian national identity. As Vivian Schelling notes, since the early colonial period in Brazil, elite and ruling classes used European culture to emphasize difference and maintain control over the racial makeup of the nation. This included education in Europe for the elite, and close ties with the colonial center—indeed Brazil only became a republic in 1889 (after nearly a century as a colony and monarchy). This helped to align elites with the "dominant metropolis," who continued to view Brazil as backward and peripheral, particularly because of Black and Indigenous influences.[5] This peripheral position is what Euclides and Mário attempt to re-align in their respective journeys.

Euclides, born in Rio de Janeiro state, was educated in military school and became a journalist and engineer, and many consider him to be one of the first sociologists in Brazil. Euclides's *Os sertões* formed a fundamental part of the Brazilian literary canon and made a major contribution to thinking on national identity.[6] In *Os sertões*, Euclides represents the backlands as a study of contrasts rooted in mixed-race characters from the Northeast who form the strength of the new nation. This publication catapulted him to fame, and in 1904 he traveled to the Amazon, writing the essays that make up *À margem da história*, eventually collected and published in 1909, the same year as Euclides's death at the hands of his wife's lover.[7] These essays formed what was to be the base of an epic narrative like *Os sertões* about the Amazon that he was never able to complete.

Like Mário, Euclides understands the Amazon specifically through travel. He sees the country in a state of transition that is more accurately depicted while in the process of journeying—also itself a transformative process. Travel to peripheral regions could allow him to engage with a specifically Brazilian cultural identity that was less influenced by the European avant-garde. Euclides also critiques the invisibility of the region's history as chronicled by previous scholars and naturalists, most of whom came from outside of Latin America.[8] As such, he often references other travel writers and comments on how they could never fully capture an Amazonian reality: "Hence this singularity: in all of the Americas it is the most sought-after place for the wise and yet it is the least known. From Humboldt to Emílio Goeldi—from the dawn of the last century to the present day, they all eagerly search for it [the Amazon]."[9] Euclides, in his Amazonian travel writings, is working to nationalize the region as both a Brazilian territory and part of the Brazilian social order through his position as a Brazilian nation-builder.

Euclides traveled to the Amazon for nine months as the head of a Brazilian-Peruvian commission to demarcate a border between the two nations along the Upper Purús river. His narrative thus has an explicit geopolitical agenda: to situate a historical and cultural precedent to Brazilian territory in the Amazon.[10] He does this through a sustained focus on the difference between *caucheros* and *seringueiros*. *Caucheros* are rubber workers residing on the Peruvian side of the border, who Euclides claims are nomadic and have no real connection to the land, in contrast to the more settled *seringueiros*, tappers in the Brazilian Amazon. This nomadism is at least partially attributed to the rubber extraction system on the Peruvian side of the border that extracts *castilloa* rather than the Brazilian *hevea* that more readily allowed for plantation-style tapping.

During the time of Euclides's travel, positivist ideals guided many intellectuals and politicians, as seen with Rondon in the previous chapter. Bringing order and progress to the peripheral regions of Brazil were key aspects of forming a united nation. Indeed, Euclides and Rondon were educated in military school together where they were exposed to these ideas. In contrast to Rondon, who fully adopted positivism throughout his life, Euclides became more skeptical. Frederic Amory traces Euclides da Cunha's relationship with positivism, arguing that while Euclides was interested in the philosophy during his schooling and in relation to mathematics, he never fully subscribed to the positivist vision of humanity (that the only reasonable knowledge must be scientifically verified or mathematically proven). Instead, Euclides, like many other Brazilian intellectuals, veered toward social Darwinism. Social Darwinism, or an idea of "survival of the fittest," differs from biological Darwinism and is essentially the idea that evolution is deterministic, where each stage of human society is a consequence of a prior, less evolved stage. Adapted from biological Darwinism by Herbert Spencer, social Darwinism in this period (Latin American nation-building) was used to scientifically justify campaigns to overcome "primitive stages of mankind."[11] In this sense, like positivism, social Darwinism was seen as "synonymous with progress, models to follow in the planning of a nation, racially and historically."[12]

Euclides's view of social Darwinism was coupled with environmental possibilism, evident in his writings about different racial and social groups.[13] Environmental possibilism understands culture as socially conditioned, where the environment can limit or foster said conditions. Within this ideology, humans are the active element within the human-nature spectrum. Environmental possibilism is different from environmental determinism—the idea that physical geography predetermines a culture's history and level of development. Euclides argues that the environment has played an important but not determinant role in human development in the Amazon. In his telling, to adapt to the environment, Amazonians have remained nomadic, as such hindering progress: "Adaptation is exercised through nomadism. Hence, in great part, the paralysis, at once disordered and sterile, of the people who for three centuries have wandered here."[14] For Euclides, nomadism has hindered the development of the region and serves to justify his argument for the migration of outsiders who would not be nomadic but establish life and society in settlements. He advocates for a kind of purposeful evolution led by the workers he envisions coming to foster economic development within the national and global system.

Several decades after the ideas of positivism were part of the prominent governing ideology, Mário de Andrade traveled in the Amazon and Northeast regions of Brazil from 1927 to 1929, writing short columns that were published together with his photography in *O diário nacional* and eventually compiled as the travel narrative *O turista aprendiz*. As a founding member of the Modernist movement in Brazil, Mário created poetry, photography, ethnography, song, and critical analysis that mirrored conflicts of racial and national identity of both the author and the Brazilian nation.

Mário, writing as a *mestiço* yet part of the intellectual elite from the South of Brazil, is himself a conflicted character. Mário's racial identity is not directly addressed in *O turista aprendiz*. However, he vocalizes his race in a poem he wrote near the end of his life called "Meditação sobre o Tietê" (Meditation on the Tietê [a river in São Paulo]) and there distinguishes himself as a "bardo mestiço," or mixed-race bard.[15] As a *mestiço* yet part of the intellectual elite, Mário laments his cultural whiteness. In his poem "Improviso do mal da América" (1928; Improvisation on America's ills), he begins with the line "Imperious scream of whiteness in me."[16] This sets the poem out as a struggle of personal identity, where whiteness assumes power or authority without justification, dominating Mário.

He ends the poem outlining his internal conflict and decrying his cultural whiteness, saying he feels neither Black nor red, but rather that he has a soul riddled with races.[17] Perhaps this internally conflicted position offers him a way to write a more inclusive vision of race and peripheral territory in Brazil that focuses on the individual experience.

Brazilian *modernismo* was itself a conflicted movement. As Vivian Schelling argues, it was defined by two intersecting ideas: synthesizing a European avant-garde and the discovery and affirmation of a differentiated national identity.[18] Traveling for three months in 1927, Mário experiences the Amazon during a relative lull in terms of resource extraction, as the rubber boom busted in 1913 and would only take on more significance in the context of World War II (as we will examine in the next two chapters). Rather than describing rubber boom migrations and processes, Mário thus seeks to distinguish Brazil through its inherent and unique characteristics. As Esther Gabara notes on Mário's relationship with modernism, "not satisfied with nineteenth-century, utopian nationalist representations of Brazilian natural phenomena nor convinced by Futurism's hyperbolic proclamations about the city, Mário combined experimental lyrics with photographic vision to create a modernist ethos."[19] This ethos, in the Amazon, creates a narrative that blends personal experience and literary sentiment, a combination of travelogue, ethnography, and imagined encounters that includes a variety of personal drawings, poems, and photography. For example, throughout his narrative he mentions the Do-Mi-Sol Indians, an imaginary group that he "documents" for their unique use of sounds rather than words, "As a matter of fact, it is worth noting that the number of sounds that they possessed was much larger than our poor chromatic scale."[20] Mário describes the imaginary tribe as sonically superior to the use of Portuguese as a language for poetry and song. This demonstrates his sardonic style that positions Amazonian culture, albeit imagined, as inspiring and perhaps even culturally more advanced.

The modernist movement in Brazil began in São Paulo, a relatively wealthy city due to a recent coffee boom (from the early nineteenth century through the 1920s). Beginning in 1922 with the Modern Art week, the first phase of modernism (1922–1930) marked a shift from cultural representations of the past and a move toward defining a Brazilian cultural tradition in the breakdown and destruction of previous, colonial, forms.[21] While taking influence from the European avant-garde, the first phase of modernism sought to create a uniquely Brazilian literary and intellectual tradition. It is during this first phase, one of breaking from the past and defining the present, that Mário travels to the Amazon. The second phase of modernism (1930–1945), focused on construction and was seen as somewhat softer than the combative reorganization of cultural norms from the generation of 1922. As a first wave modernist, Mário sought to break from representations of peripheral regions that simplified or copied a European primitive ideal. Instead, he engages with local culture through a self-reflective mixture of prose and photography. Mário produced more than four hundred photographs of his trip, along with indexes of Amazonian languages and descriptions of his travels to the North and Northeast that play with the structure and form of a travel narrative, while on a broader level exhibiting noncentral regions as central to Brazilian cultural identity.

Both Euclides and Mário approach the Amazon region with explicit purposes of incorporating the forest and its peoples into their definitions of a uniquely Brazilian culture. They are also preoccupied with the act of traveling and documenting itself. As such, they pull on travel narratives of previous European writers and purposefully distinguish their own writing as more accurate versions of the genre because of their status as Brazilians. Euclides often notes the failures of previous naturalists and geographers to fully capture an Amazonian reality. Mário explicitly pulls on travel narrative tropes to misappropriate and create an "authentically Brazilian inauthenticity."[22] Furthermore, both Euclides and Mário understand non-white Brazilians as fundamental parts of the nation, different from the governing racial ideology of their times. While they write for relatively similar purposes, I argue that Euclides focuses on the collectivity of the region's backland characters, while Mário individualizes and distinguishes the unique characters he encounters during his travels, demonstrating two differing ways of creating the Amazon region as part of the Brazilian nation.

The Amazon: A Land without History

During his travel in Amazonia, Euclides not only writes essays but also works on geographical mapping projects, defining territorial boundaries that contain an abundant nature to establish Brazil's national claims to the land. Traveling on a mission to delineate territory for the Brazilian government and help settle a border dispute, Euclides works to transform territory both literally and figuratively. As Lúcia Sá explains, in his Amazonian essays Euclides begins to move away from the blame involved in an "imperialist nostalgia" and toward more straightforward imperialism—"instead of blaming himself or his own country for eliminating cultures and the environment, he blamed other countries or the victims themselves."[23] By blaming other counties for Brazil's internationally peripheral position, Euclides justifies Brazilian dominance of South America, as it is the largest nation, yet in his telling it had been held back from harnessing its full potential. Euclides, traveling in a binational border expedition, conceives the Amazon as a space for Brazil to take over, as a land whose "destiny is to be colonized."[24] In writing essays that expound upon the different elements that make up the Amazon, Euclides is similar in some ways to Rondon in working to nationalize the region. The ambiguity of Euclides's project is found in how the land and people that he aims to nationalize also, according to him, defy categorization and collection. Euclides uses nature to write the Amazon into the Brazilian nation and reinforce a sense of inherent greatness or *grandeza*, while using archetypes of backland characters to justify Brazilian ownership of the land.

As a function of governmental control and modernization, borders, along with myths of national identity, form part of the project of nation building. In "Dreams Come Untrue," José Murilo de Carvalho posits that myths and heroes help nations "develop unity, organize the past, and face the future."[25] In Brazil, Carvalho argues, there is an overwhelming pride in nature that equates the country itself to an earthly paradise. As Carvalho explains, this myth originates in the first colonial gazes upon and writings about the "New World," when European modernity begins to be implanted in Brazil. For example, in Amerigo Vespucci's 1503 letter to Lorenzo de' Medici known as the *Mundus Novus*, he describes Brazil as an "earthly paradise."[26] As mentioned in the introduction to this book, the national myth of *grandeza* positions the country to become a great empire through modernity and development because of the sheer size and amount of its natural resources.[27] *Grandeza* posits that Eden is found within Brazil, feeding into a national myth of superiority and future promises of prosperity.

Euclides views the Amazon as a place of potential for the Brazilian nation. His remarks on the nature of the Amazon reveal a region that he views as at once expansive, varied, and at times monotonous. In the Amazon, Euclides also continually notes the encompassing natural environment: "It escapes us entirely, it can only be measured, divided up: this amplitude must be reduced in order to be evaluated; the greatness, which can only be seen, getting smaller, through microscopes: and an infinity that is dosed, little by little, slower and slower, indefinitely, torturously . . . analytical, long-term discourse is fatal. Human intelligence could not suddenly bear the weight of that portentous reality."[28] Here Euclides expounds on the expansive heterogeneity of the region that cannot so easily be documented or explained, despite previous attempts to do so. The Amazon is described by its greatness, both in terms of size and in terms of natural phenomena found within. However, as a writer from the tropics, the Amazon is perhaps less lauded for its natural features than seen as a site on which to project a mixed-race nation building.[29] It is also described here as a region in processual change ("long-term discourse is fatal"). For Euclides, it is only in breaking off small swaths that the region can begin to be understood. This is notable as he does not claim to be the ultimate authority on the Amazon, but rather another curious party who is better suited to understand and thus plot the future of the forest.

In the chapter titled "General Impressions," Euclides sardonically writes the Amazon as a place with a lack of history (a fresh, disorganized Eden): "Such is the river then, and such its history: tumultuous, disorganized, incomplete."[30] However, Euclides is fascinated by the regional (environmental) history, and in his travel, he works to write a history that can justify the region as part of Brazilian territory. Euclides is traveling at the height of the rubber boom in areas dominated by violence and conflict. This is not a land without history, but rather a land where history is rapidly unfolding. Yet by positioning the region as incomplete, Euclides can suggest that under the right guidance the Amazon could fulfill its destiny as a source of great wealth and neo-imperial power for the emerging Brazilian nation. In writing about the Amazon, much as Euclides previously did with the *sertão*, he is writing the backlands into existence within a national identity. In *Os sertões*, Euclides also calls the *sertão* history-less, a region in constant change that is modified by the environment, linking the *sertão* with Amazonia as abject, or condemned ecologies.[31] This representation as a wasteland creates a further justification for Brazilian claim to the land as it could be seen as empty and unclaimed, thus Brazil, as a neo-imperial power, can claim, harness, and develop it.[32]

Despite a rhetoric that works to incorporate and justify Brazil's claim to Amazonian territory, Euclides describes not only the strangeness of the Amazon itself but his own feeling of being a stranger, estranged from the central Brazilian state, while still within the nation. As he writes, "He [man] feels dislocated in space and in time; not outside his country but nonetheless estranged from human culture, lost in the hidden recesses of the forest and an obscure corner of history."[33] This dislocation in time and space, in a land perceived as evasive of previous implantations of Western history, points to new possibilities as a new history, according to Euclides, remains to be written. However, a void still exists within his country; it is at once foreign, new, and exciting while, most importantly for Euclides's purposes, contained within the nation. As Rex Nielson notes, "on the surface da Cunha makes a case for considering the Amazonian territory as essential to the Brazilian national project, his writing simultaneously focuses on the strangeness, the otherness of this landscape that by its very nature seems to resist identification with the Brazilian nation."[34] As seen in *À margem da história*, nature in the Amazon seems to dislocate culture, making Euclides's project of implanting culture one of the ways to lay claim to the land. This conflict demonstrates the discord between Euclides's political project of border creation with his personal impressions of the forest.

Within the Amazonian wilderness, Euclides notes the role of humans: "The overwhelming impression I had—perhaps corresponding to a positive truth—is this: humankind is still an impertinent interloper here. We have arrived uninvited and unprepared for, while nature was still in the process of setting up this vast, magnificent salon. And they encountered an opulent disorder."[35] We can once again see the idea of process—the Amazon region, and the nation of Brazil's future ascension as a neo-imperial power, is dependent on migration, settlement, and incorporation. As Hecht explains, Euclides views the landscape as "rooted in continuities of incremental change rather than divine design or simple disaster."[36] Euclides's view of Brazilian gradual change in the hinterlands hinges on internal migration and as such settlement into the nation. However, there is a constant anxiety of a peripheral modernity where Brazil, despite containing landscapes and people ripe with potential, does not achieve the modern, imperial status of other nations.

To that end, Euclides's writing situates the Amazon as a site where the tropical climate would not be a deterrence to Brazilian colonization. Indeed, as an intellectual from the tropics, Euclides cites the failure of previous colonizing efforts, again politically maneuvering for Brazilian control of the land. Euclides, in his chapter "This Accursed Climate," elaborates on the challenges facing Amazonian development as he recounts the history of imperial powers that have previously colonized in similar landscapes: "Open any regulation book of colonial hygiene. What stands out even to a cursory reading are the incomparable efforts of modern colonization and its complex mission, which, in complete contrast to that of its predecessors, do not contemplate introducing the transformed barbarians to civilization but rather transplanting civilization integrally to the primitive and adverse barbarian territories themselves."[37] Euclides expounds this strategy for colonization of the Amazon region, following a model that steadily "transplanted" civilization onto the Other. He distinguishes Brazil as especially adept at colonizing, briefly mentioning cases of unsuccessful models in English, German, and Belgian colonies where official agents had to return home after just a few years. Using Acre (a state in the Amazonian northwest, bordered by Peru and Bolivia) as an example, he argues that through the settlement of *sertanejos* fleeing drought in the Northeast, the colonization of a particularly difficult land has been successful and stands as a model of progress not just for Brazil but for the entire world. This perhaps criticizes Rondon's positivist model for gradual Indigenous incorporation examined in the previous chapter. Rather than an introduction to civilization in stages for those already living in the region, in Euclides's narrative, the Amazon requires continuous transplantation of people to the territory, thus gradually transforming the landscape. Also different from Rondon is Euclides's focus on the "barbarian territories themselves," which he views as territory that can be potentially managed through migration of mixed-race workers.

For Euclides, Amazonian land is difficult or impossible to fully know, as the naturalist or geographer can only understand small parts of a much greater whole. While mentioning his sense of the staggering greatness of the region, the land, he argues, is still irrevocably Brazilian: "In such places the Brazilian, albeit a foreigner, would be walking on Brazilian land. Which leads to an astounding perplexity: to the fiction of extraterrestrial law—country without land—is counterposed another basic physical concept—land without country."[38] Again, this passage politically maneuvers for Brazilian territorial claim. Indeed, he is here positioning his vision for increased migration to the region to transpose country onto the land. Euclides draws on occidental geographical knowledge yet translates it through a Brazilian lens, working toward building a nation both geographically and culturally.[39]

Euclides's writing about Amazonia positions the Brazilian nation to stake claim over Peru to the land. Euclides describes an emerging civilization in the tropics, one that is definitively Brazilian. He follows an imperial ideology, creating comparisons between the two nation's histories, cultures, and natural features. In this sense, Brazilians on Amazonian land needed to be written as already part of the nation. As such, he creates the landscape as uniquely Brazilian ("would be walking on Brazilian land") and begins to naturalize the Amazon region into part of the nation. Euclides's writing about the landscape is coupled with a sustained focus on migration, using sweeping poetic language to convey a space that calls for further settlement by a uniquely Brazilian cast of characters.

Migration to Build the Nation

A primary preoccupation of intellectual elites in Brazil and South America in general during this period was how to create a "civilized," that is, white, nation.[40] At the turn of the twentieth century, immigration was used as a political tool to create a modern Brazil that could gradually move toward whiteness through the settlement of "desirable" immigrants.[41] Immigration was used by elites as a means of creating a superior nation, and successful migration that had already occurred to the Amazon was used to justify Brazilian territory.[42] Against what other intellectual elites and nation builders proposed and did as a whitening project of encouraging the migration of white Europeans to Brazil, Euclides instead argues for mixed-raced Brazilians who already make up the peripheral regions as the true backbones of the country. According to Euclides, further development is conditional on the right type of migration and adaptation, or a settlement by Brazilians for Brazil. This can conveniently fit into Euclides's thesis throughout *À margem da história*: that the continued incorporation of the Amazon is dependent on increased migration and settlement of a mixed-race worker, rather than the integration of existing groups.[43]

Euclides focuses on the strong sturdiness of male rural workers, using them as an example of Brazilian exceptionality and pitting them in contrast with Peruvians. Indeed, he hardly comments on women at all throughout his narrative. Due to the Great Drought (1877–78) in the Brazilian Northeast, many Northeasterners, the majority of whom were poor sharecroppers, called *sertanejos*, were unable to maintain their land. Hundreds of thousands of these sertanejos migrated to the Amazon and transformed into *seringueiros*, or rubber tappers.[44] As seringueiros from coastal regions of Brazil had already begun the difficult process of working the land during the rubber boom, according to Euclides, they laid claim to the space in that process.

Euclides explains the great potential of mixed-race Brazilians in Amazonia, explicitly linking race and environment. As he explains, the environment itself has determined who is worthy to populate it. "It [the Amazon] has policed, it has cleansed, it has moralized. It has selected and continues to select the worthiest for life. It has eliminated—and continues to eliminate—the less able, through flight or through death. It is a climate to be admired that prepares new regions for the strong, for the steadfast, and for the good."[45] Here Euclides very explicitly lays out his ideology of environmental possibilism in the Amazon, where nature at least partially evaluates who belongs and who does not. In this telling, the environment provides a challenge that only some are worthy of surviving, where ultimately man, or the right type of man, will create "the good." For Euclides, the ideal type that should settle the Amazon is the seringueiro, most often a mixed-race caboclo, who, as a specifically Brazilian character, is the hero worthy to transform the landscape. This is reflective of the value he places on backland people, as it is the caboclo who "come in spite of the environment. . . . They have been victorious in a battle to the death."[46] Thus, within a climate described by Euclides as challenging, it is the caboclo, racially emblematic of Brazil as a whole, who can withstand and ultimately transform the wilderness. The caboclo has *chosen* and already occupied the difficult terrain, thus creating a legitimate claim to the land.

Ideas of degeneracy, pervasive at the dawn of the Brazilian Republic, characterized miscegenation within Brazil as part of the perceived backwardness of the nation, partially through the tropical environment that "reduced individuals to unproductive laziness and society to a parasitical organism."[47] However, as discussed in terms of Rondon in the previous chapter, the "redemption of the caboclo" was used as a political tool to encourage miscegenation toward whiteness, and as such a gradual national racial cleansing. Euclides's championing of the backland character of the *caboclo seringueiro* as the authentic Brazilian can be seen as one of the ways he conformed to the nationalizing project while also critiquing it. Rather than explicitly promoting the whitening project, he centers national identity around the specifically Brazilian racial mixture that already exists. Indeed, as Frederic Amory notes, Euclides's experience of the Canudos rebellion that prompted *Os sertões* led him to question his attachments to Brazilian Republicanism because of the Brazilian army's role in slaughtering the diverse residents of the rural settlement. Once he was sent to the Amazon and witnessed rubber era abuses toward workers on the Peruvian side of the border, he became more deeply convinced of the Brazilian nationalizing project.[48]

For Euclides an idea of Brazilian *grandeza* is reinforced through the landscape itself ("It is [the Amazon] nonetheless, doubtless the greatest sight in the land"[49]), and the possible implantation of sturdy, problem-solving backland characters such as the sertanejo transformed into the caboclo seringueiro. As Leandro Guimarães discusses, "the Brazilian problem, for

Euclides da Cunha, was to civilize, witness, and develop, above all, the sertanejo-seringueiros, abandoned in the forest and interior of the country."[50] Euclides purposefully writes the value of Amazonian inhabitants as dependent on their ability to function within the landscape, similarly to the sertanejos he describes in *Os sertões*. These Amazonian inhabitants are portrayed in contrast with the more nomadic trajectory of settlers living in the Upper Purús, again as a manner of staking claim to land. Individual struggle worked toward a collective goal, that of claiming and transforming Brazilian territory.[51] Rather than focusing on individuals, Euclides chooses certain peripheral characters to stand as representative of this stage of Brazilian social evolution and environmental possibilism. Euclides's perceived idea of the greater good for the Brazilian nation characterizes his Amazonian essays where he takes himself out of the picture (as compared to Mário's highly self-reflective journal). His border-creating imperial ideology emerges in his casting of Brazilian characters as the ideal pioneers of the Amazonian frontier.

Mark D. Anderson examines literary tropes of abject landscapes, primarily the Brazilian interior (*sertões*) and Amazonia. He looks at *Os sertões* next to *À margem da história*, arguing that positivist ideals lent themselves to conceptualizing abject landscapes as areas to be developed, or lost paradises that must be reclaimed. This conceptualization reflects racialized ideas about the populations in abject ecologies: "Therefore, the indigenous either became part of non-human nature, or they too required expulsion from the garden, or at the least infusion with European genes and culture to transform into civilizable, mixed-race caboclos."[52] To successfully become part of the Brazilian nation, immigration as well as miscegenation would have to occur. Immigration and miscegenation point to a land in transition, in an unfinished state of becoming. Euclides describes the region as in transition, but it is a transition that is already being led by Brazil, another means of staking claim to contested territory. The development of the Amazon would depend first on the demarcation of Brazilian borders, which itself was dependent on Euclides's trip and version of history that posits the already occurring settlement of the region by Brazilians.

Euclides advocates for the workers that he sees as the future of the Amazon. Traveling at the height of the rubber boom, Euclides spends a large part of his narrative denouncing violence against seringueiros and suggesting ways that the Amazon can become further settled: "What comes definitively to the fore is the urgent need for measures to rescue this hidden, abandoned culture: a work law that ennobles human effort; an austere justice that curbs excesses; and some form of homestead provision that definitely links man and land."⁵³ Here Euclides remarks with concern toward the culture of the seringueiros, frontier workers who have come to work in rubber plantations under dire conditions. Indeed, his use of the word *culture* emphasizes and elevates their importance. Euclides continually expresses a disdain toward nomadism, which he uses to again write for a Brazilian claim to land as, by his telling, there is far more settlement by Brazilian seringueiros than Peruvian caucheros. He suggests that the best way to settle the Amazon is to continue to import migrants from the Northeast and offer them a simple, regulated system that will facilitate settlement and "definitively link man and land." This can be seen as a way that Euclides socially advocates for the populations he sees as the future of Amazonia, or the Brazilian nation. In the above quote, Euclides notes the responsibility that the Brazilian state owes to these homesteaders through their work in establishing Amazonian settlements and thus incorporating the region into the nation.

Euclides describes the seringueiro as cunning and intelligent enough to mobilize the environment to their benefit. He shows a certain respect for the seringueiro and an admiration of their adaptability and traits necessary in the wilderness. "He is a case of psychic mimetism: a man who pretends to be a savage to defeat the savage. He is a gentleman and a Wildman according to circumstance."⁵⁴ This character trope of the Brazilian seringueiro once again represents a racialized ideal for the Amazon—as Euclides describes, he can be a man who (pretends) to be savage while also someone who can behave in polite, civilized society. This demonstrates Euclides's view of the adaptability and intelligence of the mixed-race seringueiro. This respect echoes Euclides's previous portrayals of the sertanejo as the person who can connect nature and culture. This admiration builds to Euclides's point—that with the right migrations, the Amazonian frontier is destined for greatness.

Euclides goes on to say, "a Brazilian discovered *caucho*, or, at least, established the industry of its extraction. I do not go alone in my reconstruction of this chapter in our History, which, if fully developed later by a historian, might be entitled: 'Brazilian Expansion in the Amazon.'"⁵⁵ This writing of Amazonian history establishes Brazilian precedent to the land, and credits Brazil with "discovering" rubber, further justifying Brazilian claim to the region. Coming ten years before the rubber boom busted, Euclides, much like other travelers, prospectors, and locals, believed the economic prosperity of the Amazon would be neverending. Euclides, in suggesting this reconstructed chapter of history, is producing knowledge about the region while also inserting an internal coloniality. In Euclides's configuration, Brazil, due to its history and the discovery of the wealth of the Amazon (rubber), is destined to expand and lay claim to the contested territory.

For comparison, Euclides turns to the state of the rubber industry in neighboring Peru. Amazonian *castilloa* rubber trees, more often found on the Peruvian side of the border, defied plantation style growth due to blight. This required rubber workers to increasingly move deeper into the forest, creating multiple difficulties for the rubber industry, primarily how to monitor and control their workers, which in turn facilitated a pervasive culture of violence.[56] As Euclides explains, "the exploitation of *caucho* as the Peruvians practice it, with its felling of the trees and the constant movement in search of undiscovered stands of Castilloa in an endless professional nomadism, leads them to practice all manner of abuse in the inevitable confrontations with the natives, and thus brings with it the systematic disruption of society."[57] According to Euclides, workers in Peru, linked to the environment, are nomadic, prohibiting their settlement of the area. If modernization is based on ideas of settlement, a containment that leads to growth and structure, the Peruvian rubber industry represents the opposite. The nomadic nature of the industry itself leads to abuse and "disruption," or a lack of so-called civilization, particularly on the Peruvian side of the border.

The Peruvian caucheros are then presented as nomadic and uncivilized in comparison with the more settled Brazilian seringueiros. Euclides argues that settlement is essential to spur development and end exploitative practices of debt-peonage utilized during the rubber boom. "The man who dwells there invests no effort to improve a place from which he can be expelled at any time with no right of appeal."[58] This presents caucheros as debt-peons and is used to advocate for Brazilian claim to the land because as a nation it will work toward settlement, the slow march toward "progress." In some ways this is like Rondon's vision of small-scale settlements in the Amazon with the intended outcome of incorporating the region into a burgeoning nation. In presenting Peru as an example of abuse and mismanagement, Euclides politically maneuvers for Brazil's claim to Amazonian land.

The Amazon, for Euclides, is a region where Brazil can exert its imperial potential. As such, he positions the Brazilian nation as already leading the settlement of the region and argues for the importance of mixed-race Brazilian settlers to continue to build the nation and lay claim to territory during a highly contested period. These migrations illustrate his vision of a collective Brazilian identity that thrives and should lead because of its mixed-race history and natural environmental abundance that other, non-Brazilian naturalists have failed to understand. Euclides continually puts forward a racialized argument of Brazilian exceptionalism where, because of the ability of sertanejos to survive in harsh landscapes, there is the possibility of a future settlement that those coming from European colonial centers could not manage. Migration thus works within an idea of *grandeza*, that by importing people and allowing them to improve this tropical landscape, Brazil could move beyond the process of becoming and into a fully modernized nation. Euclides's project is one of political, geographical, historical, and ultimately imperial rhetoric to strategically claim territory for the Brazilian nation. Mário, also writing toward an idea of Brazilian nationhood, positions Amazonian populations, rather than territory, as uniquely Brazilian.

The Novice Traveler with a Camera in Hand

The anxieties about modernization, race, development, and most importantly how to create a unified Brazilian nation expressed by Euclides at the turn of the twentieth century also appear in Mário de Andrade's *O turista aprendiz*. Positioning Brazil as able to use European models of imperialism and intellectual discourse while at the same time differentiating the nation through its distinct characteristics, both Euclides and Mário produce knowledge about the Amazon through travel and for the development of a Brazilian national identity. The question of whether Indigenous and Afro-descendant people could or should be citizens was a large part of building the Brazilian nation. Mário specifically uses peripheral regions, peoples, and landscapes to showcase a uniquely Brazilian identity. While Euclides focuses on the need to import and mix Brazilians from other regions to create a manageable, settled, written, and historicized region, Mário, in his travel narrative of the Amazon and Northeast, situates the individual of peripheral regions as already the most authentic and emblematic of Brazilian identity. Mário, in contrast to Euclides, uses individuals to represent the whole.

Mário's narrative style differs from Euclides's more sober essays and observations, and he also experiments with photography to showcase a modernist vision of Amazonia. He mixes poems, imagined and real Indigenous folklore, and songs with travel observations akin to other travel narratives popularized in the eighteenth and nineteenth centuries, which he often cites. *O turista aprendiz* is divided into two parts; the first documents his journey to the Amazon from May to August 1927, and the second describes his journey to Northeast Brazil from November 1928 to February 1929. Here I focus on Mário's Amazonian journey. Mário presents his life onboard a steamship, highlighting the Amazonian landscape in motion while also writing about cities and architecture. There are several photographs of the author and people living along the river. This variety of photography and narrative represents the diversity of both Mário's experience and the area itself. Mário also characterizes the Amazon region in movement; however, this movement, different from Euclides's vision, is not in a straightforward evolutionary trajectory, but rather made up of a variety of crossings.

The travel narrative and visuals Mário created give insight into the ways a Brazilian modernist viewed the Amazon. Mário's use of the camera and insistence on his position as a tourist in the region point to how both the camera and the tourist experience frame and transform his idea of self and nationhood. As Nancy Stepan notes, "by becoming an apprentice tourist, Mário experiences a transformation much like Macunaíma's, from racialized peripheral modernist looking toward Europe into 'whitened' city dweller in the interior of Brazil. Perhaps because of his occupation of multiple racial categories, Mário creates a genre of Brazilian primitivist portraiture in which he includes himself as both subject and object."[59] Having already culturally whitened himself as a member of the intelligentsia, in travel to a peripheral region, Mário whitens himself further through travel. In becoming and explicitly calling attention to his role as a tourist in the Amazon, along with photographing himself, Mário relocates the idea of center. However, in Mário's case, as Stepan notes, he is both subject and object, a self-described tourist who also occupies peripheral spaces.

The modernist movement in Brazil sought to create a national cultural identity to differentiate from European cultural models, often drawing from the periphery. In *Errant Modernism*, Esther Gabara focuses on the modernist aesthetic created by Mário in *O turista aprendiz*. She deems this modernism "errant" because it critiqued nationalism, set up a new way of thinking about nationality, and strayed from conventional, colonial representations: "Errant modernism therefore pictures a broad and varied set of practices that continue to circulate among artists at the beginning of the twenty-first century. No longer contained by objects, these practices actively engage popular culture, decenter the authorial subject, undermine scientific truth, and interrupt the forward motion of progress—social, individual, and even narrative."[60] An interruption of forward progression can be seen in the disruption of the traditional travel narrative that Mário creates. He both puts himself into the narrative and decenters himself by focusing his camera and imagination outward toward the people he meets. He engages with not only the elite that greet him in Amazonian cities, but with villagers on city streets or rural peasants in riverine communities. In *O turista aprendiz*, Mário also invents entire cultures, which undermines the supposed scientific truth of natural histories and instead focuses on cultural crossings and imagined communities.

Through critique and a concentration on underrepresented regions and peoples, *modernismo* could reframe Brazilian national culture and thus contest turn-of-the-century anxieties about racial degeneracy. Mário centers rural populations in *O turista aprendiz*, focusing on a particularly Brazilian brand of beauty that highlights Black and mixed-race people. This diverges from travel narratives during the nineteenth and early twentieth centuries that categorized Indigenous and Black people in remote regions using scientific racism, where non-white races were conceptualized as biologically inferior. Dain Borges emphasizes the importance of hygienization, or the medicalization of racial claims in Brazilian social thought from 1880 to 1940. Degeneration, or deterioration, was "a psychiatry of character, a science of identity, and a social psychology," meaning that much more than just being conceived as racial, hygienization was tied to and backed up by the science of the day, shaping policy and the Brazilian social-welfare state into the present.[61] In the Amazon, Mário, within the ideology of *modernismo*, works to create a more nuanced vision of different racial identities that make up the Brazilian nation.

Modernismo, in designing an explicitly Brazilian culture using previously ignored peoples and regions, could reject a history of colonial oppression. However, *modernismo* as a movement was created and accessed almost exclusively by the elite and as such, it was "innovative but inaccessible," a critique that Mário himself made in a 1942 lecture.[62] For Mário, modernism made up a "critical nationalism" that "critiqued the colonial history of the Americas and its twentieth-century formation, yet did not obediently serve the interests of the increasingly centralized and homogenizing modern state."[63] This innovation yet lack of accessibility speaks to the travel experience, where travel is a bourgeois activity only available to the select few. In experiencing the Amazon through travel, Mário is a step removed from his surroundings, able to portray them though photography and prose, yet not fully accessing life in the Amazon. Mário connects with local populations while at the same time being removed by his status and literal position on board a traveling vessel. He performs a sort of proto-ethnography where he observes and interviews his subjects, but also frames himself as an apprentice tourist. Furthermore, in his self-designation as *apprentice tourist*, Mário negates his own authority—he is in the process of learning how to be a tourist, photographer, and traveler.

In his collection of stories and images of the Northeast and Amazon, Mário creates national patrimony. In the 1930s, after this journey, he worked for Brazil's Serviço do Patrimonio Histórico e Artístico Nacional, or the National Historic and Artistic Heritage Service, an agency that listed and preserved buildings and sites of national heritage.[64] In the Amazon, he appears as a consumer and creator of heritage by photographing and cataloguing yet gazing from the other side. In his later work as an archivist, Mário vocalizes his approach to preservation as picking up on specifically Brazilian elements, such as a watermelon added to a depiction of the Last Supper in a church in São Paulo.[65] Cultural hybridity and the multiple elements that composed Brazilian culture across the racial and class spectrum formed part of Mário's vision of modernism. As Barbara Kirshenblatt-Gimblett remarks on the relationship between heritage, tourism, and preservation, "heritage is a mode of cultural production in the present that has recourse to the past. . . . Heritage not only gives buildings, precincts, and ways of life that are no longer viable for one reason or another a second life as exhibits of themselves. It also produces something new."[66] Through his travel and documentation as an "apprentice" tourist, Mário creates the Amazon as a destination and brings back emblems of cultural heritage in the form of his photography and travel diary.

Mário collected over four hundred photographs during his travels in the North and Northeast, contradicting his self-designation as a "novice." His photography is wide-ranging and often features people, himself, and the landscape of Amazonia.[67] He uses a technique of double exposure to further disorient the viewer and create his specific, parodical version of a travel account. As seen in Figure 3.1, Mário leisurely rests on board the *S. Salvador* ship with "sun in his face in the middle of Peru." In photographs of Mário on this trip he either creates self-portraits with his shadow blending into the landscape or is shown in this type of pose, usually with a smile on his face. Mário dominates the scenery, differentiating himself through his dress, stance, and use of technology. Mário's ability to travel and document (being a tourist) positions him as an outsider. His clothing draws on typical explorer garb (like the outfits worn by Roosevelt and Rondon as seen in the previous

FIGURE 3.1 Mário leisurely rests with his face in the sun aboard the *S. Salvador*, the boat he traveled on throughout the Amazon. Courtesy of the Arquivo do Instituto de Estudos Brasileiros USP – Fundo Mário de Andrade, reference code: MA-F-0305

chapter), but rather than a military pith helmet, he dons a wide-brimmed hat, and rather than holding a rifle, he carries a camera, underlining his leisurely position as tourist. Mário's work is centered on photography and tourism, and he even creates a neologism for photographing—*fotar*. While photography had been in existence in Brazil since the mid-nineteenth century, a major difference in the twenty-four years between his voyage and that of Euclides was the creation and propagation of a visual culture that encouraged and fueled travel itself.

The photographs of Mário communicate his ease and enjoyment of the trip, and his images at once appear artistic and modern, and at times flippant and ironic, particularly through his use of captions, where he plays with the themes of his narrative—what constitutes culture, beauty, and nature? For Mário, it seems, beauty, and Brazilian identity, lie in the people he encounters in Amazonia. His approach to the region aims to produce a historical knowledge that is differentiated from broader observations of the vanguard. Mário expands ideas about high culture to include the Amazon and its peoples, thus addressing his own later critique of the modernist movement. In a similar fashion to Euclides, Mário found that European models did not fit the Brazilian experience and thus wrote toward a particularly Brazilian brand of culture. Of course, he (and other *modernistas*) could not escape their European thinking and educational formation entirely, hence creating concepts such as cultural anthropophagy, or a cultural cannibalism that chewed up outside influences and "spit out" something uniquely Brazilian. Modernist primitivism seized on indigeneity as a marker of differentiation. Certainly, modernists used the idea of cultural anthropophagy to create a Brazilian culture where indigeneity could compare, mix with, or even exceed Western forms of knowledge and culture.

Before taking off for his months-long trip, Mário, in reference to other travel narratives of the Amazon, reflects on what he expects upon beginning the journey. He repeatedly voices a reluctance to travel and characterizes himself as a homebody. His reluctance sets up his tourist experience as a sort of sarcastic self-sacrifice, as he is actively pushing himself beyond his comfort level to incorporate Amazonia and the Northeast into the Brazilian nation, while obviously enjoying himself. Before leaving his home in São Paulo, Mário voices his expectations: "I know well that this trip that we're doing contains no adventure or danger, yet every one of us, beyond their logical consciousness also has a poetic consciousness. Memories of readings led me beyond reality: savage tribes, alligators, and fire ants.

And I imagined: cannon, revolver, walking stick, pocketknife."[68] Mario's imagined violence and subsequent excitement point to the outsider perspective of the Amazon. The Amazon was often conceptualized as a place to demonstrate man's potential to dominate the wilderness, and an area of violence not just because of the dangerous flora and fauna but because of the infamous violence of the rubber trade. Mário dialogues with previous travel narratives of the region, the focus of which have been savage tribes, alligators, and fire ants—threats both big and small. These elements make up an imaginary, exotic wilderness—much like Roosevelt's "hostile wilderness" described in Chapter 2. As a response, Mário then pictures weapons with which to confront the wilderness, the outlier of which is certainly the *bengala*, or walking stick, often used for promenading in urban public space. Associated with elegance and city life, why should a *bengala* be listed amongst these other tools? Indeed, this points toward the self-referential, sarcastic approach that Mário takes, and the public, city image that he invariably carries. Again, we see how, like Euclides, Mário also transforms the travel narrative genre through critiquing previous iterations written by non-Brazilians.

Once on his journey, Mário also uses his camera to showcase Amazonian landscapes. The photograph in Figure 3.2 of a small town on the Madeira River gives us a different vision than that set forth by Euclides. Rather than a land in need of increased settlement, this town is a picturesque, managed landscape. Figure 3.2 is a photograph of a town called Bom-Futuro, in Rondônia, captioned for its gothic church, yellow flowers (*sumanúmas*) and "agua de Narciso." The photograph, along with the caption, describes the beauty of the landscape to the point that the viewer can perhaps fall into the trap of Narcissus, gazing at themselves until drowning. Or perhaps the caption refers not to the viewer but instead the town itself. Picturesque despite a slight rightward tilt, the town, gazing at its reflection, could drown in its own beauty. Once again, it appears that Mário ironically engages with European art and architectural periodization, along with Greek mythology, in so designating a humble building and landscape in the furthest reaches of the Amazon. The name of the town and his description in the caption engage with differing temporalities—modern/pre-modern, future and progress/stagnation—and spaces—civilization/wilderness. In this reflection a separation between the town and the water, culture and nature, blurs and ultimately disappears. In this photograph, the wilderness has been transformed into civilization in the form of a pretty, quiet town on the banks of a calm river. Here Mário harnesses classic Western ideals of the

FIGURE 3.2 Bom-Futuro Bonita, a small town on the Rio Madeira, photographed by Mário and captioned for its sumanúma flowers and "agua de Narciso." Courtesy of the Arquivo do Instituto de Estudos Brasileiros USP – Fundo Mário de Andrade, reference code: MA-F-0379

picturesque, yet features typically Brazilian flowers, creating a specifically Brazilian piece of national patrimony.

André Botelho offers an interesting point of comparison between Euclides and Mário. While analyzing *O turista aprendiz* as a travel narrative in which Mário attempts to create an image of Brazil where he recognizes a cultural plurality and conceptualizes civilization as multi-faceted, Botelho compares Mário and Euclides in their portrayals of the river itself. Both remark on the monotonous nature of the Amazon River and a certain sense of build-up and then personal disappointment rooted in previous representations of the region, yet there is an important distinction in the outcomes of Euclides's and Mário's commentary. Mário remarks on the monotony of the river to highlight the intrigue of Amazonian populations and cities. Euclides, on the other hand, imagines the Amazon as a monumental landscape coupled with a land (and people) that seek fixity. Thinking back to the quotations at the beginning of this chapter we can again see distinctions in how Mário and Euclides treat the idea of the river, and more generally the Amazon. Mário characterizes the alligator bringing him closer to God, while Euclides concentrates on the overwhelming, destructive, and all-powerful force of the river. Nature, for Mário, is representative of an approachable part of the nation as he focuses on an alligator, and his personal, spiritual connection to the animal, despite the potential danger that this animal represents.

Individualizing Amazonian Culture

For Mário, the underlying idea in both his landscape and portraiture is the beauty and elegance of the Amazon region and its peoples. In his descriptions of the riverscape, Mário repeatedly describes the Amazon as feminine, and largely features women in his photography. Amazonian beauty, according to O *turista aprendiz*, revolves around the feminine body. This is different to Euclides, whose depictions of nature (while still following the trope of nature as feminine) demonstrate anxieties about man's potential when faced with the task of harnessing and developing the wild. It is the sturdy backland character of the (male) seringueiro who can tame the jungle. Mário instead highlights the attraction of the feminine space of the Amazon region. In 1920s Brazil, the unerring standard of beauty was white; thus, in Mário's photographs and descriptions of beauty in the Amazon as Black, Indigenous, and *mestiço*, he departs quite radically from convention.

In one image from his trip, Mário showcases life on the riverbanks of the Solimões (part of the upper Amazon River from its confluence with the Rio Negro at the border of Peru) as well as life in transit. I do not include this image here because the archive in which it is housed at the University of São Paulo prohibits the reproduction of photographs that depict Indigenous or riverine peoples. While this is part of an effort to confront the unequal power dynamics involved in image creation, the image is still worth describing as it is emblematic of Mário's specific approach toward the region. Framed by a dark doorway, the photograph shows a mother and child gazing directly at Mário's lens, sitting on their porch elevated from the river by stilts (a type of house prominent in riverine communities generally called *palafitas*). Geometric shapes of dwellings usually index modern planning and construction, but here they appear in the context of a *palafita*—an unregulated, unplanned housing structure, integrated closely to the river, and sitting directly atop the water. The lifestyle of this family is thus defined by the proximity of nature and culture. This mother and child can sit and watch the world float by. The image's caption, "sobre as ondas" (above the waves), directly references where the subjects are while also possibly pointing to their position above or away from the chaos of city life. The mother and child's position "above the waves" also causes them to gaze down on Mário. This is a different perspective than we have seen with photography from the previous chapters in which Roosevelt and Rondon gaze on the landscape while Indigenous subjects look up toward the camera. Here Mário's subjects look down on him, elevating them to a position of power. However, while Mário moves on, creating this tourist snapshot, they are static. The image does not appear posed, although it is also not entirely candid. It is emblematic of the mobile tourist gaze, or a shot taken while in transit itself.[69] These are "glances" that passersby can achieve through the creation of modern technology that showcase the photographer's mobility. Mário, aboard a steamship, can create these images with a quick snapshot, capturing a moment of quotidian life, with or without the need to interact with his subjects.

As mentioned briefly in the introduction to this book, Carolina Sá Carvalho puts forward a theory about a photographer's point of view through an analysis of Roger Casement's photography of Huitoto people and their abuse at the hands of rubber barons in the Putumayo region of Peru that has some bearing on Mário's photography. She posits that because of Casement's position as a colonized subject of the British empire (he was Irish), he works to visibilize aspects of violence that are not easily seen by others. This point of view is thus determined by "past experiences and affective dispositions."[70] This also emerges in Mário's photography. As a non-white Brazilian, Mário sees the Amazon from the perspective that many other explorers at the time could not. He purposefully points out and highlights the racial mixture of the region that forms a point of pride for him and perhaps better situates himself within a national culture.

In Figure 3.3 Mário photographs typical scenes on the river that highlight riverine people in a semi-candid manner. In this photograph, Mário captures two people in a canoe, and he captions it "Corpo lindo de tapuia linda," or "beautiful body of a beautiful *tapuia*." Identified in the caption as a *tapuia*, a term used to describe Indigenous people who did not speak Tupi, the woman on the right of the photograph has captured Mário's admiration. This caption highlights Mário's repositioning of the female body, in particular the non-white female body, as beautiful and distinctly Brazilian. The woman in the photograph has adopted language and dress of the center, while remaining a peripheral subject. The canoe appears at a distance, part of the snapshot of daily life that he seeks to capture, while also demonstrating a closer relationship with nature than Mário has perhaps experienced in his own travels aboard a steamship. These images framed through Mário's specific point of view show an Amazon made

FIGURE 3.3 Photograph from the banks of the Amazon River captioned "Corpo lindo de tapuia linda," or beautiful body of a beautiful *tapuia* (Indigenous person who does not speak Tupi). Courtesy of the Arquivo do Instituto de Estudos Brasileiros USP – Fundo Mário de Andrade, reference code: MA-F-0286

up of a wide variety of individuals against backdrops in various stages of development.

Figure 3.4 showcases some of this Amazonian development. Mário's photography includes quite a few shots of workers at the various ports where he stops. This image captures men moving wood at a *porto de lenha*, or firewood port. The photograph demonstrates the partial development of this Amazonian town where men are collecting wood for trade. There are organized stacks of felled trees that also nod to the deforestation of the region. The photographs of these workers mirror Euclides's descriptions of sturdy Northeastern men who come to the Amazon to work in the rubber industry. However, in this case, the men at the port remain at a distance, and appear almost faceless. The men are in motion and their activity rather than their faces or bodies characterizes them. Mário captions one of the photographs in this series as "homens levando lenha para o vaticano," or "men carrying firewood for the Vatican." We can again see Mário's sarcastic, modernist style as he connects European "high" culture to the activities of workers at a riverine port deep in the Brazilian Amazon.

Mário writes Amazonian places into comparisons with world capitals (linking Belém to a tropical Paris, for instance) to incorporate the region into a global discourse and to showcase its cultural production and charm.

A Novice Traveler in a Land without History 121

FIGURE 3.4 On the banks of the Solimões River, men gather firewood into stacks for trade. Courtesy of the Arquivo do Instituto de Estudos Brasileiros USP – Fundo Mário de Andrade, reference code: MA-F-0228

Mário's journey through the Amazon took him down several different rivers, where he describes the monotony of life aboard a steamship but also details city life in the Amazon, breaking from previous travel narratives where the journey only begins when the city is left behind. Mário spends much of his narrative detailing the pleasures of Amazonian cities like Belém and Manaus. This situates these capitals as centers of cultural production comparable to Western tradition. For example, Mário includes a photograph of a colonial building on stilts on the Tapajós River that he captions "Veneza em Santarém" (Venice in Santarém). Links with high culture imagine an Amazon not entirely rooted in wilderness but a place with traditions and history worthy of esteem and as part of a nation. In describing Belém, the capital of Pará state, Mário writes a poem again comparing Amazonian capitals to the United States and Europe:

> There is more enjoyment here than in New York or Vienna!
> Just one look from one *morena*
> Mixed type, a Brazilian cocktail,
> Nourishes more than an açaí tree,
> Man's sweet enjoyment of woman!

> In Pará it doesn't stop, nothing is lacking!
> Try Tucupi! Try tacacá!
> What a happy port,
> Belém of Pará.[71]

Reading almost as an advertisement for potential tourists, this poem invites guests to try the Amazon as they will undoubtedly like it and stay. Mário portrays Amazonia as a bustling metropolis, filled with beautiful women whose gaze makes the traveler drunk on a distinctly Brazilian cocktail. He mentions some of the most important and regionally specific food staples—açai, tucupi, tacacá—distinguishing the area from the rest of Brazil as culturally unique, important, and delicious. This also points to an idea of consumption of the Other employed by the *modernistas*. Here Amazonian life revolves around the easily consumable fruits of the landscape, the culture of its inhabitants, and the cities.

While in Belém, Mário passes through markets, meets with local politicians, and remarks on the beautiful mangroves that line the city, creating what he deems a tropical Cairo. On one of his walks, he details a woman he comes across:

> Sitting on the ground, there was a white white blouse on a black black woman who, raising to us angelic teeth and eyes, all white, offered with a black hand outstretched a black stained wood gourd with white smoke billowing from a white white *munguzá*. . . . I have enjoyed myself too much. Belém was made for me and I fit into her like a hand into a glove.[72]

A woman, seated on the ground (a marker of her lower social class), looks up toward Mário and his party with "angelic" eyes and teeth, extending out a gourd with food (presumably to sell). The woman offers food to be consumed, but Mário instead consumes with his gaze. The gaze of the woman is up at Mário rather than down. However, the gaze is described as angelic, again creating a spiritual element and balancing the power scale. Furthermore, this is not the usual consumption of the Black female body by the lighter skinned male, the gaze is exchanged both ways and the entire scene is more of an apparition that gives Mário a sense of spiritual well-being, contradicting the subordinate position the woman occupies on the ground looking up. His repetition of black black (*preto, preto*) against white, white (*branco, branco*) places emphasis on the colors that make up the Amazonian and Brazilian landscape as a study in contrasts. In this momentary exchange, Mário prostrates his "civilized" self before the perceived purity of beauty that he communicates through repetition. Mário concludes his remarks on this interaction by stating that Belém suits him perfectly, perhaps because of these differences. It is in between contrasts, the grey area of identity and cultural production, that Mário situates the Brazilian periphery. This in turn highlights aspects of culture that were previously deemed undesirable. Mário's trip in the Brazilian interior focuses on individual peoples and their unique identities. Whether it be a group of women in a small town, typically Brazilian flowers, or the angelic gaze of a Black woman offering food, Mário portrays the Amazon as an area more "Brazilian" than the cities of the South, and a study of appealing contrasts.

Conclusion

In these two texts the writers—traveling in a foreign, yet domestic region—create the Amazonian periphery as a site where Brazilian nationhood can flourish. Both Euclides and Mário attempt to nationalize the space of the Amazon through travel. It is a space that they acknowledge as difficult, exotic, and enticing. Both authors are on missions of knowledge production about the region that originate or are inspired by European epistemes, but that they situate as uniquely Brazilian texts. These authors are attempting to create a new, Brazilian way of thinking that engages with territorial demarcation (in Euclides's case) or the people and cultures of Amazonia (as with Mário), aspects that can only be found within Brazil. These productions thus attempt to propose something novel and authentically Brazilian, while drawing from a history of Western knowledge production.

Both Mário and Euclides write travel narratives about the Amazon for similar purposes—to differentiate and distinguish Brazil as a unique and superior nation. However, they go about this in strikingly different ways. Euclides employs a territorially and geographically based argument using Amazonian resources to develop Brazil into an imperial power. He focuses on generalized mixed-race male backland characters who can work hard to settle the land. Mário, also working toward a collective idea of Brazilian nationhood, concentrates on the ways the Amazon connects to known cultural production while conceptualizing the space as unique because of its socio-culturally diverse inhabitants. Mário challenges ideas of racial degeneracy in peripheral areas by conceptualizing people and land as vital to a uniquely Brazilian experience. Through an attempt at engagement with local culture, Mário seeks to highlight the individual and create a complex quilt of the Brazilian nation.

Indeed, Mário critiques Euclides, as Gabara notes: "Mário explicitly rejects da Cunha's philosophy of identity grounded in these landscapes and writes a scathing condemnation of this foundational text [*Os sertões*] of Brazilian national identity."[73] In Mário's critique of Euclides, we see the shift of idealized national identity between the two authors. Euclides concentrates on the environment and its effect on people, while Mário contemplates the people who make up the environment of Brazil. Euclides focuses on swaths of generalized backland characters that can be portrayed as heroic, where Mário's characters, including himself, are often flawed and multidimensional, in personal processes of becoming.

Both Euclides and Mário's travel narratives explore how to conceptualize and incorporate a land and people marked as peripheral. Euclides's concentration on the potential of migration versus Mário's focus on Amazonian peoples demonstrate two different yet similar preoccupations: how to fully incorporate the region into a national identity that in Euclides's case is marked by contested territorial borders, and in Mário's case patches together a nation of different racial makeups and identities. Underlying these projects is an anxiety about both the land of the Amazon and its inhabitants. Euclides's encouragement of migration and settlement to lead to the development of the Amazon is used as a justification of Brazil's claim to territory. At least partially due to Euclides's previous journey, the Amazonian borders are marked as a solidified part of the Brazilian nation by the time of Mário's trip. Euclides demarcates Brazilian borders while Mário creates cultural patrimony. Mário's position then is somewhat different, as rather than justifying Amazonian land as part of Brazil, he tasks himself with representing Amazonians as Brazilian.

Settling the Brazilian Amazon

Both Euclides da Cunha and Mário de Andrade were preoccupied with situating the Amazon region within a Brazilian national culture. This depended on increased integration into the national fold as well as, per Euclides's suggestion, expanded internal migration and small settlements. As an addendum to this chapter, we will take a brief, sweeping look at the history of settlement in the Brazilian Amazon from the 1920s until today to see how these visions have been realized, thus building toward a "history of the present."

After Mário's travels in Amazonia, the region was increasingly conceptualized as an area for settlement. In 1938, President Getúlio Vargas created the "March to the West" campaign, which sought to colonize the interior of the country. Although at the time the March to the West did not quite reach Amazonia, it shifted the popular ideology toward "national interiorization to stimulate a national project of physical territorial occupation based on science."[74] The March to the West also depended on increased technological resources such as the airplane that allowed access to previously difficult to reach territories. Along with more remote areas, already well-established cities like Manaus and Belém continued to grow.

By World War II, when United States rubber markets from Asia closed, a renewed interest in Amazonian rubber and thus interest in the region re-emerged. This second Amazonian rubber boom caused waves of migrant workers from the Brazilian Northeast to move to the region. They were recruited as "rubber soldiers" and fashioned as patriotic heroes because of their role not only in the wartime effort but in settling Amazonia.[75] This migratory wave followed Euclides's vision for the future of the region as being settled through the internal migration of Northeasterners. As rubber was mostly harvested to supply the US, the role of the increasingly imperial neighbor to the north caused anxiety among Brazilian decision makers. Without the region being fully integrated into the Brazilian nation, it could be more easily taken over by a foreign power.[76]

In 1948, to combat attempts at a potential Amazonian takeover by the US and others and to further the economic and social development of the region, the Brazilian government declared all nine Amazonian states (Amazonas, Roraima, Pará, Mato Grosso, Acre, Rondônia, Amapá, Maranhão, and Tocantins) part of the Brazilian Legal Amazon. As Susanna Hecht and Raoni Rajão explain, projections of how to settle the Amazon (land use models) from the 1920s through 1950s created the groundwork for the increased occupation of the region: "It [land use models] transformed Amazonia, an 'unknown and invincible jungle,' empty and isolated from civilization, into Legal Amazon, a space for transformation and rural development in a predictable, calculable and legible way."[77] As part of the Legal Amazon, the region could more easily be conceived of as a settleable frontier.

The Brazilian military dictatorship from 1964 to 1985 once again turned to the Amazon's resources and how to exploit them, and as a result proposed the environmentally destructive and still unfinished Trans-Amazonian highway. This highway would (quite literally) pave the way for increased export of goods like timber, ores, and minerals. The government offered free land along the highway, sparking a land rush of immigrants from other regions of Brazil who were given grants to settle. These migrants turned their land into pasture and as land was rendered unproductive, they moved onto neighboring plots, creating an arc of deforestation along the southern border of Amazonian territory. As international demand for meat grew, Brazil began using this land to produce soybeans and raise cattle, pushing the arc of deforestation further north.

Relatively quickly these migrants abandoned their lands due to low crop yield, distance to markets, poor soils, and lack of credit, among other challenges. As migrants retreated, the Brazilian government gave cheap credit and tax breaks to large-scale enterprises, paving the way for the creation of massive cattle ranches and soy farms within the Legal Amazon.[78]

Running counter to these trends of deforestation and beginning in earnest in the 1980s, international eyes once again turned toward the Amazon Rainforest as deforestation numbers spiked and the murders of environmental activists like Chico Mendes were reported in international headlines. That level of international pressure and activism within Brazil led to stricter policies on deforestation and increased land protections, and during several progressive governments from the early 2000s through 2014, deforestation trends were halted and even reversed. Under President Lula da Silva, or more importantly, environmental minister Marina Silva, the Brazilian government created a plan to stop deforestation and expand the amount of rainforest under legal protection, as well as increase Indigenous lands and extractive reserves. As a result, by 2006 deforestation had massively dropped, at least partially due to a soy and beef moratorium. By 2012 almost half of the Amazon was put under protection through strengthening the forest code.

While protections against deforestation increased, representatives of large-scale farming banded together and slowly gained power within congress. *Ruralistas*, or ruralists, who represent the interests of large-scale farmers and ranchers, ultimately pushed Lula's successor, Dilma Rousseff, to weaken the forest code and slash the forest monitoring system, the Brazilian Institute of Environment and Renewable Natural Resources (IBAMA).

After several years of political turmoil, with corruption from large-scale agriculture and cattle ranching right at the center, Jair Bolsonaro, supported by the *ruralistas*, was elected in 2018. Immediately he began to spout a rhetoric of increased economic development in the Amazon. Consequently, deforestation increased, even in protected areas. Some of Jair Bolsonaro's first actions as president of Brazil were to roll back protections on Indigenous and *quilombo* lands in the Amazon. He shifted power away from FUNAI, the organization that Rondon started, to the agricultural ministry, which represents the interests of large-scale, often monoculture, farming. The rhetoric surrounding these moves was frighteningly familiar—to "integrate" Indigenous peoples toward becoming "true Brazilians" (actual words from Bolsonaro's' tweets). During his time in office, Bolsonaro also amplified a military presence and emphasized unhindered development to the region—like the goals of the brutal military dictatorship.

And as mentioned in the introduction to this book, by the summer of 2019, images of the Amazon on fire spread across social media, intensifying international concern over Brazilian sovereignty of the forest while fueling national concern about *cobiça internacional*, or interest from foreign countries in taking over Amazonia. Illegal logging and ranching, a major cause of these fires, rapidly rose during Bolsonaro's tenure. By 2021, deforestation hit a fifteen-year high, with over 5,110 square miles of rainforest cleared between August 2020 and July 2021, primarily due to soy and cattle farming but also because of illegal logging, mining, and harvesting palm oil, açai, and ayahuasca.[79] Bolsonaro narrowly lost reelection in 2022 to the returning Lula. Thus far, this transition of power has marked a more environmentally conscious turn for the country and the Amazon region, with deforestation rates continuing to drop.[80]

The past century in the Amazon has been characterized by trying to fit the region into a national but also global cultural ideology. Often, the region has been characterized by those from outside it to the detriment of Amazonian peoples and land. Euclides and Mário in their writing and work see the Amazon as a place of possibility that should be valued for its diversity and potential. The region is still ripe with possibility, but it requires collaborative work with native Amazonians and political mobilization against governments that are antithetical to environmental progress and equality.

CHAPTER 4

Learning from the Other

*Theodor Koch-Grünberg
and Richard Evans Schultes*

"Dreams are reality for the Indian, actions independent
from the free shadows of the body, the soul."[1]

THEODOR KOCH-GRÜNBERG

German Theodor Koch-Grünberg and American Richard Evans Schultes traveled to the Amazon in service to their countries of origin. Seasoned anthropologists, their work spanned decades, from the era of imperial exploration and rubber exploitation to the Good Neighbor period of heightened United States–Latin America relations, and post–World War II 1960s and '70s counterculture. Their writing has inspired many, including Mário de Andrade and the Colombian director Ciro Guerra (whose film *El abrazo de la serpiente*, which fictionalizes the two explorers and brings them together via their Indigenous informant, is the subject of Chapter 5).[2] Their photographs, ethnographies, and botanical classifications developed the reputation of the Amazon as a repository of rare and valuable plants, ethnobotanical knowledge, and a wealth of Indigenous traditions and cultures. Their research and publications demonstrate an evolution of anthropological approaches and allow us to reflect on the creation of knowledge about plants and folklore. As seen in the epigraph to this chapter, Theodor Koch-Grünberg positions himself as an expert on the Amazon through his anthropological relationships with various Indigenous groups. Where Koch-Grünberg interprets what he deems as cosmological realities for a generalized Indigenous subject, Schultes positions Indigenous peoples as unique interlocutors of knowledge about plants: "The Indians' botanical knowledge is disappearing even faster than the plants themselves."[3] Both explorers emphasize ways of understanding the world that they have witnessed and learned from Indigenous peoples. Koch-Grünberg and Schultes both attempt to learn from Native Amazonians and in return to become advocates for Indigenous peoples and the environment. In this chapter, I analyze the confluence between nature and culture via sympathetic interlocuters like Koch-Grünberg and Schultes. As such, the chapter contributes a reading of the ways the structures of modernity can begin to be reworked, even in highly asymmetrical contexts.

Theodor Koch-Grünberg was an ethnologist and explorer who spent years (1896–1924) living among and documenting various Indigenous peoples and their customs. Written in five volumes (from 1911 to 1913), the travel narrative and account of Indigenous folklore *Vom Roraima zum Orinoco* (From Roraima to the Orinoco), was Koch-Grünberg's most influential piece of writing. In the first volume, the author offers a personalized account of traveling the Roraima and Orinoco rivers in the northwest Amazon (primarily through Colombia, Venezuela, and Brazil), detailing his time conducting anthropological fieldwork with various groups such as the Pemon, Wapischána, and Yekuná, among others. Koch-Grünberg's approach was to be a "participant observer" engaging in day-to-day life with his Indigenous counterparts. He recorded languages, customs, and folktales throughout the Amazon and in the process created a large photographic and material archive.[4]

Richard Evans Schultes was a botanist who also spent decades (1940s to the 1990s) dedicated to the study of Amazonian plants and peoples and was one of the first explorers to sound an alarm about deforestation of the region in the 1960s. He collected over twenty-four thousand plant samples, including hundreds of novel specimens that have been used in a variety of medications.[5] Schultes often draws on Koch-Grünberg's work in his own. He is considered the "father" of ethnobotany, or the study of how Indigenous peoples use local plants.[6] Schultes argued that Indigenous people could guide Westerners in their use of plants as potential remedies. He incorporated various disciplines into his ethnobotanical approach including anthropology, botany, geography, and biology. Schultes documented his findings in academic journals and books, including his account of Indigenous plant-use, *Plants of the Gods* (1979), which influenced writers including Aldous Huxley, Alejo Carpentier, and William Burroughs. Although he never wrote an explicit travel narrative, travel features prominently in his ten books and 496 scientific articles. An influential professor at Harvard, many students and mentees went on to be notable themselves (Mark Plotkin and Wade Davis, among others).

Both explorers traveled at periods of increased international attention toward the extractive potential of the Amazon. Koch-Grünberg traveled at the height of the first Amazonian rubber boom and commented on the abuses of Indigenous peoples at the hands of rubber barons. Traveling at a time of violence, resource extraction, and the influx of massive investments into the region, Koch-Grünberg remarks on the very real threat of human and environmental destruction. Schultes's travels in the northwestern Amazon were also heavily influenced by rubber. He was involved in rubber exploration, primarily in the Colombian Amazon, for the United States during the World War II secondary rubber boom. While he found and collected many samples of rubber plants, his findings did not result in a revived rubber industry as instead the markets turned toward synthetic rubber.

The rubber boom backdrops of these two explorers once again recalls the Amazon as a site of El Dorado. As Charlotte Rogers explains, the concept of El Dorado epitomizes the potential wealth that could be found in the Americas.[7] As the "world's medicine chest," the metaphor of El Dorado carries on. The myth of El Dorado in this context relies on the Amazon as an inexhaustible site of natural resources and botanical potential that could lead to a plethora of medicinal cures. Plants, if found and used correctly, could become incorporated into the global economy, likely to foment the wealth of colonizing countries. Koch-Grünberg and Schultes work on an axis of knowledge extraction while also seeking to be advocates and educators to a Western public about Indigenous peoples and the environment.

As ethnographers, both Koch-Grünberg and Schultes participate with the people they observe and document, cultivating empathy while also maintaining "objectivity," or professional distance. As Pratt puts it, the ethnographer can be seen as a scientific observer, fixed on the edge of a space looking down, where the subjective experience is mobile, or as down in the middle of the action, participating.[8] Through their ethnographic work participating in daily life, in the "middle of the action," they became advocates for Indigenous peoples and cultures.

There is an evolution in Koch-Grünberg and Schultes's methods from a more voyeuristic journey (such as the case of Theodore Roosevelt) into long-lasting, reciprocal relationships with Amazonian peoples. Certainly, relationships were freighted with the tradition of anthropologists and subjects, and a history informed by patriarchal and dominant power structures, but it is fair to say that Koch-Grünberg and Schultes actively listened to Indigenous people. Even as their depictions can echo or return to elements of the imperial visions we have examined in previous chapters, their shift is in the direction of advocacy, rather than exploitation. Both began to incorporate Indigenous approaches into their thinking and subsequently tried to explain those approaches to a wider audience within their countries of origin and beyond—adding a kind of pedagogical drive to their work. In this chapter, I argue that their studies demonstrate various degrees of involvement with Indigenous peoples that they attempt to translate for their Western audiences as a means of educating about the value of Indigenous cultures and the Amazonian environment.

Koch-Grünberg's Anthropological Approach

Born in 1872 in a small German town, aptly named Grünberg, Koch-Grünberg studied the humanities, and later went on to earn a doctorate with a thesis focused on Guaicuruan, an Indigenous language family spoken in Argentina, Paraguay, and Brazil. His first visit to the Amazon was in 1898 on an expedition to the Xingu River in Brazil. Throughout many subsequent trips, Koch-Grünberg meticulously cataloged his surroundings, bringing detailed notes, diaries, photographs, artifacts, and film back to Europe, or to museums in Brazil. With continual exploration and publication, Koch-Grünberg's renown grew, and he was able to find governmental funding for his various missions, as nations like Brazil sought knowledge of the Amazon that might lead to increased profits during the first rubber boom. Koch-Grünberg had to broker relationships with a variety of actors, including other European explorers, Brazilian governmental agents, rubber barons, and the various Indigenous peoples he studied.[9] Throughout his chronicles, he notes the disappearance of the cultural wealth of the Amazon with encroaching "civilization." The anxiety of losing peoples, plants, languages, and cultures is a clear motivating factor behind his multi-volume publications. Koch-Grünberg attempts to create a narrative and visual rhetoric of value, liveliness, and conviviality of and with the people he describes.

As a European explorer who nurtured human connections, Koch-Grünberg obtained deference and access which allowed him to develop his research and build his body of work. However, as anti-German sentiment increased during World War I, the opportunities that German explorers had in Latin America faded.[10] Funding for exploratory missions, especially during the war, was difficult to obtain and Koch-Grünberg turned to public speaking tours as well as negotiating with museums to support his ambitious and multifaceted journeys.[11] Koch-Grünberg was drafted by the German army in 1917, and despite his objections, he was sent back to Europe to serve as a cartographer. Due to his chronic malaria, Koch-Grünberg was quickly relieved of military duty and was able to return to his true passion of Amazonian exploration.

In examining Koch-Grünberg's work, I consider his entire corpus but focus on the fascinating series *Vom Roraima zum Orinoco*, particularly the first of the five volumes.[12] That volume was written on his third trip to the Amazon between 1911 and 1913. It details his travels to Mount Roraima and the Orinoco River in Brazil and Venezuela and includes extensive photographic depictions of Amazonian people and land. Each of the five volumes carried a different purpose, and the first volume is the travel narrative itself, while the other volumes focused on mythology, languages, and so on. In this first volume, however, he also documents Indigenous folklore as well as plant usage, language, rituals, and ceremonies. Echoing Octavie Coudreau, it is the "authentic" Indigenous person that should be protected at all costs, and as a European explorer he situates himself as a paternal protector to Indigenous peoples. As Thomas Beebee explains, Koch-Grünberg viewed the people that he meets throughout his travels in a hierarchy: "Taking first place are the unspoiled First Nations; then the common people, nearly always racially mixed; then the local economic and political powers, often international in composition and out-look; and finally the national government, distant and ineffective, entering the scene mostly to deny or delay visas or to extort outrageous duties on imported equipment."[13] Like Euclides da Cunha, Koch-Grünberg recognizes that European models of civilization do not necessarily fit a new world or a Brazilian cultural identity, and he often contrasts people whom he characterizes as "pristine natives" with the perceived mismanagement of the development of the Amazon by the Brazilian government. Where Euclides constructs a *mestiço* backland character as the ideal to forge the future of the Amazon, Koch-Grünberg argues for the inherent value of Indigenous peoples themselves.

Koch-Grünberg's travel diaries offer his views on various groups of Indigenous people, often with an emphasis on women and children. The diaries are self-reflective as he writes about the act of documenting itself. During his stays in different villages, Koch-Grünberg made efforts to learn

Indigenous languages. He describes the difficulty of language learning and his own exasperation after sitting for hours with village leaders attempting to engage in dialogue. Koch-Grünberg comes to rely on his multilingual informant, a caboclo man named Manduca, who helps him navigate the area, build trust with Indigenous communities, and better understand their languages and cultures. Through a combination of contact due to multiple voyages, repeated gift giving, and physical and linguistic adaptation, Koch-Grünberg becomes known and able to communicate with different groups throughout the Amazon.[14]

A typical day in the field for Koch-Grünberg would consist of waking up from a night's sleep in a hammock, wandering about a small village, interacting through gift exchange with children, observing cooking, hunting, or working on his language acquisition. He was also expected to acquire and bring back pieces of Indigenous material culture, much of which is still housed today in the Museu Goeldi in Belém, Brazil.[15] Toward the end of the day, as the smells of different spices filled the air over a fire, he would pick up his pen, chronicling the day's observations before potentially moving on to the next, neighboring village. He often notices how intrinsically connected the people he sees are with their surroundings, particularly animals, and Koch-Grünberg, in turn, also attempts to connect. Upon arrival in an Indigenous setting, Koch-Grünberg settles in rather than confronts a series of new sights and experiences:

> Once again I am in a genuine domestic Indigenous environment, with its typical acidic smell of fermented yucca, of caxiri, pepper, and many other things, with its mess of baskets, pots, and various instruments, with its many xerimbabos [domestic animals], that at first are timid but then become as intimate as their masters, and I have to admit I feel much better in this savage environment than I do in the caricature of civilization that I left just a while ago.[16]

This scene is from one of the first stops of the journey, with the Wapischána in the Roraima area of southern Guyana and northern Brazil. Koch-Grünberg emphasizes the authentic nature of his surroundings, painting a tangible picture of the smells, noises, and sights of the village. His description is a delightful chaos of the senses that makes him feel more at home than in what he deems the constricted "caricature" of civilization that he has recently departed—again an appraisal on the established hierarchy. He equates the shy animals to their masters, who at first are reserved but quickly warm up. This also sets up his ongoing critique of Western civilization in comparison with "this savage environment" where he feels more comfortable and where he perceives a more balanced way of life. Despite his voiced respect for Indigenous culture, Koch-Grünberg's interactions with the people he studies are informed by a kind of paternalistic noble savage ideal. This comment places Indigenous people as inside nature and himself as outside. Developing comfort and intimacy with the Wapischána, he becomes an expert on them in the dominant Western discourse. He sets the scene for his European reader, gaining credibility by his openness to the setting, and his personal perception that he belongs there.

Koch-Grünberg's narratives and photographs demonstrate a sense of curated cultural immersion. As Deborah Poole explains, photography was a tool of ethnography that helped create a narrative about racial order. Photographs could be used as proof of contact, intimacy, and veracity, yet they are also clearly posed and manicured for the photographer's specific aims.[17] Photography itself was also useful in that Koch-Grünberg could show pictures of different Indigenous groups to each other, thus gaining insights into neighbor's customs, appearance, and ways of life.[18] As Paul Hempel explains, one aspect of nineteenth-century German anthropology was the notion of the inseparability of photography and science.[19] As photography emerged, there was a perceived and unquestioned ability on the part of the photographer to depict, define, and then mobilize facts. Photography became associated with modes of collection, a tangible, indisputable representation of what the anthropologist had observed. Koch-Grünberg's photographs are staged, and his interactions brokered with gifts, facts that he forefronts in his work.

In some instances, Koch-Grünberg puts himself into the frame, demonstrating said intimacy and a sense of belonging with the people he studies. In the carefully composed photograph in Figure 4.1, we see the anthropologist, dressed in Western attire but with bare feet, on a higher plane than the young Taulipáng man with whom he is talking. The caption states that the man is telling the explorer "fairy tales," presumably recounting his community's stories and belief system. They sit comfortably perched on boulders, framed by the branches of a tree overhead. This image reimagines the Victorian explorer through a pedagogical interaction where Koch-Grünberg learns from the young man. Furthermore, Koch-Grünberg's bare feet, harkening back to Octavie Coudreau's barefoot romps, intentionally show that he is acclimated and even at home while doing his fieldwork—emphasizing a convivial relationship with the people he studies. His hat

FIGURE 4.1 A Mayuluaipu boy "tells fairy tales" to Koch-Grünberg. Courtesy of the Ethnographic Collection of the Philipps-University of Marburg, Legacy of Theodor Koch-Grünberg, KG-H-III, 122

and walking stick hanging on a tree branch demonstrate a level of comfort and even relaxation. The title "fairy tales" places whatever the young man is saying within a European literary category, one favored by children and entirely unscientific and thus easily understandable to a European audience. The image still falls back on a patriarchal dynamic where Koch-Grünberg's higher placement within the frame creates him as an authoritative figure over both the landscape and the young man with whom he is interacting.

Koch-Grünberg's approach to fieldwork demonstrates a shift in anthropology from collection and categorization toward participant observation. The aim of participant observation is to become ingrained within the culture of study over an extended period. The ethnologist immerses themself into the community of study and takes part in all aspects of day-to-day life.[20] In this sense, Koch-Grünberg becomes both the subject and object, one who acts but who also watches himself acting. There is self-reflection, and certainly a forthrightness when it comes to disclosing his methods. As Poole notes, participant observation allows a certain openness to the humanity of those being observed while still retaining a distance over a racialized Other, as can be seen in Figure 4.1.[21] As Jennifer French explains about this era of anthropological work, "Simultaneously, the emergent field of ethnology 'scientific' knowledge produced in the service of the new colonial powers represented a hardening of attitudes with regard to racial and cultural difference, ranking the peoples of the world in terms of their relative 'advancement,' their 'progress' in developing precisely those forms of technology that constituted the economic (and epistemological) advantage."[22] For Koch-Grünberg, rather than ranking Indigenous peoples on their technological advances, the adoption of Westernized approaches or new technologies by Indigenous communities is something that equates to a loss and tragedy. This of course also carries a paternalistic weight as Koch-Grünberg attempts to manage ways Indigenous people can or cannot be.

Figure 4.2 stands in contrast to Figure 4.1 and quite literally repositions Koch-Grünberg's status and relationship with the people he studies. Here he is directly posing for the camera rather than setting up a more candid shot as in Figure 4.1. He squats down to pose with a group of Indigenous men and boys. While they carry wooden spears, Koch-Grünberg carries his rifle, pointed up in a less-threating manner. In *El abrazo de la serpiente*, the film analyzed in Chapter 5, the director reimagines this very image as a representation of Koch-Grünberg's amicable style of exploration. In contrast to Teddy Roosevelt, with his gun always at the ready, the rifle here comes

FIGURE 4.2 Koch-Grünberg surrounded by a group of Indigenous people. This same photograph was used in *El abrazo de la serpiente*. Courtesy of the Ethnographic Collection of the Philipps-University of Marburg, Legacy of Theodor Koch-Grünberg, KG-H-III, 88

across as nothing more than a Western version of the Indigenous peoples' wooden weapons. Koch-Grünberg forms the focal point of the image—he is directly in the center and stands out in a white shirt and straw hat. He appears perhaps more relaxed here than in Figure 4.1, despite his previous lack of shoes. Taken together, the two images embody Koch-Grünberg's self-fashioning of his version of participant observer. On the one hand, as seen here, he is the friendly, beloved explorer who happily learns from the locals he stays with; on the other hand, as shown in Figure 4.1, he is the meticulous observer and chronicler, uniquely suited to document Indigenous life as he places himself on a higher plane.

Another aspect that can be read in this photograph is how Koch-Grünberg positions himself surrounded by this group of Indigenous men and boys. Anne Cheng puts forward a theory of ornamentalism in relation to Asiatic femininity in Western modernity by examining ornamental personhood or the relationship between subjects and objects. Cheng addresses the racial aspect of both the Oriental and the ornamental, as she explains, "ornamentalism often describes a condition of subjective coercion, reduction, and discipline, but it can also provoke considerations of alternative modes of being and of action for subjects who have not been considered subjects, or subjects who have come to know themselves through objects."[23] She traces alternative subjectivities following Mbembe's "aesthetics of superfluity," or a "mediation between indispensability and expendability that informs labor and life, especially at the height of imperialism and the subsequent global movements of bodies and things."[24] The Indigenous people which whom Koch-Grünberg surrounds himself serve to ornament him and add legitimacy to his work as an anthropologist. Furthermore, Indigenous groups within the Amazon, as seen throughout this book, were most often caught in this duality between indispensability and expendability. Koch-Grünberg, alternately, portrays the people he studies as entirely indispensable.

Koch-Grünberg's self-styling of his exploration demonstrates an anthropologist-traveler who, through common tactics such as gift-giving, immersed himself in his communities of study.[25] As Thomas Beebee notes, "To a greater extent than his predecessors, Koch-Grünberg placed a high priority on living with and becoming friends with the peoples he was observing and collecting."[26] His work emphasizes his interest in learning and his connection and bond with most of the Indigenous groups he encounters, as well as important cultural traditions and language that he learns from them. We can see an emergent pattern of a kind of pedagogical patriarch where Koch-Grünberg works to better understand and learn from his surroundings and the people he interacts with while still falling back on dominant power structures with himself in the center. However, he uses his position as a documenter to advocate for the importance of Indigenous peoples through his written and visual work.

Fashioning the Other: Depictions of Women and Children

Ethnography is, as James Clifford describes, "the science of cultural jeopardy," meaning that ethnographers place themselves and their work as a method of saving cultures that they position as in peril.[27] As such, ethnographers often describe the people they study as on the verge of extinction. This gives their practice importance while also taking agency from the people they study—solidifying their way of life as rapidly disappearing and thus, in a sense, justifying that actual disappearance. Therefore, part of creating an authoritative or meaningful stance is stressing the possibility and rapidity of the disappearance of the culture being studied. This also misses or negates the survival strategies and continued resilience of Indigenous peoples. However, in the time and context that Koch-Grünberg was creating anthropological studies, particularly in the Putumayo region, a genocide of Indigenous peoples was being carried out by the Peruvian Amazon Company, and Koch-Grünberg's positioning of cultures in peril is a means of exigent advocacy.

In the context of his time, Koch-Grünberg is rightly preoccupied by the rapid disappearance of Indigenous cultures. While he accounts for his perception, he also continually makes note of how Indigenous people perceive him, with an emphasis on their affection or preference for him and the special place he occupies for both women and children of the various groups he encounters. This focus once again throws him into the role of patriarch, giving him an authority and perceived ability to manage that is superior to the people he is studying, while gift-giving creates a power dynamic of dependence. His relationship with women and children establishes him as a patriarchal authority, but his claims of friendship and reciprocity show a more nuanced, transformative, educational relationship.

Photography worked hand in hand with ethnography as the "science of cultural jeopardy." As Sá Carvalho explains, this was also the era of "salvage anthropology" where "ethnographers felt their subjects were rapidly disappearing from the globe as a result of the expansion of civilization, and photography was a way of preserving 'difference.'"[28] In his photographs of Indigenous peoples, Koch-Grünberg attempts to create a sympathetic appreciation from Western audiences while also preserving a "difference" he worries is rapidly diminishing.

Figure 4.3 is carefully posed, perhaps remarkably so given how many children are in the frame. One can imagine that Koch-Grünberg had to convince the children to be patient as he set up his camera and made sure that the different rows were arranged to showcase the sheer volume of kids that he was photographing. The children appear fascinated about being photographed, with some looking at the camera, some smiling, others (the majority) frowning, some attentive, some curious or doubtful, a few making faces or fiddling with one thing or another. Shot straight on, this photograph recalls a modern-day portrait of a sports team. Perhaps this is an overly apt metaphor, as a sports photograph can demonstrate simultaneously the potential and the prowess of the team being photographed. The image showcases a sense of "salvage anthropology" by visually depicting Indigenous children, photographically locking-in their traditional hair,

FIGURE 4.3 Photograph of Indigenous children whom Koch-Grünberg describes as his dear friends. Courtesy of the Ethnographic Collection of the Philipps-University of Marburg, Legacy of Theodor Koch-Grünberg, KG-H-III, 191

clothing, and jewelry that stand in contrast to Western conventions. Given the subject of so many children, the image may naturally raise questions for the Western observer about what this next generation's future will look like. Thus, the photograph explicitly appeals to a Western viewer, sounding an alarm about their possible assimilation or disappearance.

Indeed, Koch-Grünberg is particularly concerned about this next generation and often writes about his special relationship with Indigenous children. Children were likely the most welcoming and easy inroad for Koch-Grünberg to establish himself in a village. In his words,

> Once they get over their initial shyness with a stranger, these children are the most confident and happy little creatures one could imagine. They accept all of my jokes with joy and they never behave badly. They are loving and polite with me and they live in great harmony with each other. If I give a piece of chocolate to one of them, they immediately divide it with the rest. I've never seen them fighting or hitting one another.[29]

Brokered with gifts, the children's curiosity about this outsider gives him a benefit where they can be innocent informants. Most noteworthy, to him, is that they "never behave badly," a generalization that expresses awareness that such behavior might interest or even surprise a Western audience, and, more profoundly, points to Indigenous people having or offering a better, more communal way of being. The children chose to share and divide gifts, illustrating the benefits of a communal structure. Koch-Grünberg jokes with the children, and it seems as though their relationship is in harmony.

Also demonstrated in this quote is how Koch-Grünberg uses gift-giving to establish his importance within various Indigenous communities. There is a sense of reciprocity, where, in exchange for beads, chocolate, or other trinkets, Koch-Grünberg was given masks or other articles of importance to daily life in Indigenous settlements that he left at local museums or took back to Germany. As Koch-Grünberg explains, "It has already been a month since I've been here in Koimélemong and I'm good friends with all the residents. I'm likable because I always have time for everyone, I'm nice to all, never angry, and I reward each small service with beads, tobacco and small fishhooks."[30] Highlighting a kinship or connection with one's subjects can be a show of soft imperialism, or, pushing against the grain of an "objective, scientific" approach. This "friendly" approach was common among German ethnographers of the early twentieth century, as they often portrayed themselves as friends and advocates of Indigenous peoples to broach the distance between self and other, while also creating a fortified sense of paternalism.[31] Koch-Grünberg's methods, particularly in relation to children, position him as a benefactor or patriarch to those he interacts with.

Like his descriptions of children, Koch-Grünberg's visual depictions of Indigenous women in relationship to their surroundings emphasize their cultural differences to European conventions, positing that Western society could have something to learn from these other cultures. The photograph in Figure 4.4, captioned "um filho adotivo" (an adopted son), from *Vom Roraima zum Orinoco*, shows the closeness to nature that Koch-Grünberg wants to demonstrate about the Indigenous peoples he documents. There is an easy, convivial relationship between the girl and the deer, her "adopted son" who eats at her feet. Even if she is just avoiding the gaze of the photographer, it appears as if the girl is confiding in the deer; with her head tilted slightly down, both deer and woman are interested in the same thing. The deer is a fawn, which in Western literature is commonly associated with a pastoral innocence. This image transfers that same association; the girl and her fawn appear calm, innocent, and fully comfortable with each other. The deer has obviously been domesticated, demonstrated by the collar it wears, its familiarity with people, and eagerness to eat the food being provided. Koch-Grünberg has positioned himself

FIGURE 4.4 A young Indigenous woman interacts with a deer. Courtesy of the Ethnographic Collection of the Philipps-University of Marburg, Legacy of Theodor Koch-Grünberg, KG-H-III, 16

on an equal footing and framed the shot at eye level. Taken as a whole, this image shows an approachability and innocence, and an intimacy between the photographer and subject, garnered through Koch-Grünberg's specific approach. Portrayals such as these worked to create a sympathetic vision of Indigenous peoples to protect them—part of Koch-Grünberg's stated mission. This photograph also showcases some aspects of ornamentalism, or a lack thereof. In the lack of material objects shown in the photograph, the viewer is instead prompted to understand a simplified closeness between nature and culture.

The three Indigenous women in Figure 4.5 are posed as they make clay pots, showing the skillful and enterprising nature of daily life. Here we can also see aspects of an ornamentalism where the women are interacting with objects, in the process of creating material culture. Rather than the Oriental fetishism that Cheng describes in her theory of ornamentalism, here we see an Indigenous fetishism that revolves around the women's "lack" of clothing, their ornamentation instead with beaded necklaces and, most importantly, their proximity to the earth that they are wielding to create pottery. Although the women are sitting on the ground, Koch-Grünberg

FIGURE 4.5 Three Indigenous women engage with Koch-Grünberg as he photographs them making pottery. Courtesy of the Ethnographic Collection of the Philipps-University of Marburg, Legacy of Theodor Koch-Grünberg, KG-H-III, 196

has again put himself at eye level. As with the photograph of the girl with her deer, the three women are not far from nature, in the dirt, near brushy plants, and, given their scant clothing, exposed to the sky. The effect of this framing is twofold; first, it shows the women bringing together the elements of their surroundings, and second, it brings the viewer intimately into their sphere. The photograph thus creates a narrative of Indigenous women as closer to nature, like Figure 4.4, but one where the objects they create are not just ornamental but also practical.

Koch-Grünberg's photography is often accompanied by descriptions of how he achieved his shots. For instance, in photographing a group of women he explains, "I asked residents to paint themselves festively, because I wanted to take some pictures. I asked everyone to line up. Some girls wore European cotton dresses. I explained to them that I do not find them [the dresses] pretty at all. Immediately, they dropped their dresses and showed off beautiful pearl-aprons that they were wearing underneath civilization."[32] European cotton dresses, a veneer of "civilization," hinder Koch-Grünberg's goal of portraying an "authentic" Indigenous scene. In his telling, they immediately appease his wishes as the girls drop their dresses to reveal their non-Western attire. What is interesting here is the acknowledgment that Koch-Grünberg makes of his own direction, and how this scene is heavily manicured by his hand. It is impressive that he informs the European reader that he has staged the picture to create a scene that will be "authentic," which also speaks to creating a type of "salvage anthropology," where some aspects of Indigenous culture are already lost. As Tuhiwai Smith explains, arguments toward authenticity reinforce an idea that Indigenous people are static, unmovable, and unchanging. Photography was a means to demonstrate an "authentic" Indigenous way of life. In reality, that life was one that was rapidly changing and incorporating outside influences, beginning to take on syncretic, unisolated terms, "what counts as 'authentic' is used by the West as one of the criteria to determine who really is indigenous, who is worth saving, who is still innocent and free from Western contamination."[33] Prompting the women to wear their traditional clothing was one method that Koch-Grünberg was employing to make the argument to the world that they were "worth saving." He is thus explicitly appealing to a Western public's worldview. But he does so self-consciously and informs the reader of this choice.

While Koch-Grünberg is visiting the Taulipáng, more commonly called the Pemon, who live in the inland mountain savannahs of Venezuela and northern Brazil, he relishes the perceived sexual freedom he witnesses from the women of the community.[34] He writes, "It seems that feminine innocence is as lost here as in Vaupés and elsewhere. I can see this from conversations with my workers. Two of them even left their own hammocks for an offering of love! But what sensible person can blame these girls? They are an extraordinarily robust and fiery breed, endowed with a healthy sensuality, and the excess of the women is great. Let them have fun!"[35] Koch-Grünberg congratulates the sexual appetite of the women, particularly as they have chosen *his* workers. This sets a scene that shatters Western conventions but is ultimately entirely satisfying and "fun" for all involved. Again, he positions himself as a happy patriarchal observer who understands, supports, and manages from afar. There is also an implicit critique of Western ideas about sexuality and feminine "innocence," where these Pemon women appear uninhibited. Rather than a condemnation or judgement, Koch-Grünberg applauds and supports their perceived sexual freedom. Indeed, this quote even positions the women's behavior as something to learn from, as their described sexual appetite is portrayed in a positive light that perhaps Koch-Grünberg's mostly European audience could benefit from.

To that end, Koch-Grünberg continually emphasizes a perceived preference of Indigenous women for the "white man." For example, by his telling, Indigenous women prefer a white man to the *mestiço* Brazilians who come to villages and then take away Indigenous men to work:

> The women love the white man who came from far away to their land, so different from the mestiço Brazilians who, from time to time, visit their village and take away the young men to work for them, who then only come back after some years and no longer want to know about the old customs. They love the white man because he does not think himself better than them, because he lives with them like one of their own, he hunts with them, he drinks with them, he dances with them.[36]

According to this passage, Koch-Grünberg's participant observation places him above the Brazilians he describes, and his interactions and the purported joy and acceptance with which they are met give him an authority. That celebration places Indigenous culture as aspirational and something that is worthy of full participation by a European outsider. Koch-Grünberg is essentially saying that *mestiço* Brazilians come to rob the village women of their culture, while he, the white man, is there to celebrate it. This sets up a dichotomy of extraction versus participation, where the Brazilians are extracting labor and the white man is participating in culture. However, Koch-Grünberg is partaking in a kind of cultural extraction as a white anthropologist placing himself in a position of authority through documentation. Here Koch-Grünberg positions himself explicitly as an advocate for Indigenous peoples, particularly over Brazilians looking for workers. As he has experienced village life and, by his telling, has been fully accepted by various Indigenous communities, he claims to be better suited to understand, empathize, and thus advocate for them.

Working within the "science of cultural jeopardy," Koch-Grünberg would most want to preserve a perceived authentic vision of women and children as the potential future of Indigenous peoples. While this reinforces his patriarchal position, it also works to educate an outside audience about the customs, cultures, and potential future of the Indigenous Amazon. Koch-Grünberg views acculturation of Indigenous groups as an egregious error, and something that takes away from their inherent value, a tension that we will return to in Chapter 5. However, Koch-Grünberg also seems to reject European culture, and instead positions Indigenous ways of being as something that Europeans should study and learn from.

Advocating for Indigenous Peoples in a Rubber Boom Context

Naturalists, botanists, and collectors like Koch-Grünberg and Schultes were extremely important in the circulation and production of knowledge about plants while participating in the propagation of a "scientific colonialism," or a "process whereby the center of gravity for the acquisition of knowledge about the nation is located outside the nation itself."[37] In these two case studies, both explorers worked for their national governments on trips to acquire Amazonian flora and information about the region's inhabitants.

Furthermore, the disparate power dynamics of a cultural contact zone carry over to the economy of plants. As mentioned in the introduction to this book, Londa Schiebinger presents the idea of biocontact zones, building on Pratt's conceptualization of contact zones, as a place of disparate contact "between European, Amerindian, and African naturalists in a context that highlights the exchange of plants and their cultural uses."[38] Plant-based knowledge and potential cures moved up a food chain, so to speak, where Indigenous peoples learned from observing animals interact with plants, and the colonizer learned from the Indigenous peoples, and then that knowledge was transferred to the rest of the Western world, often via travel narrative and botanical categorizations.[39] This was used to demonstrate the supposedly natural link between Indigenous peoples, animals, and plants—subjects that could serve as potential sources of knowledge when it came to forms of life that were considered "less perfect than animals and humans."[40] Most plant-based knowledge from the New World was passed on from Indigenous guides or informants. In turn, plant collectors renamed and repurposed their findings to export and turn into capital, using plants as another tool of empire within the colonial project.

Beyond plant taxonomy, the demand for particular cash crops like sugar, tobacco, cotton, or rubber developed systems of slavery, organization, and control based on the subjugation of peoples and landscape.[41] A social and juridical discourse is "naturalized," where a hierarchy of inequality becomes "part of nature," and a Western grid of knowledge is implanted on nature to justify systems of economic exploitation based on racial difference, such as the slave plantation; forced labor in the creation of roads and railways to transport exploited minerals, plants, and resources to markets; and so on.[42] In the Amazon, rubber fueled the exploitation of Indigenous peoples and mixed-race workers whose relegation to enslavement or debt peonage was justified by their race. The international demand for rubber at the turn of the twentieth century and later during World War II massively impacted the region with internal and external migrations, widespread environmental destruction, and the decimation of peoples and cultures.[43]

Koch-Grünberg, like the Coudreaus, Rondon, Roosevelt, and da Cunha, traveled during the first Amazonian rubber boom. With this background context, he had to become an expert in brokering difficult relationships. He received some funding from rubber barons and thus had to carefully navigate his criticism of them.[44] Despite this potentially compromising relationship, he did document the violence that he witnessed. This passage, which Schultes quotes in an article eighty years later, is from a 1910 expedition where Koch-Grünberg noted the rapid changes taking place in the region due to the rubber demand:

> Hardly five years have gone by since my last visit to the Caiary-Vaupés. Whoever comes here now will no longer find the pleasant place I once knew. The pestilential stench of a pseudo-civilization has fallen on the brown people who have no rights. Like a swarm of annihilating grasshoppers, the inhuman gang of rubber barons continue to press forward. . . . Raw brutality, mistreatment and murder are the order of the day.[45]

His language here recalls Octavie Coudreau, although instead of her anxiety about mocambeiros overtaking the jungle, it is the "swarm of annihilating grasshoppers," the rubber barons, that he fears. He explicitly calls out the racialized nature of this violence against "the brown people who have no rights." Koch-Grünberg describes the rubber barons' treatment of workers as inhumane and destructive of not just Indigenous people but also the environment that he so enjoyed. Rubber boom extraction brought increased settlement, or "pseudo-civilization," that Koch-Grünberg also sees as a type of violence. Thus, there are three types of violence described here: first, the tangible and extreme culture of terror being implemented by the rubber barons, second, the exertion of a colonizing "civilization," and finally, the environmental destruction of a formerly pleasant place.

As such, Koch-Grünberg again positions himself as the protector of Indigenous groups, and one of the few people capable of managing all interested parties. By his telling, Koch-Grünberg must step in to stop the potential "continued press" of rubber baron brutality. In another passage, also quoted by Schultes, Koch-Grünberg uses descriptors such as "vigorous," "bright intellect and gentle disposition," and "human material capable of development," to describe the value of the Indigenous peoples he is seeking to protect:

On the lower Caiary, the Brazilians are no better. The Indians' villages are desolate, their homes have been reduced to ashes, and their garden plots deprived of hands to care for them are taken over by the jungle. Thus a vigorous race, a people endowed with a magnificent gift of bright intellect and gentle disposition, will be reduced to naught. Human material capable of development will be annihilated by the brutality of these modern barbarians of culture.[46]

According to Koch-Grünberg it is the Brazilian's mismanagement of the rubber trade that has driven Indigenous people out of their villages, and the jungle, once dotted with peaceful clearings, is now creeping back in. His appeal to the potential "development" of Indigenous peoples can be read to decry the violence of the rubber boom and appeal to a European sensibility that there is a future potential worth saving. This quote, coming from 1910, is also emerging in a context in which there is an increased international consciousness about the atrocities being committed to extract rubber in the Congo and the Amazon.[47] Koch-Grünberg's descriptions of violence work on an international scale to advocate for Indigenous peoples, like his descriptions of women and children, which place him as an amicable patriarchal authority.

Koch-Grünberg's work shows a complicated yet dedicated anthropologist who immerses himself in participant observation and takes on the task of educating a European public about Indigenous issues. His approach begins to create a reciprocal pedagogical relationship where he acknowledges the difficulty of learning yet still strives to gain knowledge from the Indigenous peoples he studies and then educate a wider, non-Indigenous audience. He pushes against the pillars of the coloniality of power while still writing in a Eurocentric manner for a Eurocentric audience. Although his educational impulses may not be entirely reciprocal as he positions himself at the head of the figurative classroom, his work did leave behind a new, more sensitive approach toward learning from, advocating for, and interacting with Amazonian people. Koch-Grünberg's last journey, in 1924, was taken alongside Dr. Hamilton Rice and Brazilian cinematographer Silvino Santos, resulting in the film *The Trail of El Dorado*. The expedition, met with a great deal of press and chronicled through Santos's photography and filmmaking, resulted in Koch-Grünberg's death at fifty-two years old from malaria.

Ethnobotany and a New Perspective from Richard Evans Schultes

Just a few decades later, a new explorer/ethnographer would pick up where Koch-Grünberg left off, this time dedicating himself wholly to the study of human and plant interaction in the Amazon basin. Richard Evans Schultes was born in Boston, Massachusetts, in 1915 to a middle-class family.[48] During a childhood illness, he read Richard Spruce's *Notes of a Botanist on the Amazon and the Andes*, which he said led to his interest in the region and the potential medicinal applications of Amazonian flora.[49] During his undergraduate work at Harvard (1933–1941), he began to study peyote, conducting fieldwork with the Kiowa in Oklahoma. Soon thereafter, he won several grants that funded trips to the Amazon, the region that would become the subject of his life's work. Like Koch-Grünberg, Schultes also spends extensive time living among various Indigenous peoples, and he adopts a viewpoint of learning from these different cultures and worldviews. Schultes often uses Koch-Grünberg as a reference point, citing him at the outset of many of the chapters of his most famous book, *Plants of the Gods* (1979), and drawing on his approach of participant observation, reciprocal pedagogy, and advocacy. However, his work imagines the Amazon region as the world's medicine chest and considers Indigenous peoples as the gatekeepers of this knowledge through the discipline of ethnobotany, reworking the human-nature paradigm an explicit step further than Koch-Grünberg.

Schultes first went to the Amazon in 1941 on a ten-month grant from the United States' National Research Council to identify plants that Indigenous peoples used in hunting.[50] He focused on curare, a common name for various plant-extract-alkaloid arrow poisons from Central and South America. According to him, the northwestern Amazon, where he conducted the bulk of his fieldwork (primarily in Colombia), was the most interesting part of the basin because of the richness of flora.[51] Schultes thus spent his most famous and academically fruitful trips in the northwest Colombian Amazon, traversing areas where "no outsider had ever been."[52]

As a field, ethnobotany refocuses the ethnographical approach toward the cultural importance and usage of plants by local peoples. By the mid-twentieth century the Amazon became a site of plant possibilities explicitly for the purposes of modern medicine.[53] Could the cure for cancer lie in the heart of the Amazon? As a distinct possibility, this has become a consistent argument for the importance of "saving the rainforest." This popular point for why the Amazon region is worthy of conservation tends to privilege plants over people, rather than listening to the knowledge that local people have about plants, a pattern Schultes critiqued and attempted to reverse. Schultes worked with Indigenous peoples, and shamans in particular, as the gatekeepers of knowledge central to understanding the healing potential of the forest.

The overarching questions that ethnobotanists seek to answer are how and why local people select plants for use, and what the conservation and livelihood implications of plant use are. Throughout Schultes's career, he advocated for the study of how Indigenous peoples use the natural world to gain a greater understanding of the ways Western medicine and Indigenous knowledge could combine or reformulate around the study of plants. As he describes,

> Ethnobotany is sometimes considered by people who have no contact with Indians as a rather sentimental discipline, a form of scientifically sanctioned nostalgia for simpler ways of life. I would argue, however, that it is a thoroughly practical discipline. The human species depends on plant species for its own welfare and ultimately for its survival. Each living species is the repository of organic molecules that are the products of the plant's irreproducible evolution. Science should intensify its study of these chemicals, because there is little time left to learn; when a plant becomes extinct, the opportunity to learn is lost forever. It is only common sense that we who can apply technical analyses to problems should learn from peoples who are intimately familiar with their floral environment and its useful properties for the benefit of all mankind.[54]

As Schultes explains here, humans and plants on every scale are intimately connected. Combining Indigenous and Western approaches creates new possibilities. Ethnobotanists seek to understand the relationships between people and plants, thus in a sense making cultural understanding a scientific object of study. By Schultes's telling, what is necessary is a combination of skill sets—that of technical analyses coupled with on-the-ground knowledge—for the benefit of all mankind. Indeed, Schultes's advocacy helped center Indigenous knowledge and link the conservation of cultural diversity with environmental conservation.[55]

Like Koch-Grünberg, Schultes empathizes and relates to the Indigenous people he studies and works with. Schultes's focus is on how Western culture can better learn from Indigenous practices, particularly in relation to plants. This attention toward plants and their properties could be considered a continuation of a botanical colonization where plants were taken from colonies to be grown, studied, cross-pollinated, and dispersed to serve the interests and economies of colonizing groups. Yet the focus on plants also creates new pathways for prioritizing Indigenous knowledge and engaging in meaningful cross-cultural collaboration. Kelly Enright notes how Schultes, like Koch-Grünberg, situated himself as a learner: "Rituals were not curiosities to him, but central pieces of a vast web of botanical knowledge. Rather than objectifying indigenous people, he valued them for what they knew about the complex forest around them."[56] As Schultes himself describes in a 1994 article decrying deforestation and titled "Burning the Library of Amazonia,"

> A few Western botanists have a "taxonomic eye," the gift of recognizing significant morphological variation in a plant. But only the Indians are well acquainted with the various properties of the plants as well as with their external appearance. Why not enlist that vast, intimate knowledge? Why not regard the Indians in the Amazon Basin as a kind of phytochemical rapid-assessment team already on the ground, which could help locate the most promising plants for chemical and pharmacological evaluation?[57]

This passage illustrates Schultes's ethnobotanical approach toward understanding Indigenous peoples and their various knowledge systems. As Schultes recognizes, Western and Indigenous knowledge are not inherently antithetical; they both rely on consistent repetition, observation over time, inference, and prediction. While Western systems rely on binary categorizations, Indigenous knowledge employs elements of a scientific method. As a "phytochemical rapid-assessment team," Schultes advocates for Indigenous-led science that employs collecting and an already intimate knowledge of the environment to educate or cure others. This proposed method of bioprospecting took cues from the progressive movement happening in the United States at the time to move from a fully extractivist model into a softer, scientific extraction which included some Indigenous participation.[58]

As Schultes nods to above, plants play an important and sometimes unrecognized role in the production of culture and the project of empire. Ethnobotany seemingly considers the disparate power dynamics involved in cultural and botanical exchange while still operating within a biocontact zone and the larger geopolitics of plants. As a disciplinary approach, ethnobotany explicitly seeks to learn new methods and usages of plants from Indigenous peoples through understanding their cultural context. Anthropological fieldwork seeks to learn about different cultures, and ethnobotany seeks to learn *from* and thus implement practices within a biocontact zone. However, the question remains of how that knowledge is used and whom it serves. While ethnobotany privileges Indigenous knowledge and practice, it can still be used as a tool of extraction for the purpose of commodification within an unequal power dynamic set up to benefit the extractors, a continuation of a scientific colonialism.[59] Schultes recognized these pitfalls and attempted to use ethnobotany as a tool of advocacy for environmental protection as well as respect and deference toward Indigenous knowledges from Western scientists.

Schultes's purpose for fieldwork in the Amazon shifts from Koch-Grünberg—from a comprehensive overview of culture and folklore—toward a more focused study of plants, what they have to offer humans, and plants' role in medicine and culture. Like Koch-Grünberg, Schultes's Amazonian discoveries were mediated and created through work with Indigenous informants. The crux of ethnobotany is a local informant, preferably a shaman, or *payé*, who can explain the area's plants and their properties to Westerners.[60] The shaman's sacred knowledge is then translated for a Western audience. Like Koch-Grünberg, Schultes argued that with encroaching modernization, Indigenous knowledge of medicinal, narcotic, and toxic plant species and varieties was being quickly lost. He advocated for Indigenous rights in the context of gaining knowledge that the Western world desperately needed to unlock the so-called medicine chest.

Schultes was fascinated with Indigenous ways of using plants as hallucinogens to explain the "magic" of the world. He would earn the trust of a community through participation in ritual ceremonies including *yage*, or ayahuasca, in a sense "going native."[61] "Going native" is an originally derogative expression from the colonial period. However, as scholar of anthropology Danny Jorgensen explains, for early anthropologists the concept of "going native" meant that they were attempting to reorganize their Western viewpoint and adopt a more subjective vantage point through full participation in daily life.[62] Indeed, although Schultes fashioned himself in the tradition of Victorian explorers, he advocated for researchers to fully immerse themselves in Indigenous communities as a means of respecting and conserving both nature and culture.[63] It was through one of his Indigenous informants, Salvador Chindoy, that Schultes gained access to his subjects and a greater understanding of plants and their properties.[64]

Through work with Chindoy and other Indigenous informants, Schultes was able to develop his method of ethnobotany and in turn, find some pharmaceuticals that are still used today. He argues for conservation of

Indigenous land and people because of the latter's knowledge of the different medicinal properties of local flora and fauna, and looming Western encroachment:

> It behooves scientists who are interested in biological diversity to seek out the knowledge of local natives and country people who live and work with their flora. In many instances, this valuable knowledge will not long be available; for it will soon disappear with westernization. It is for this reason that ethnobotanical conservation is so urgently significant as a vital link in the conservation of biological diversity.[65]

Schultes's advocacy for Indigenous knowledge merged with Western science, like Koch-Grünberg's, is still steeped in a desire for extraction. While the ends—creating science or products that could better human health—is admirable, the means continue an imperialist structure of extraction despite importantly reconfiguring knowledge production to include and center Indigenous voices. This presents a power structure where Indigenous peoples and their land are only valuable in their knowledge of resources that Western science needs. For example, Schultes was employed as an explorer on behalf of the United States' quest to find high quality Amazonian rubber during World War II.

A Wartime Explorer

The beginning of Schultes's Amazonian travels took place during the Good Neighbor Policy period of relations between the United States and Latin America, from 1933 through the end of World War II. This period of "good relations" spurred more cooperation, particularly regarding trade and technology. As Barbara Weinstein notes, modernization theory assumed that those in Latin America would welcome and were seeking the same way of life as the United States.[66] In the case of the Amazon this progress was plant based, the region deemed a "tropical treasure trove" that, rather than requiring industrialization, needed the guiding hand of science to develop its foliage into riches.[67] Schultes's ethnobotanical approach inverts the assumption that the tropical regions of the world needed the guiding hand of Western science. Instead, it is Western science that needs the knowledge contained within the forest, and Indigenous intermediaries to translate that knowledge, making them conduits to capital gain.

Complicating this inversion, during World War II attention once again turned to Amazonian rubber, and Schultes was an important figure during American war efforts to secure it. In 1942, he was in the Putumayo region of Colombia, and after Pearl Harbor was bombed, he promptly reported to the closest American embassy to enlist. He was instead directed to a mission to work for Franklin D. Roosevelt's Rubber Reserve Company (RRC) meant to ensure US rubber supplies remained intact after access to rubber colonies in Southeast Asia were cut off. As Schultes describes in a field notebook from 1952, the American government organized this initiative to assist local governments in restarting their long-since abandoned rubber outposts to support the US war effort. According to Schultes, he was employed in the following: "I joined this organization and immediately plunged into the rubber forests of Colombia as an explorer, searching out the densest and best type of rubber, mapping rivers, and reporting on their navigability and other tasks preparatory to the rebirth of the wild rubber industry."[68] The RRC, formed in 1940, sought to meet wartime demands by resurrecting wild rubber reserves, recycling scrap rubber, and reopening wild rubber tapping in South America.[69]

The US government sent plant collectors and biologists throughout Latin America to establish blight free plantations for the benefit of the country's wartime effort. The US government also argued that this would benefit Latin American countries. According to a 1940 news report from the *Christian Science Monitor*, "the United States Government is trying to establish this industry not in its own territory but in Latin-American countries which will be vastly benefited if the enterprise is successful. They will grow rubber and sell it to the United States; they will profit and so will their northern neighbor."[70] This "mutually beneficial" agreement was bolstered by arrangements with each country where exploratory missions were deployed. Of course, those profits, if ever brought to yield, would likely land squarely in the hands of outside investors or the wealthiest people within the countries of extraction. By early 1942, the United States had negotiated agreements with fifteen Latin American countries to buy all their surplus and natural rubber production.[71]

Rather than growing effectively in neat plantation rows, *hevea* trees naturally grew far enough apart to keep rubber blight at bay. Schultes's research focused on the northwest Amazon, primarily in Colombia, a less traveled area where there were rumored blight-resistant species of *hevea*. Schultes, as part of a USDA-run rubber cooperative, worked for over a decade searching for blight-free rubber trees while also collecting other botanical specimens. Schultes actively helped start rubber stations where researchers investigated techniques to combat blight—many of which looked quite promising.[72] This decade-long search for an almost magical plant is again akin to the enduring search for an Amazonian El Dorado.

As part of his RRC mission, Schultes established a home base in Leticia, Colombia (on the triple frontier border between Brazil and Peru), where he would travel to the interior of the jungle collecting seeds. Eventually, Schultes selected 120 clones to dispatch to research stations in Costa Rica to aid the US wartime effort for rubber. By 1944 he had collected three tons of clones, which he paid locals to help find and store. Despite the RRC's findings, after the war ended and synthetic rubber manufacturing took off, there was less of a need to create blight-resistant rubber plantations in the Americas. Indeed, when all was said and done, the RRC had only stockpiled one million tons of rubber, while the military consumed around six hundred thousand tons per year. Lacking governmental support and funding to create a comprehensive report of his findings, Schultes never published them. Like other failed missions to find El Dorado, Schultes's quest for rubber gold ran dry. Perhaps this experience led him toward an increased focus on the value of an ethnobotanical approach as the best way to merge Western and Indigenous knowledges.

At the same time the US was sponsoring rubber stockpiling in Latin America, they were also heavily funding the development of synthetic rubber, and by 1944 there were fifteen privately run rubber plants that manufactured four different grades of rubber, quickly transforming the United States from the largest global rubber importer into its main exporter.[73] Once again, the Amazonian rubber boom had busted. Schultes remained in the northwestern Amazon until 1953, when he returned to the US and became a renowned professor at Harvard. After his many Amazonian adventures, Schultes stayed active in advocating for rainforest conservation and the importance of Indigenous peoples' plant-based knowledge until his death in 2001.

Conclusion

The explorers of this chapter break from overtly dominant rhetorics of modernity and imperial exploitation and work toward learning from the Other. This occurs against dramatic historical backdrops of stark inequality, global rubber exploitation, and world war. Ultimately this chapter, as the rest of this book, deals with the creation and proliferation of knowledge.

In the Western tradition of knowledge production, meaning is achieved through scientific and "objective" research methods. Western knowledge is taken as the center of legitimate knowledge through globalization.[74] This dismisses a whole world of alternate approaches and different ways of looking at the natural world that seek to holistically heal or just exist. Koch-Grünberg and Schultes both acknowledge these distinctive ways of interacting with the world that occidental approaches have too often dismissed. Their work laid the foundation for important later strides toward listening to, learning from, and advocating with Indigenous peoples.

A major connective tissue between these two explorers and their engagement with Indigenous peoples of the Amazon is the concept of transformation. As Lúcia Sá notes, Amazonian stories demonstrate a nature in flux, in a constant state of transformation and growth, and hardly ever an untouched, virgin forest.[75] Throughout their studies, both explorers seem to find a deeper, transformational meaning in their own lives due to the stories they learned from the rainforest and its peoples. Furthermore, they use what they are taught in the Amazon to reach a broad Western audience and teach about issues facing Indigenous peoples and a rapidly changing natural environment. Rather than directly imposing a scientific approach over nature, they begin to reexamine the relationship between nature and culture, particularly through Indigenous practices and worldviews.

However, an inherent flaw in these explorers' contributions is who the knowledge created serves. Western outsiders, despite noble intentions, are still operating on an axis of extractivist power, within a biocontact zone. While both Koch-Grünberg and Schultes reimagined and reconfigured this axis, their work also mobilized arguments for the value of Indigenous peoples based on their knowledge or a perceived inherent goodness, rather than a shared, global value as human beings. These explorers move us into the subject of Chapter 5, director Ciro Guerra's film *El abrazo de la serpiente*. We will explore Guerra's reimagining of Koch-Grünberg's and Schultes's work in the next chapter, a testament to the enduring appeal of the two anthropologists and their dynamic yet complicated accomplishments.

Ethnomuseology: Material Culture and Preservation

One method of a decolonizing approach is creating opportunities for collaborative research in the process of documenting culture. As such, this addendum presents a brief study of the legacies of anthropological collection and contemporary attempts to reformulate the collection of material objects and museum science. Koch-Grünberg's collecting formed part of his practice of "salvage anthropology,'" where objects, like the documentation of language, folktales, and photography, worked to represent cultures that were perceived to be in earlier stages of evolution and that were rapidly disappearing. While doing anthropological fieldwork, explorers like Koch-Grünberg engaged in the collection of material artifacts. Explorers were most interested in objects that they believed to carry a sense of cultural authenticity or ritualistic importance. Even if the objects were not necessarily the most beautiful, their importance for the community was taken as a sign that it would also be an significant artifact of cultures perceived to be disappearing.

Koch-Grünberg left behind not only a plethora of written material and photography but also actual material culture from the Indigenous peoples he visited. Many anthropologists from the early nineteenth century on worked with ethnographic museums, which would help sponsor their trips, and as part of the funding, they would bring back material artifacts. Throughout his more than twenty years of working in the Amazon and documenting various Indigenous groups, Koch-Grünberg collected objects both sacred and quotidian to Amazonian life. Some of those objects he sold to the Royal Museum of Ethnology in Berlin, and another swath of objects were purchased by Emílio Goeldi, a Swiss-Brazilian naturalist who started the Museu Paraense in Belém, now called the Museu Paraense Emílio Goeldi. Today, the museum houses the largest repository of Amazonian collections and is the most important ethnographic museum in Brazil, particularly after the fires at the National Museum in Rio de Janeiro in 2018. Of that collection, Koch-Grünberg's contribution from the Rio Negro region is the largest in the museum, including four hundred pieces from eighteen Indigenous communities. The collection is made up of "textile, clothing, ceramics, basketry, toys, music instruments, feather work, household objects, head and body ornaments, archery, whipping for dance and masks."[76]

As discussed in this chapter, at the time that Koch-Grünberg was doing this collecting work, a time rife with conflict and violence, navigating relationships between different interested parties (including rubber barons, government officials, and Indigenous peoples) was difficult. Like the other actors Koch-Grünberg negotiated with, the Indigenous groups he worked with were interested in managing power relations to achieve their own purposes. A major way they could do so was via exchange with the anthropologist who was eager to collect various artifacts and as such would make political promises (that, at times, he did not keep).

Word quickly spread among different Indigenous groups about Koch-Grünberg's political connections and eagerness to collect material from their various cultures. There were even times when communities would hear of his imminent arrival and arrange items that they wanted to sell or trade with him.[77] This essentially means that Indigenous peoples helped to curate their own collections by specifically deciding what artifacts they would present to the explorer. However, Koch-Grünberg at times exaggerated his connections or lied about meetings with regional governors to acquire items that he perceived were integral or sacred to these groups. For example, among the Tukano, there was a sacred drum that Koch-Grünberg invented a meeting with the governor of Amazonas to acquire. The Tukano wanted to gain governmental aid and goods, and as such agreed to trade the culturally important drums despite misgivings.

Koch-Grünberg's work and collections have obviously had a lasting impact. A new approach toward material collected by anthropologists and explorers has recently emerged. Like ethnobotany, ethnomuseology attempts to actively partner with Indigenous peoples to combine knowledge and create a new, more equal approach toward knowledge production and preservation—part of a decolonizing praxis. Ethnomuseology is "an approach to museum science that seeks to put indigenous people in dialog with their own heritage, whether it is already part of museum collections or in the process of being converted into cultural heritage."[78] This innovatative approach can connect Indigenous peoples with objects from their past that were taken in circumstances of extreme inequality, or in the case of Koch-Grünberg, occasional exaggeration. This more contemporary approach aims to "make the Other present within institutions, placing peoples in a new dialogue with (and about) their heritage."[79] This requires collaboration and partnership between museums and Indigenous peoples.

Recently, the Museu Goeldi has undertaken this process of ethnomuseology in a project of exchange and dialogue with the Mebêngôkre-Kayapó, from the Xingu River and tributaries, and the Baniwa, from the upper Rio Negro, in relation to collections of materials from their ancestors. This project incorporates collections from Koch-Grünberg among other anthropologists who studied the region. Anthropologist Glenn Shepard, a researcher and curator with the Museu Goeldi, started this project and has published on some of his Indigenous counterparts' experiences upon interacting with objects housed within the museum.

As part of this ethnomuseology practice, both the Mebêngôkre-Kayapó and Baniwa visited the ethnographical collections held at the Goeldi museum. Researchers from the Goeldi museum also visited their communities, and Indigenous youth were offered opportunities to learn video recording techniques to document the experience.[80]

The Mebêngôkre-Kayapó have had a long and sustained relationship with the Museu Goeldi and have participated in exhibits from 1938 until the present day. When they visited the collection, community members found many objects that they still use in daily life. They also noticed an unpleasant smell that they called *moja tum*, or "old things"—objects that belonged to people who had already died.[81] Because objects are seen as still tied to people after their deaths, the smell of old things and physical touch was viewed as capable of causing illness and prompted at least one Indigenous visitor to stop coming. As Shepard explains, "the meaning of the Museum and its collection for them is not primarily as a repository of memories and 'old things', but rather an extension of their ongoing forms of ownership and capacity for cultural renovation."[82]

The Baniwa had a slightly different experience than the Mebêngôkre-Kayapó during their ethnomuseological visits to the Goeldi collection. The Baniwa were heavily affected by missionaries, losing "much of their ritual life and associated material culture during the time period separating the historical collections of Koch-Grünberg, in the early twentieth century, and the present day."[83] As a result, they encountered objects like bracelets and ritual headdresses that they had only heard about from their grandparents. The Baniwa were reported to have an overall positive interaction with the collection's objects, with one notable exception. Koch-Grünberg collected a sacred Kowari (Jurupari) flute, which is currently housed in Europe, but the Goeldi museum has a photograph of the instrument. The Baniwa participants voiced anger at the desecration of a sacred object that was only meant to be seen by certain people during ritual ceremonies. The Baniwa also showed a good deal of interest in repatriating their material culture. Shepard carried this out with a digital repatriation trip where he left behind the Goeldi's entire digital photographic record with the Baniwa communities he visited.

Overall, this practice of ethnomuseology helps to understand continuities between when the material objects were collected and their use, manufacture, and importance for communities in the present day. The project also helped to recognize cultural differences between the two groups involved. To end with Shepard's takeaway from the project: "in its broadest spirit, the project has instigated a critical reflection on the relationship of indigenous peoples with their 'museified' material culture, and on the historical processes that distance or unite them with objects preserved in ethnographic collections."[84] As such, practices like ethnomuseology can rework the legacies of knowledge and material extraction, moving toward increased reciprocity, access, and equity.

CHAPTER 5

The Reconfigured Travel Narrative
Indigenous Representation and El abrazo de la serpiente

Bursting forth out of greyscale, light emerges from a young man's eyes and mouth, drowning the screen in white. His large stone necklace fades as the scene shifts from human face to an otherworldly nature. Sound reverberates and begins to throb, and images of the starry cosmos pan in and out while swirling, multicolored shapes against a black backdrop slowly tick forward. The colors—hazy blue, a vibrant red, and neon yellow—are particularly bright, their light shattering the previous two hours of black and white Amazonia. In these brief moments, the viewer is swallowed whole, transported into outer space, or perhaps another dimension. The universe opens through a gatekeeper, an Indigenous man named Karakamate, who is the last of his fictionalized people, the Cohuiano. As both a young and old man, he is shown guiding two semifictionalized Western explorers through the Colombian Amazon in pursuit of an imagined and mystical *yakruna* plant during the first rubber boom and later World War II secondary boom. As the travelers move through the jungle, the viewer is prompted to question Western structures of narrative, nature, and culture.

Colombian writer and director Ciro Guerra's 2015 epic travel film *El abrazo de la serpiente*, or *The Embrace of the Serpent*, centers Karakamate in youth and maturity in his interactions with two Western outsiders. The first explorer, a fictionalized version of Theodor Koch-Grünberg, a German

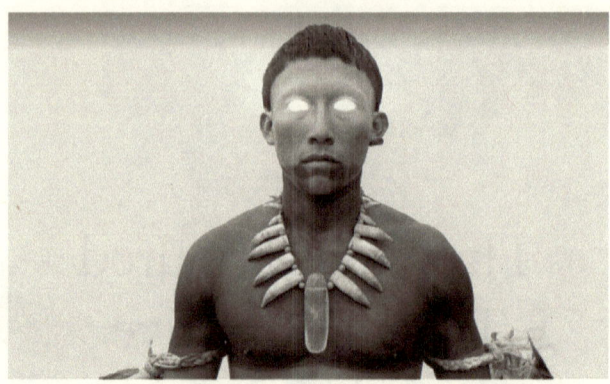

FIGURE 5.1 Young Karakamate's face harkens the beginning of Evan's psychedelic trip. Courtesy of Oscilloscope Laboratories

called Theo, travels in 1909, during the height of the first rubber boom. Theo is already familiar with Amazonian territory and has been writing diaries and taking pictures to document plant life in the region. He enlists a young Karakamate to help him find the *yakruna*, the only cure for a disease he has contracted. Theo also travels with a formerly enslaved man named Manduca, who provides some points of conflict with Karakamate. The *yakruna* drives the plot, and it is through Karakamate's association with the plant that he gains importance for the explorers. The film flickers back and forth between Karakamate's interactions with Theo and into the 1940s with the American explorer Evan, based on Richard Evans Schultes, who has come to the Amazon also in search of *yakruna* because of its ability to purify rubber. He is seeking this high-quality rubber to aid the American effort in World War II. Throughout travels with both Theo and Evan in their different decades, Karakamate experiences periodic, violent encounters with outsiders in the jungle. The film pinpoints two eras of heightened economic extraction of rubber from the Amazon while keeping a primary focus on an alternative plant, the *yakruna*.

The film is director Ciro Guerra's take on the travel narrative genre. Through months of exploration and filming, *El abrazo de la serpiente* uses Indigenous concepts to create a travel-narrative film designed for contemporary, international audiences. This is demonstrated by the ways the film interprets time and chronology and its character's relationship with plants. Despite stories that take place in different chronologies, the characters in the film are connected in their search for the *yakruna* plant, a mystical cure-all that both explorers seek and of which Karakamate, as a shaman, has advanced knowledge. The *yakruna* is what induces the other-worldly trip and what propels the travelers throughout the film. By following the *yakruna*, the traditional travel narrative's chronological form is stripped, and the film instead cycles back and forth between times, resisting a Western order. Past, present, and future blend in a synchronous contact zone. Time within the film is malleable and connected to nature, which the travelers experience as they move throughout the jungle and engage with the environment. Furthermore, the Western cultural touchstones that the film employs are all aspects of the genre of travel literature. This chapter analyzes Guerra's film as a reconfigured version of the more traditional travel narrative explored in previous chapters as a new way to approach the genre—one that engages with Indigenous cosmovisions and alternative ways of being.

Within the Amazon of this film the three main characters are united by a desire for knowledge and discovery of both the self and Other. The production and preservation of this knowledge is central to the film and, more broadly, central to representations of the Amazon. As Joey Whitfield explains, the film demonstrates a shift in the order of knowledge, namely "the loss of aspects of indigenous thought through the culturecidal activities of Christian missionaries and the genocidal violence of the rubber industry."[1] While outside forces like missionaries and the rubber industry threaten to completely disappear Indigenous knowledge, the film problematically elevates the two explorers as heroes of knowledge salvation. According to the film, it is through their studies and actions that the vanishing Indian's plant-based knowledge is saved. However, as others have argued, the film also demonstrates a rupture in the colonial narrative of knowledge extraction. Camilo Jaramillo Castrillón explains that the film can only be understood in terms of knowledge exchange in that it subverts the idea of Western ways of thinking as superior, instead demonstrating how Western thinking has been informed through negotiations and interactions with Indigenous knowledge.[2] Elaborating on this argument, Castrillón writes that the film's use of Indigenous dialogue makes the film itself a cultural register and archive of Amazonian communities. The film, as a take on the travel narrative, complicates the idea of knowledge production, circulation, and extraction through its periodic demonstrations of exchange and acknowledgment of the debt that Western knowledge owes to Indigenous knowledges, particularly when that knowledge is plant-based. However, these complications fall back on problematic tropes of an Indigenous character who only appears in relation to Western outsiders.

An Indigenous-centered Amazon is created through the director's use of two reimagined Indigenous concepts to guide the film, the *yakruna* and the *chullachaqui*. As previously mentioned, the *yakruna* is a fictional plant that serves as a metaphorical stand-in for the Edenic hope of plants in the Amazon and is a loosely disguised version of ayahuasca. In the film, the *yakruna* is sacred to Karakamate's fictionalized tribe and he is the gatekeeper to the plant. It has medicinal and hallucinogenic properties and grows as a flower that resembles an orchid. The *yakruna* is also attached to rubber as it is said to grow on trees creating a higher quality, blight-free rubber. The *yakruna*, in its rarity and potential as a product, is thus representative of the extractive hopes of outsiders in the Amazon. Instead, the plant is entirely managed by Karakamate who would rather destroy it than see it grown in plantations or used for export.

Like the *yakruna*, the *chullachaqui* is also based on Amazonian concepts, however Guerra changes its meaning in the film. A *chullachaqui* is thought of throughout the Amazon basin as a transformative being. The *chullachaqui* can take on a human form, often appearing with bodily disfigurements and is also inherently solitary, yet finds solace in growing trees and other plants, demonstrating a deep connection with nature. Indeed, as the Amazon region has become increasingly developed, the conception of the *chullachaqui* has also transformed, this time into a being that takes on deforestation, becoming a "protective spirit of the jungle."[3] In *El abrazo de la serpiente*, the *chullachaqui* is recast as a soul without a body—a kind of empty doppelgänger. In old age, Karakamate worries that he has become a *chullachaqui*, a spirit wandering the forest rather than an actual human with tangible memories. While the *chullachaqui* of the film wavers between human and spirit, the *yakruna* is part of a wider ecosystem of knowledge, mysticism, and a plant-centered narrative. The *chullachaqui* is thus between being and non-being and the *yakruna* between knowledge and mysticism, occupying spaces that confound rigid categories.

The categorical distinction between nature and culture, for many non-Western cultures, is nonexistent, as nature is considered an extension and integral aspect of culture itself. Both the *chullachaqui* and *yakruna* represent what Eduardo Viveiros de Castro terms an "Amazonian perspectivism" that puts forth an Indigenous worldview that understands nature and culture dynamically. Perspectivism maintains that knowledge always depends on the perspectives of those observing and that no human or culture has access to an absolute view of the world. Within Amazonian ontologies, perspectivism explains how different beings "see," or how humans, animals, and spirits perceive each other as different beings. Indeed, all beings of a species perceive one another as human or person, and other species as not-person, meaning that beings have a shared culture with different natures. This opens a possibility of environmental equity where nature and the non-human can be considered a being of equal status, the beating heart of a symbiotic system.

In this chapter, I argue that the film takes strides toward presenting an alternative travel narrative by stripping the narrative form itself and instead taking a nonlinear approach through engagement with Indigenous cosmologies. To examine *El abrazo de la serpiente* as a project that pushes certain Western conceptions of time, space, race, and a plant-based cosmology, this chapter first discusses the ways that Guerra has chosen to rewrite travel literature for a new cultural market—that of contemporary international film. The chapter then moves into an overview of human-plant interaction and the contact zones within the film itself where characters interact based on plants, and concludes with an examination of memory and the interaction between Indigenous and Western cultures. While others have examined the pedagogical imperative of the film, its negotiation between different types of knowledge, or its employment of a posthuman ethos, a specific focus on the film as a travel narrative propelled by plants furthers a reading of the decolonial impetus (and its pitfalls) within the film.

Constructing a Deconstructed Travel Narrative

Production on *El abrazo de la serpiente* took place in the Colombian Amazon where director Ciro Guerra consulted with local communities and cast Indigenous actors to play central roles. Guerra uses his personal travels in the Amazon to create the film, relaying his experience to a wide audience, with the goal of bringing Indigenous knowledge closer to Western audiences, much like the real explorers upon whom he based his study.[4] Young Karakamate was played by Nílbio Torres of the Cubeo, and Antonio Bolívar, an Ocaina elder, was cast as old Karakamate.[5] The tone of the movie is dark and somber, the dialogue is limited, and where it exists is presented in Indigenous languages with the occasional German, Spanish, Catalan, or Portuguese conversation. It is notable that both Western actors had to learn to speak and act in Indigenous languages. Overall, it is an art-house film shot in black and white that reached a predominantly international, specialized audience. Despite its niche qualities, the film received accolades including an

Academy Award nomination for best foreign film in 2016 (the first ever for a Colombian production). It has elicited frequent comparisons to Amazonian travel films such as Werner Herzog's *Aguirre, the Wrath of God* and *Fitzcarraldo*, and narratives that explicitly decry abuse or focus on the rubber boom era such as *La vorágine*.[6] Yet, *El abrazo de la serpiente*, in contrast to these other narratives, has a sustained and explicit focus on an imagined Indigenous perspective (however mediated through contact with Western explorers).

As explained in the previous chapter, Ciro Guerra drew inspiration for *El abrazo de la serpiente* from two Amazonian explorers who worked in different periods and capacities to expand plant-based knowledge of the rainforest. Guerra knew he wanted to shoot in the Amazon, so he consulted with an anthropologist who suggested looking at travel narratives for inspiration.[7] In so doing, Guerra landed on Theodor Koch-Grünberg and Richard Evans Schultes. These explorers, in Guerra's view, demonstrated the most humane approach to the jungle and Indigenous peoples and he was attracted by the wealth of photographic images they created. He explicitly states this inspiration in a slide at the end of the film, clearly connecting this imagined story with the two travelers. As seen in Chapter 4, Koch-Grünberg and Schultes prioritize the role of Indigenous informants particularly in an ethnobotanical approach that operates through interaction and knowledge exchange. *El abrazo de la serpiente* uses this concept and layers information and informants.[8]

To construct his deconstructive travel narrative, Guerra relies on Koch-Grünberg and Schultes's works as a point of reference, as outsider informants about Indigenous cultures. However, Guerra explains how he chose to fictionalize the explorers to have creative freedom:

> It's fiction, but these events are inspired by real acts. Koch-Grünberg and Schultes as characters are also not exactly themselves; they're inspired by them but are a construction that also borrows from other anthropologists. It is a fictional work ... through fiction one creates to be able to speak. It is not a documentary, it's a story inspired by events and also a way of approaching those who do not understand this [way of life].[9]

In using creative license and taking bits and pieces of travel diaries and photographs, Guerra can reject a fact-based approach, fashioning the film as a work of artistic translation and sidestepping critiques of authenticity. As Ana María Mutis explains, the film uses layering of time, experiences of real explorers, and imagined fictions to create an "andamiaje metaficticio" or metafictional scaffolding that can cycle between temporalities and utilize some reflexivity in its approach.[10] Although Guerra drew inspiration from real-life explorers, his recasting creates characters that can serve as stand-ins for almost any outsider intervention in the Amazon. In that sense, Guerra imagines the explorers as a shadowy interpretation of Koch-Grünberg and Schultes, perhaps as *chullachaquis* themselves.

In the fictionalized narrative of *El abrazo de la serpiente*, Koch-Grünberg and Schultes are Guerra's informants that he then uses to translate to a wider audience, much as the explorers did in their initial writings. Guerra also employed the local men cast as Karakamate and Manduca to shape the Indigenous languages and their character's portrayal in the film. Giving voice to informants by having their dialogue in their own languages and put on film works toward upsetting the Western order. The film explicitly ties itself to real events, particularly through quotations from the actual explorers and their own photography, as well as the use of authentic Indigenous languages. However, these ties to an "authentic" Amazon become problematic as this level of poetic license can result in the audience confusing fiction with fact.[11] The dreamlike quality of the film and the blending of fact and fiction create an illusion, an essentialized glance at an extensive set of complicated realities. Guerra reimagines imperial contact with competing visions, languages, and sounds and in the process, relativizes the notion of Western scientific truths.

Through *El abrazo de la serpiente* Guerra puts forward a nuanced Indigenous character with the presence of Indigenous language, critical thinking about the imperial project by the Indigenous person, and a consideration of ways to respond, reject, and survive it. As Charlotte Gleghorn notes, the film creates a pedagogical imperative where Indigenous culture becomes interpretable and as a result commodifiable through Guerra's lens. This pedagogical relationship echoes the real explorers, as detailed in the previous chapter. However, the film also propagates and revamps the disappearing Native trope, taking away from some of the film's decolonial impetus and fomenting cliches of the inevitability of Indigenous disappearance.[12] Indeed, Karakamate is the self-proclaimed last of his people, and as an old man he struggles to remember his culture, representing an overall loss of Indigenous knowledge.

Karakamate lives through two key eras in the history of Amazonian extractivism, represented by Theo and Evan. Theo experiences the Amazon with a utopian idealism that is marred by the violence of the rubber trade, and Evan comes to the Amazon driven by capitalistic pursuits of re-establishing mass exports of rubber from the region. The film is framed as contingent on contact with two Western outsiders with a desire to extract knowledge from Karakamate yet, as Maria Chiara D'Argenio explains, the Western explorers are portrayed in consistent states of lacking. They rely on Karakamate for assistance, elevating the Indigenous protagonist to a position of power or at the very least exchange. While the position of peril or the inadequacy of the Western explorers falls back on colonial tropes, and constructs Karakamate's character always in relation to the explorers, it also restructures the power dynamic of the film and highlights the Indigenous protagonist's importance.

The Geopolitics of Plants and the Nature–Culture Divide

As discussed in the Chapter 4, the geopolitics of plants examines the role of plants in a geopolitical power structure. Furthermore, biocontact zones help us understand the unequal power dynamics involved in the exchange of plants and their cultural usage. Throughout *El abrazo de la serpiente*, Karakamate's interactions with other Indigenous characters and the white explorers revolve around plants and their cultural usage, creating an Amazonian biocontact zone within the film. In the Amazon of *El abrazo de la serpiente,* characters have purpose through their relationship with plants, and the Indigenous actor has equal billing because of his plant-based knowledge. The two explorers are interested in collecting and circulating information about plants, while throughout the film rubber fuels a backdrop of violence.

The geopolitics of plants works on an axis of extractivism, which once again separates nature and culture. Indigenous leaders such as Ailton Krenak have remarked on the interconnectedness of nature and culture, and how a separation demonstrates man's ego, as, in his words, "humans are not the only interesting creatures of the world."[13] He argues that the act of depersonalizing nature and denying its sentience creates nature as a resource—something that can then be extracted, commodified, and used.[14] Krenak's critique of Western viewpoints is similar to Phillipe Descola who examines Indigenous cosmologies for their approach toward what Western thought has portrayed as a dichotomy between nature and culture. He finds that

> in contrast to modern dualism, which deploys a multiplicity of cultural differences against a background of an unchanging nature, Amerindian thought

envisages the entire cosmos as being animated by a single cultural regime that becomes diversified, if not by heterogenous natures, at least by all the different ways in which living beings apprehend one another. The common referent for all the entities that live in the world is thus not Man as a species but humanity as a condition.[15]

In other words, the human condition is part of a broader way of being that is intricately interconnected with all living things. Nature, for many non-Western cultures, is not opposed to culture but rather an extension and integral aspect of culture itself, like ideas of Amazonian perspectivism as put forth by Viveiros de Castro. *El abrazo de la serpiente* attempts to show some of this cosmology to a Western audience, using the importance and inseparability of plants to rethink not only the travel narrative but the supposition that nature and culture are inherently at odds. To that end, when viewed as a new interpretation of the traditional travel narrative, *El abrazo de la serpiente* opens a discussion of non-dichotomous, linear, or Western trajectories.

Indeed, the practice of interrogating Western systems of knowledge and research has been a part of Indigenous methodologies for decades. Scholars such as Linda Tuhiwai Smith, Marisol de la Cadena, Silvia Rivera Cusicanqui, Davi Kopenawa, and others have been analyzing the nature/culture divide and the importance of Indigenous research methodologies to decolonize Western epistemologies.[16] This can open space for alternative voices and approaches to knowledge production that give equal billing to both nature and culture, and to historically underrepresented peoples, which *El abrazo de la serpiente* certainly attempts to do.

One method of a decolonial approach is speaking the world differently through practices such as the pluriverse. Marisol de la Cadena, in "Indigenous Cosmopolitics in the Andes: Conceptual Reflections beyond 'Politics,'" interrogates the nature-culture divide by looking at current Indigenous social movements and elaborates on the emergence of the pluriverse as a political tool. This plural political engagement uses Indigenous epistemologies to understand nonhumans as actors in the political arena—including animals, plants, and the landscape.[17] She deems these relationships "earth-practices" that do not fit the "dominant ontological distinction."[18] Reorganizing the political sphere to incorporate alternative ways of thinking would give more autonomy to Indigenous peoples.[19] For example, de la Cadena explains a Peruvian protest about a potential mining project in the Ausangate mountain, outside of Cusco. Beyond viewing the mine as environmentally destructive, Indigenous protesters were wary of the destruction the mountain itself would cause as a reaction to human intervention at a sacred site. Articulating the sentience of nature and its importance within an established system of laws that does not use the same vocabulary or understand the world in the same way demonstrates the importance of creating a dialogue across different cultural practices. Similarly, Cusicanqui notes that "the possibility of a profound cultural reform in our society depends on the decolonization of our gestures and acts and the language with which we name the world."[20] Decolonial thinking would necessitate speaking the world differently. Part of this process is renaming and reconfiguring current streams of knowledge.[21] This is what Guerra attempts in *El abrazo de la serpiente*, creating a filmic travel narrative that reshapes the genre and speaks the world differently using Indigenous languages (literal speech), an alternative time-space relationship, and a reconstruction of the human-nature relationship.

The fictional Karakamate in *El abrazo de la serpiente* assumes a spokesman-like position for Indigenous peoples and, more broadly, the Amazon Forest itself, as an emissary of insider knowledge about the land. In many ways Karakamate negotiates between cultures, as he is critical and skeptical of the Westerners and others he encounters, while still taking the time to recognize their humanity and interact. He is, though, tasked with speaking as a stand-in for all Indigenous peoples and the environment itself, and his persona in the film appears as dependent on his interactions with the two explorers that bookend his life in youth and maturity. The film begins and ends with the first and final encounters with Western explorers, constructing Karakamate always in relation to these outsiders. He ultimately never fully exists on his own terms, serving instead as a point of contrast and a guide for Western civilization.

El abrazo de la serpiente is one of the few contemporary representations with relative commercial (and abundant critical) success where an Indigenous character even has a name, let alone a full story, dialogue in an Indigenous language, and equal billing. As previously mentioned, the film creates a pedagogical imperative that is aimed at teaching non-Indigenous audiences about Indigenous knowledge.[22] And indeed, it is non-Indigenous audiences who should be educating themselves about Indigenous issues and ways of thinking. However, this comes at a cost of orienting the film toward outsiders and mediating an imagined Indigenous experience through the lens of Western explorers. Thus, the question becomes how to create stories that center an Indigenous character and avoid tasking them with demonstrating their value through ties with Westerners' thirst for knowledge or a potential product.

Initial Encounters and a Plant-Based Cosmovision

The explorers chosen and reimagined by the director interact with Karakamate in different ways. Karakamate's initial encounters with both Theo and Evan demonstrate why the explorers seek him, and how he can wield his power over the two, upsetting a narrative of immediate Western dominance. The first shot of *El abrazo de la serpiente* opens on a young Karakamate staring at his reflection in the river. He hears something in the wind and stands alert as a canoe slowly approaches, the camera centering his body and closing in on his facial expressions. The paddler introduces himself as Manduca and asks if Karakamate is a shaman healer of the world. He presents the ailing Theo, explaining that Karakamate is their only hope of curing the man, because of his knowledge of the *yakruna* plant. Theo also tells Karakamate that he has seen members of his community, the Cohuiano, and will lead Karakamate to them if he agrees to help. Theo's life is placed in Karakamate's hands, shifting power because of his plant-based expertise. Karakamate appears masculine and strong and in decided contrast to the ailing Theo who is entirely dependent on his Indigenous counterparts. The mise-en-scène follows Karakamate's gaze, once again disrupting the Western order.[23] Throughout the film there is little direct interaction between Karakamate and other non-Westernized Indigenous peoples, he is presented to the viewer as the last hold out against Western encroachment, embodying a type of final frontier within the film.

Karakamate initially refuses to help the explorer, explaining that both Manduca and Theo killed the last of his people. Karakamate is resistant, angry, and vocal about the ravages the Western world has wrought on his home. Despite this anger, he is ultimately willing to listen and dialogue. As Karakamate ponders joining the explorers, the viewer is presented with a glimpse into his life. The camera reveals that he lives in a large, open hut with a palm frond roof and markings on the sides. He makes an entrance as a solitary, complex character, both flawed and otherworldly, while also constantly changing. Karakamate's identity is grounded in his solitary being, in contrast to other Indigenous characters who have in some ways assimilated as guides and workers in religious missions or rubber plantations, and the white explorers with whom he engages.[24] This scene of initial greeting within the biocontact zone demonstrates some key elements of a reimagined travel narrative such as Karakamate's initial reluctance, vocal anger, and solitary life. Rather than the Indigenous peoples who the real Koch-Grünberg wrote about as his friends and confidants, and who lived together in collective harmony, this man initially rejects the explorer's advances and clearly vocalizes his reluctance and rules, upsetting the power balance.

By the next day, Karakamate returns to Theo and Manduca and agrees to help them based on a set of conditions. These conditions include asking permission to each animal they eat, not cutting down any trees, and if they encounter a woman, waiting until the moon cycle changes for intercourse. In setting the terms of their agreement Karakamate takes control of the narrative. He asserts his language and his rules, while also having something to gain for himself. D'Argenio, following de la Cadena, argues that how Karakamate explains the rules and relationship between nature and human beings in the film demonstrates the jungle as an "earth-being": "Unlike, and in opposition to, European travellers and conquerors, Karamakate can 'conceptualise' the jungle, relate to it and even 'verbalise' it. The relationship between human and non-human beings is not one of dominance but one of respect: the jungle is a being which needs to be 'respected,' is 'fragile.'"[25] Karakamate fully interacts with the jungle and lives his life in dialogue and relationship with his surroundings. Furthermore, he communicates the ways the forest should be treated by outsiders, directly and clearly stating how to respectfully travel through the jungle and how to best interact with the environment. Rather than travel on the Westerner's terms, Karakamate's set of rules push the narrative forward following an Indigenous cosmology.

His rules reflect a worldview that is characterized by interaction with the environment, reconfiguring the power dynamic of the biocontact zone. As Viveiros de Castro notes on Amazonian perspectivism, there is a malleability between human, animal, and spirit within Amazonian ontologies.[26] This way of knowing is based in nature where "relations between society and nature are themselves natural" and "human society is one natural phenomenon amongst others."[27] Karakamate's set of conditions shows a reciprocal relationship between the environment and the ways they as humans interact with it. The travelers will be able to move forward if they respect and pay attention to the world around them. Again, this upsets the order of a traditional Western travel narrative, where rather than being mapped or traveled over, nature is traveled *through* and interacted *with* in a symbiotic, respectful, and evolving relationship.

The film continually shifts between the early 1900s and the 1940s, blurring the lines between time and space, creating a story woven together with the fabric of a plant. As the film goes forward into the 1940s, we see the first encounter between Evan and Karakamate. In a long shot the camera focuses on a snake writhing in the water, moving toward a small cove where the viewer sees large rocks covered in carvings.[28] The music is ominous as the camera slowly pans out revealing more carvings on the rock side.[29] The snake reaches the shore, and the viewer is presented with an aged Karakamate busily carving until he suddenly drops his tool, gazing up the river toward Evan, who enters the scene paddling a canoe. The film takes shots from the bottom up, reversing Mary Louise Pratt's analysis of the traditional travel narrative viewpoint (and something we've seen with explorers like Roosevelt): the "monarch-of-all-I-survey scene."[30] Evan holds up a book with young Karakamate on the cover—written by Theo, the protagonist from the 1909 parts of the story. He explains that he is following Theo's tracks to find the plants that he wrote about thirty years before. This connection between the two times hinges on the explorer's interactions with Indigenous peoples. It is because of Theo's informant Manduca that his work was published posthumously, as Mutis argues, making the diffusion of knowledge a collective production. It is also because of the publication and proliferation of this travel narrative that the two Westerners relate to Karakamate. Evan has come to verify if the writings are true, stating that he has "devoted his life to plants." Karakamate responds with, "That's the most reasonable thing I've ever heard a white say."[31] The plant Evan seeks, of course, is the *yakruna*.

Karakamate agrees to help Evan find the *yakruna*, although his memory has faltered and he has forgotten its location. Their relationship is based on a curiosity and interest in the natural world. However, the two men have entirely different motivations. Evan wants to monetize and extract the *yakruna*, while also searching for rubber that could be used in the war effort, facts that he does not share with Karakamate until the end of the film. Karakamate, conversely, wants to remember and rekindle his relationship with the environment through the *yakruna*. Karakamate's loss of memory suggests a larger idea of the loss of Indigenous voice, record, and self-representation, which is also central to Guerra's study of the two explorers. At the end of their initial encounter and before they leave, Evan photographs the rock surface that Karakamate has been writing on and questions the meaning of the inscriptions. Karakamate explains that he is empty, with no memory, but that the rocks used to speak to him, and to regain some memory he continues to draw on them; by his telling, this lack of memory and overall confusion make him a *chullachaqui*. Karakamate produces and stores precious knowledge in his body and in nature itself through his inscriptions on the rock and in the way he reads the river. This scene shows aspects of a decolonial approach where the world is spoken differently through interactions rather than extractions. Karakamate creates knowledge in relation to the environment, as nature is intertwined with his memory. The texts that Karakamate writes are inscribed within the environment, and the environment is inscribed with a sacred meaning. Through Guerra's telling, this once again rewrites the travel narrative to directly focus on the layering of knowledge through the environment itself.

El abrazo de la serpiente questions knowledge production, and how that knowledge is preserved. Thirty minutes into the film, Theo, Manduca, and Karakamate encounter an Indigenous group that Theo knows. After a happy night exchanging food and talking, Theo departs only to realize his compass is missing. An angry Theo confronts the chief, explaining to Manduca that he cannot leave without his compass. Karakamate, watching this exchange, responds with "You are nothing but a white." Theo then responds, "Their orientation system is based on the winds and the position of the stars. If they learn how to use a compass, that knowledge will be lost." Karakamate counters with, "You cannot prevent them from learning. Knowledge belongs to all men. But you can't understand that, because you're nothing but a white."[32] This brief scene creates a discussion about preservation, knowledge, and paternalism. In attempting to "save" this group from the use of a compass and thus loss of their traditional knowledge, Theo prevents an exchange of ideas. This is akin to Theodor Koch-Grünberg's actual approach, and his preoccupation with Indigenous "authenticity" and the looming threat of encroachment of Western cultures (for example, when he asked the Indigenous women he was photographing to take off their European-style dresses), detailed in Chapter 4.

As Gleghorn writes about this scene, young Karakamate's response critiques essentialist ideas about Indigenous peoples that attempt to freeze a certain idea of what it means to be Indigenous.[33] Young Karakamate argues that learning is for everyone and stopping the proliferation of knowledge is futile, pointing out and pushing against Theo's paternalistic approach. Karakamate is not interested in the idea of isolation or the static preservation of Indigenous knowledge. Instead, he understands that knowledge is fluid and that there are different ways of gathering information that can be a combination of both Western and Indigenous concepts. Furthermore, freezing knowledge or halting interactions is unrealistic, and mixture does not ruin an outsider's definition of what is authentic. Theo's reservations about losing or changing this group's knowledge system demonstrates a kind of imperial nostalgia where through contact alone, he destroys how things were before.[34] The concept that knowledge belongs to everyone is a central idea throughout the film. That knowledge is communicated in a wide variety of ways, including through writing, photography, and speech, as well as the meta-filmic aspect of the audience watching these exchanges unfold.

These first meetings initiate the overarching idea of the malleability of time. Through reworking a linear chronology, the travel narratives within the film echo each other thematically rather than temporally. In this journey story, there is no destination beyond increased enlightenment, despite the united goal of the *yakruna* for both explorers. The film moves between times, with the past informing the present but never separated from it. A humanistic, Western approach to time sees it as linear and straightforward, where knowledge grows as a practice in incremental learning. In the imagined world of the film, time is cyclical, and rather than being, the world is in a constant process of becoming.

Within Amazonian perspectivism, where individual points of view are located within the body (that body could be plant, animal, or spirit), the concept of time is also mutable. In this sense, bodies are merely a vessel that the spirit performs through, where a *chullachaqui* could be the inner spirit escaping the body. This is a process that relates to the way the Western explorers are portrayed in the film. Separated by thirty years, they spiritually carry on in a similar manner, where their bodies are only their souls performed, their own *chullachaquis* exchanging form. Thus, not only does Karakamate embody an Amerindian cosmology, but the entire structure of the film puts forward this same ethos. This also speaks to the intertextuality of the characters. They each read and learn from each other in different ways; creating a participatory and integrated approach toward knowledge production.[35]

Rubber and Violence within the Biocontact Zone

The *yakruna* facilitates the interaction between Western and Indigenous cultures, while rubber creates a violent backdrop within the contact zone represented in the film. As others have noted, the film directly addresses the adverse effects of the rubber industry on the Western Amazon, which caused massive destruction, death, and torture throughout the region. In the geopolitics of plants, and as seen throughout this book, rubber is an exemplar of the extractivist nature of the imperial project. In a scene thirty-five minutes into the film the viewer sees Manduca, dressed in linen pants and a shirt, walk into the jungle where he encounters a set of trees that have been tapped for rubber. Accompanied by Theo, Manduca angrily reacts to the marked trees, dumping out the rubber tap. As he does so a rubber tapper, missing an arm, appears extremely distraught and begs for help after seeing the spilled tap. He asks (in an Indigenous language that Karakamate interprets) to be killed.[36] Manduca runs over with a rifle to the man begging on the forest floor, who says that if he does not kill him the rubber barons will torture and murder him. Theo and Karakamate plead with Manduca not to kill the man and Manduca replies, "No one deserves this hell." The rubber tapper then takes the barrel of the gun and points it to his forehead. Here, we see the Amazon through a necropolitical lens where capitalism is the driving force behind the infliction of death and destruction. In this scene, the Amazon is portrayed as a green hell, not for the innate nature of the land itself, but because of human interventions.[37] The scene is gripping with palpable violence and desperation. Manduca fires the rifle on the ground rather than at the man and begins to sob—demonstrating his personal experience of enslavement in the rubber trade. The scene ends with Karakamate, Theo, and Manduca reentering their canoe, leaving the rubber tapper behind. As they continue down the river, they hear a shot and scream, as the fate of the tapper is seemingly decided. The shroud of the forest can perhaps enable violence to occur out of sight, yet the violence of the rubber boom looms throughout the film, demonstrating the necropolitics of this biocontact zone and creating an intense element of terror.

In the next scene after these horrific events, Karakamate, in reaction to the shotgun and previous tension, tells Theo that he will not continue the voyage. He sits down and refuses to carry on, stating, "Whites can't be trusted. . . . Is this your knowledge? Shotguns? All your science only leads to this, violence, death."[38] Karakamate takes a stand against the capitalistic system, linking science and thus the type of exploration that Theo is engaged in with violence and death. This violence, perpetrated because of the geopolitics of plants, demonstrates the peril of the culture-nature divide. With rubber used as an extracted resource, the respectful relationship Karakamate is shown to have with the environment is shattered—a culture of terror takes its place. In this scene, Guerra recreates for his audience the violence of the rubber extraction industry without explicitly showing that violence.

This ambiance of terror is used throughout the film. The lines between identities are continually blurred as Manduca, Karakamate, and the two foreign explorers encounter others in the jungle. With each interaction, they are forced to examine why they are there and what their intentions are. In a later scene, they come across what Theo at first thinks is another rubber plantation, but Karakamate intuits otherwise. What they find is a Catholic mission, and a group of four boys dressed in white run forward to meet them. They take the travelers to a Spanish priest, who is leading a larger group of boys in song.

After dinner in the mission mess hall (where fish is served, in direct defiance of the conditions Karakamate proposed upon agreeing to travel with Manduca and Theo), the camera pans to a plaque that reads, "'In recognition of the courage of the Colombian rubber pioneers who brought civilization to the land of cannibal savages and showed them the path of God and his holy church'—Rafael Reyes, President of Colombia, August 1907."[39] This rewrites the way that Karakamate (and Manduca) have lived and experienced the rubber industry. It also grounds the mission within a national border and wider international interest. According to the plaque, the rubber workers are the heroes of the Colombian frontier, who evangelized and brought so-called civilization. This is a site where man has intervened on nature; as D'Argenio writes, this scene showcases "examples of how the jungle is not depicted as a nature deprived of history but rather as a nature that has been 'intervened, written and re-written.'"[40] The plaque itself serves as a Western method of knowledge preservation and national memory. Rather than storing knowledge in the physical body or reading the landscape, the plaque publicly puts forth a false history and inscribes the landscape with a one-sided narrative of the success of man over nature.

In a beautiful act of defiance, Karakamate teaches this group of young boys on the mission about their natural environment and as such cultural heritage. After stopping to read the plaque, Karakamate takes the boys to some of the plants growing on the outskirts of the property. He points out a plant called *chiricaspi* and recounts the origin story of how the gods intended it to be used. Karakamate tells the boys his story in their shared language over a fire, "Priests picked me up too, when the rubber barons killed my people. They didn't surrender to them, they fought. Don't believe their crazy tales about eating the body of the gods. They give you food, but they don't respect the prohibitions. One day they will finish all the food of the jungle."[41] This conversation demonstrates the importance of listening to the environment and the hypocrisy of what was written on the plaque.[42] It also creates a pedagogical relationship based in plant-knowledge. Karakamate repeatedly points out the flaws of Western knowledge production and, in this scene, explicitly criticizes extractivism. This speech by Karakamate is meant to empower the next generation of Indigenous boys who have been subjected to the strict life of the mission and into a forced assimilation, while carrying on an important biolgical knowledge—part of a the decolonial impetus within the film.

Here, Karakamate can bond with the boys through plants, actively educating them in their cultural traditions. On a meta-filmic level, *El abrazo* seeks to educate a Western audience about Indigenous cosmovisions; in the film the Indigenous protagonist shares his knowledge and engages in dialogue with the Western explorers as well as the boys he encounters in this scene. Since Karakamate has been alone in the Amazon, there is no sense of a collective memory, where his experiences can be passed on to his family or other members of his community. Through the interaction with the boys, he mediates the silent world of plants for the next generation, fighting against an imposed rule of only speaking Spanish and helping them read the environment around them in their language, carrying on a pedagogical legacy, and defying the taxonomic naming process of colonialism, in the process rewriting a travel narrative that considers an Indigenous view.

Listening, Memory, and the Elusive Yakruna

Throughout the film there are different and conflicting visions of how to produce, listen to, and store knowledge. Indeed, the entire film is a meditation on knowledge production and loss within a plant-based travel narrative. This surfaces in how the two Westerners place value on material things while Karakamate seems to have no material possessions. For Karakamate, as previously mentioned, knowledge is tied to the natural environment, which he never possesses but rather interacts with. Both Theo and Evan, conversely, cart around their books, cameras, photographs, or record players, symbols of connection and preservation, as well as proof of what they have experienced and witnessed in the Amazon.

For example, in a scene toward the end of the film, the viewer is privy to Evan accusing Karakamate of fake amnesia and Karakamate's subsequent charge that Evan is greedy and too attached to his material things. As a result, Evan quickly throws his suitcase into the water, leaving behind only one small box to prove his lack of attachment. By separating from his material goods, Evan works to gain Karakamate's trust. Evan had kept his material goods to provide a source of comfort and a sense of connection to his home in this strange new place—something that Theo was also doing earlier in the film with his letters and diaries. Karakamate displays some curiosity about Evan's possessions and asks him what is in the remaining box. Evan opens a portable record player and plays Handel's *The Creation*, explaining that it takes him back to his father's house in Boston. This metaphorical transport spurred on by an attachment to an object prompts Karakamate to ask, "What do you see? The world is like this, huge. But you choose to see just this. The world speaks. I can only listen. Hear the song of your ancestors. This is the way you're looking for. Listen for real. Not only with your ears."[43] Karakamate urges Evan to move beyond the world in front of him, to listen not only to Handel's music but also to the way the earth responds to it. Here he is Evan's guide, opening him up to the cosmos, falling back on the trope of an Indigenous person's role in opening the mind of a Westerner. Harkening back to the real-life Richard Evans Schultes, the Indigenous informant serves as an intermediary to explain the world more deeply from an Indigenous perspective and cure the ills of Western society. As Gleghorn writes about this scene, "The rapprochement of varied vehicles of knowledge—music, story, dream—reconciles the 'rational' Western world and the Indigenous world of dreams. Evan's realization of the location of the *yakruna* flower emerges because of his own learning process and experience; the process is depicted as Karamakate's unlocking of the possibility to dream for Evan."[44] In this sense, Karakamate is the shamanic guide to better the Westerner, by giving him the ability to dream and pointing him toward what he seeks.

There appears to be a growing conviviality between Karakamate and Evan, and the music, although seemingly out of place within the broader cacophony of insects, monkeys, and distant birds, seems to sooth them both. In this scene, sound connects Evan and Karakamate, as well as Theo, working as a conduit to ancestors and the layers of the past. Where Karakamate uses the natural environment as a source of connection and a path toward memory, Evan's material goods offer a similar purpose. Rather than classical music guiding a cultural Other, the Indigenous person is shown reinterpreting and reimagining a new blend of cultures albeit as the spiritual guide to the Westerner.[45] This demonstrates the primary pitfall of the film, which echoes the travel narrative genre (or an ethnobotanical approach): the Indigenous person is continually tasked with guiding, teaching, and thus proving their worth to the Western outsider.

As the camera pans toward the sky, Handel playing, Karakamate goes to the water's edge where, in a complete blend of temporalities, he sees a bedraggled Theo stumble forward. He begins talking to the image, explaining what Cohiuano men do to become warriors:

> On that journey he has to discover, in solitude and silence, who he really is. He has to become a vagabond of dreams. Some get lost and never come back. But those that do are ready to face whatever may come. Where are they? Where are the chants that mothers used to sing to their babies? Where are the stories of elders, the whispers of love, the chronicles of battle? Where have they gone?[46]

This lament about memory, time, and tradition wavers between dreams and so-called reality. Cohiuano men must take the *yakruna*, altering their state of mind with nature, imbibing, and becoming in the process. A key aspect of becoming is the journey and solitary movement, following dreams and learning to listen to the environment, at least partially through the practice of travel itself. In Guerra's telling, the voices of the Cohiuano explicitly stand in for a host of Indigenous groups in the Amazon that have been lost, which he states in a slide at the end of the film. As Tuhiwai Smith remarks on the act of remembering as part of a decolonizing methodology, "the remembering of a people relates not so much to an idealized remembering of a golden past but more specifically to the remembering of a painful past, and importantly, people's responses to that pain."[47] Karakamate does not necessarily seek to remember the violent processes of colonization, but rather laments loss through the colonizing process. This juxtaposes classical music with the lacuna of Indigenous voice. Through setting the narrative in the past and using travel as an approach to Amazonia, the film focuses on the loss of Indigenous voice despite the continuity of those very voices.

As Karakamate reflects on his people's journey, Evan passes out, and in the next scene, the viewer is taken back to the 1909 version of the story. In this last scene of 1909, Theo grows increasingly sick, shown occasionally delirious and convulsing. They finally arrive at the last of the Cohuiano's village, only to find a forest burned and what remains of a settlement. Karakamate wears a full headdress for the first and only time, which stands out against the Westernized attire of the remaining Cohuiano. Thus, when Karakamate encounters his own people, with his headdress and lack of Westernization, he is still a cultural Other. In the center square, a group of Cohuiano villagers drink the *yakruna* and toast to the end of the world.

Karakamate has retained an "authenticity" or cultural knowledge, yet he is isolated, whereas the last of the Cohiuano have acculturated to dire ends. Karakamate leaves in disgust as he witnesses his own people disrespecting nature's rules by getting high on *yakruna*. Theo, Karakamate, and Manduca find *yakruna* on the outskirts of the village, where it has been grown in rows. Karakamate is visibly angry and screams that the *yakruna* should never be cultivated and immediately blames Theo.[48] Next a military group of Colombians arrive, shooting and scattering villagers. Violent encroachments continually threaten and gradually close in on Karakamate. During this chaos Karakamate sets the *yakruna* on fire. He destroys the *yakruna* rather than see it misused and exploited. As the town erupts into flames, Manduca paddles away with a sick Theo, disappearing from the frame and film itself. Karakamate chooses to preserve the purity of the *yakruna* in its destruction, once again making him the mediator of the plant. He becomes the voice of the *yakruna* and its gatekeeper, asserting his importance and power.

The image of the *yakruna* is again employed to move the plot forward and shift between temporalities as the flower burning gives way to Evan and old Karakamate reaching a mountain in the jungle. They climb to the top and the terrain changes completely; instead of an engulfment in a riverscape, they gain perspective, and Evan sits in awe. For the first time, the jungle appears flat from above. They find one *yakruna* flower that Karakamate plucks to make *caapi*, a drinkable hallucinogenic. This flower is the last in the world, according to Karakamate, and he tells Evan that its preparation will be his gift. Evan admits that the *yakruna* is not what he came to the Amazon for, and that there is a war going on and his people need high-purity rubber, finally disclosing his economically driven purpose in the jungle, much like the real Richard Evans Schultes.

As night falls, Karakamate prepares the plant for consumption. This scene explicitly places Karakamate as the purveyor of knowledge to Evan. His role, previously complicated and intricate, is again quickly reduced to an Indigenous person with the burden of educating a Westerner. It is important to note that even in this reduced role, Karakamate is vocal about his desire to teach Evan, even if it is because he has lost his people due to Western incursions. While Karakamate retains control of the last flower, Evan still gains knowledge and experience to take to a wider audience. Evan takes a sip of the *caapi* and Karakamate breaths some powder into his face. The camera spans up and over the treetops, down to the river, over to the mountains, pulling together an entire Amazonian topography while bird calls drown

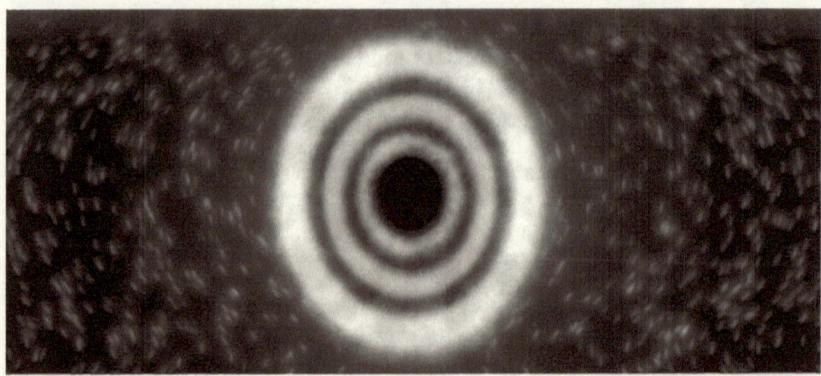

FIGURE 5.2 The psychedelic drug trip is the only moment where the film uses color, taking the viewer on a journey through space and time. Courtesy of Oscilloscope Laboratories

out an ominous score. This is the embrace of the serpent that the title alludes to—a psychedelic trip that winds in snaking contortions like the river itself. The last shot in this series focuses on young Karakamate's face where he opens into a galaxy of a thousand pieces. Once again, the Westerner's pursuit of knowledge disappears the Indigenous person.

In an extreme close up, the camera concentrates on a young Karakamate's face (Figure 5.1) and a blinding light bursts through until the screen is drowned in white and then fades to black with different shots of slowly rotating symbols in color appearing against the black backdrop. This scene breaks from the rest of the narrative in its trippy, nonnarrative form. A visual rhetoric emerges and shatters the rhetoric of empire that produces the body in a Western imaginary. Karakamate's body explodes, becoming nonexistent. Music that thumps like a beating heart plays as what appear to be the carvings that Karakamate put into the side of the rock come to life and pulsate with color. This brief scene further pulls apart ideas of linearity and narrative, breaking into a cosmos of color. The film becomes a game between being and knowing that decenters the human experience. This plant-induced trip is about seeing beyond what is immediately there and engaging with light, enlightenment, color, and knowledge separate from time. Seeing comes into being through a visual exploration of the cosmos. This scene reconfigures the travel narrative once again as it takes the viewer on a different kind of trip, a visual and aural experience through the cosmos.

This thirty-second interlude ends, and in the next shot Evan slowly comes to in the middle of the day, the previous nights' fire dying next to him. He walks around a barren mountaintop, yelling for Karakamate. Evan rows his

The Reconfigured Travel Narrative 183

FIGURE 5.3 Evan (bottom right) is engulfed in white butterflies as he searches for Karakamate. Courtesy of Oscilloscope Laboratories

canoe back to the initial spot where they first encountered each other, looking fruitlessly for him until he is engulfed in a flood of white butterflies (Figure 5.3), echoing an earlier scene where Karakamate was also surrounded by butterflies. This is perhaps reflective of some Indigenous ontologies where a body is part of a larger metamorphosis as spirits or souls move through bodies, in the process of becoming. Viveiros de Castro explains, "The performative rather than given character of the body, a conception that requires it to differentiate itself 'culturally' in order for it to be 'naturally' different, has an obvious connection with interspecific metamorphosis, a possibility suggested by Amerindian cosmologies."[49] Metamorphosis is a central theme in the film, as each character and the environment itself are shown in stages of processual change. For example, Figure 5.3 shows Evan as a miniscule part of the larger environment. The use of the butterfly, a creature that itself goes through metamorphosis, suggests that Evan has experienced a life cycle of growth. This suggestion is strengthened by the previous psychedelic drug sequence where the audience goes on a trip with Evan, as perhaps all of this was just a product of imagination, a nostalgic trip back to a lost world. Karakamate appears as part of an Amazonian fever dream for the two Western explorers, guiding them in their various pursuits. At the same time his disappearance feeds into an idea of Amazonian perspectivism, where his bodily presence has now been transferred or translated into the environment. Perhaps, with the ingestion of the last *yakruna*, Karakamate must inevitably vanish because of his deep connection with the plant.

Ultimately, Evan finds and participates in the knowledge he sought and Karakamate disappears, recreating a problematic narrative of Indigenous disappearance. This connects to the same frame of coloniality and extraction where knowledge, plants, and bodies are taken and used, ultimately leading to their destruction or disappearance while negating their continued resilience and current existence. The rhetoric of modernity suggests that if Indigenous peoples do not become modern or assimilate, they seemingly cease to exist.[50] Karakamate's entire being is based in non-being, and while he has human emotions and actions, he appears as a nonhuman figure, as a gatekeeper of nature and the cosmos. The Indigenous person vanishes, problematically creating room for the spiritual growth of the Westerner. Throughout the film we see Karakamate as the guide and key to knowledge about the flora and fauna of the forest who wavers between being a complex human character while also being decidedly non-human—a mystic capable of transformation, in dialogue with the cosmos as seen in the psychedelic trip he induces and his overall ephemerality.

A final slide in the film states that it is dedicated to "la memoria de los pueblos cuya canción nunca conoceremos," or "the memory of the peoples whose song we will never know." This dedication, as Gleghorn argues, invites the film's audience to become part of a community of explorers, pushing them to seek out Indigenous knowledges that were "legitimized in the film's staging of Evan's epistemic inheritance. The dedication at the end of the film emphasizes framing devices that condition the ways in which knowledge is represented."[51] However, this dedication also negates the continued resilience of Indigenous peoples. Together with this final caption comes a series of seven photographs primarily from the diaries of Koch-Grünberg with one photograph from Schultes. These photographs, two of which appear in this volume's Chapter 4 (Figures 4.1 and 4.2), situate the film within a tangible reality, creating a touchpoint where the director clearly states his inspiration. The film transforms the photographic snapshots created by the real explorers into a fully visualized world. That these images showcase Koch-Grünberg in various degrees of interaction with Indigenous peoples is used as Guerra's justification for reimagining him as a model of exploration. However, like the caption, the use of the photographs also adds to the narrative of Indigenous disappearance. These black and white images taken from the early twentieth century act as a lasting symbol of what was—a glimpse of the song that we will never know. Indeed, in promotional stills for the movie, Guerra recreates an almost exact replica of the photo shown in Figure 4.2, of the actor playing Koch-Grünberg posing in the center of a group of Indigenous men and boys. This once again plays with the fictional narrative by giving the film a kind of pseudo-documentary authority and placing it within the travel narrative genre.

Conclusion

The final caption about the loss of Indigenous song explicitly frames the film as a narrative of loss. Karakamate's ephemerality casts him as a mystical character, running the risk of reformulating a narrative of Indigenous peoples as less than human. His final disappearance operates similarly. In showing Karakamate as the last of his fictionalized group, there is a sense of loss and nostalgia that both Theo and Evan engage in, and presumably the audience as well. Furthermore, Karakamate's passage of knowledge to Evan seemingly gives a greenlight to the concept of Indigenous disappearance and the role of a Western outsider in disseminating it. The documentation of travel journals and ethnographies, while part of a larger system of Western dominance and control, can also be important ghostly traces of Indigenous knowledge, which the film explicitly states by showing images from Koch-Grünberg's diaries together with its final caption. This frames Guerra's intervention as a mediation of knowledges about the Amazon that privileges the education of non-Indigenous Westerners.

El abrazo de la serpiente marks a representational shift where Western chronology is reworked and plants and Indigenous peoples are given equal billing with the white explorers, and certainly there is a firm questioning of the rhetoric of modernity and imperialism. The dreamlike quality of the film and the fictionalization of real events creates a separation that can allow the viewer to at once think critically about power and dominance without engaging further with present-day realities. As Gleghorn aptly argues about the problematics of this fictionalization, "authorship and authority count in the singing of the 'canción' precisely because Indigenous voices have been ventriloquized, excluded from public discourse and from the possibilities of creative self-expression."[52] The final caption that marks Indigenous cultures as lost negates the thousands of groups who are alive and fighting. The film reworks some key problematics of the travel narrative genre by centering an Indigenous character, using Indigenous languages and temporalities, as well as plants as a pedagogical tool, yet it is ultimately a film produced for Westerners that depends on Western interaction to think about Indigenous stories.

As a take on the travel narrative, the film's reconstruction of time, place, and emphasis on the importance of plants and Indigenous voice provides a new, modern reading of movement through a foreign space. Despite these important strides, the framing of *El abrazo de la serpiente* around imperial tropes, and the vehicle of an international film almost explicitly for export written and directed by an outsider in the Amazon engages with a decolonial approach yet falls short. The Indigenous protagonist is consistently framed in relation to Westerners and his knowledge continually extracted. Solving these issues would mean creating an entirely different film; one that rewrites Western epistemologies, perhaps ignoring the need for marketability and, beyond just using Indigenous languages, incorporating Indigenous voices in ways that acknowledge their present-day realities.

Knowledge Loss and Indigenous Self-Representation

Chapter 5 examined a filmic travel narrative about Indigenous peoples and how the film reflects on knowledge production. Antonio Bolívar, the Ocaina shaman who played old Karakamate in *El abrazo de la serpiente*, was dedicated to promoting Indigenous self-representation, a cause he highlighted with his participation in the film. Sadly, Bolívar passed away due to COVID-19 in May 2020.[53] This addendum will address the loss of Indigenous knowledge represented by Bolívar's untimely death, along with ongoing efforts of Indigenous self-representation.

Like his character in the film, Bolívar was one of the last remaining members of his tribe, the Ocaina. There are currently only fifty-four speakers of the Ocaina language, scattered throughout northeastern Peru and the Amazonas region of Colombia. The Ocaina, or the People of the Center, are no strangers to outsiders causing devastation to their community. The Ocaina were victims of the rubber boom, and their entire community was almost wiped out by enslavement, violence, and disease. Only a very small number of Ocaina people still identify as members of the group. Bolívar recalled how the rubber boom was still taboo among his people and many chose not to talk about it. Because of this, he was initially reluctant to join *El abrazo de la serpiente*. He wanted to be sure of Guerra's intentions and was ultimately swayed by the idea of storytelling where he could play a key role in constructing the narrative. Furthermore, to ensure his participation, he urged Guerra to bring the film back to be shown in the different Indigenous communities where it was shot.[54] Bolívar was working to revive his native language and culture through his acting.

Bolívar lived in Leticia, Colombia, the same town where Richard Evans Schultes spent a good deal of time collecting rubber. When Bolívar fell ill (April 2020), residents had to go all the way to Bogotá to get a COVID test, and Leticia had no access to ICUs.[55] The lack of resources to combat the disease within his community led to his death.

The effects of COVID-19 on Indigenous communities throughout the world and in the Amazon has resulted in a loss of invaluable knowledge and leadership but has also demonstrated once again the resilience of Indigenous communities. In Peru for example, Indigenous organizations advocated through public protest in front of government offices to demand their right to participate in COVID-19 response efforts.[56] Other groups organized early to block off their lands and ensure that there was limited contact at the height of the pandemic. The impacts of COVID-19 on the Amazon basin (and the world) will remain for years to come but they also grant an opportunity to rebuild and reconfigure the ways we interact with nature and how we consider humanity. The pandemic and subsequent loss of Indigenous knowledge points to the importance of knowledge creation in a more equitable manner.

One decolonial method of knowledge production and preservation has been explored with a long-standing project within Brazil. Across the border in the Brazilian Amazon, Video nas Aldeias (Video in the Villages, which I will refer to as VNA) has been working to facilitate Indigenous self-representation since 1986. Started by Vincent Carelli, a Brazilian documentary filmmaker, VNA works with Indigenous communities to provide video production training, workshops for Indigenous filmmakers, equipment access, post-production support, and international distribution. Over the past thirty years they have worked collectively to create an extensive amount of audiovisual documentation by Indigenous filmmakers.

For VNA, images and films constitute a process of political engagement and cultural revitalization through filmmaking between Indigenous villages and non-Indigenous peoples. The films themselves are not only an archive of diverse cultures and cultural practices but reveal multifaceted and complicated worldviews that work against the historical invisibilization of Indigenous peoples. VNA, in a similar manner to Projeto Nova Cartografia Social (described in "Poetic Justice for the Residents of Cachoeira Porteira," the addendum to Chapter 1), invites Indigenous groups to approach them and then offers several week- or month-long workshops that train community members in filmmaking and editing techniques.

The films carry an explicitly political purpose and have been used to educate outsiders about Indigenous life with work created by the communities themselves. Films are also used to educate and create increased contact among different Indigenous villages. As Zoe Graham describes, "since its inception, Video in the Villages has contested abuses of state power and control over indigenous communities in Brazil, while also celebrating their distinctive cultural worlds."[57] The films that VNA has produced have been shown around the world, and in the 1990s there was even a short-lived television program about the project that was broadcast throughout Brazil.[58] VNA films are created in a process of collective authorship where interested community members are trained in production and then invite people from their village to be characters in the videos. Community members then decide if they want to participate and what story they want to tell. It becomes a collective, interactive storytelling process.

There is a notable difference when the camera is in the hands of an Indigenous filmmaker. For example, *Awotsi Yorenkatsi Tasori*, a 2016 short film by Ashininka participants in VNA, shows some Indigenous filmmakers traveling across the border to Peru to connect with Peruvian members of their group. They participate in several touristic activities such as stopping at a church, taking pictures of mountains with their smartphones, and going on brief tours. In this video, technology, travel, and photography are shown as integral to Ashininka culture, and a means by which community members can connect between themselves and their surroundings. This demonstrates the nonstatic nature of Indigenous communities and how they have adapted to technology to suit their purposes.

Throughout the film, the Peruvian and Brazilian Ashininka go to various sacred spaces and comment on how they can help preserve them. Two community leaders laugh over stories of hunting tapir, but comment on the fact that there are hardly any animals left. The film is a brief but powerful commentary on the ways national borders separated a once unified community and the struggles that both communities face in continuing their traditions while some of their sacred spaces are fenced off or inaccessible to them. In one portion of the film, we see an Indigenous leader address the Ashininka from both sides of the border, saying, "That is why we say: the death of the great is the death of the small and Nature is the mother of all human beings. If we do not take care of her, we will die victims of our own actions."[59] Conceptualized, shot, and participated in by Indigenous peoples in their own language, the brief film is just one example of the many created by the VNA project that firmly places the power of visualizing into the hands of Indigenous peoples.

Like the work that Bolívar was doing in Colombia, the VNA is focused on self-representation, and films are always accessible in the communities of origin. This kind of collaborative project between Indigenous and non-Indigenous people as well as across different Indigenous communities changes the power dynamic and works toward a decolonial praxis. Indeed, this type of self-representation locates cultural difference within a universal humanity.[60]

CONCLUSION

Transnational Perspectives on the Rubber Boom Frontier

Every object of cultural representation is a product of its time, inseparable from the social, environmental, and political history of its production. The way we read these objects depends upon our own temporality and positionality, again pointing to a "history of the present"—a means of tracing the ways that the past became the present, a genealogy of history. The material considered in *Eyes on Amazonia* included natural histories, travelogues, biography, fiction, photographs, and film that were read with acknowledgment to the context of their production but, inevitably, with a twenty-first-century lens. Their creation reflects the ideologies of their time as well as the position of their creators—most often outsiders to the region with objectives ranging from botanical collection to geographical mapping to nation building. The legacies of these writings about the Amazon are demonstrative of the continuity of representations about the region, which have been used to differing political ends. The narratives examined in this volume illuminate how each author in their specific context contested, challenged, or contributed to imperial/national formations and modernity.

This book has provided five case studies of Amazonian representation at the intersections of economic exploitation, nationalization, and personal narrative, exposing through biographical history the loci of enunciation of travel writers. These diverse texts in effect define, categorize, represent, or collect Amazonian territories and peoples through the act of travel to a foreign place. Overall, the book focuses on travel writing by providing a comprehensive description of the ways a variety of intellectuals have attempted to understand Amazonia as an Other space, along with justifications of their place within it. I have explored the topics of Amazonian representation and the inscription of empire onto a forest frontier particularly through travel writing in different languages. In transnational movement conflict occurs, and these texts portray clashing visions of the transnational contact zone of Amazonia. While the gaze on the region has only intensified with the mounting threats of climate change, it is more important to consider the gazes and voices of those from within.

In selecting the objects of analysis contained in the previous pages, I was attracted to characters that demonstrate a complexity in both their personal identitities and representational choices. These characters include people such as Octavie Coudreau who, in her photographic and cartographic Amazonian incursion, displayed ambiguities of gender and race. Or Theodore Roosevelt, who co-led an imperial exploration in the Amazonian wilderness that he was interested in both preserving and exploiting, and that ultimately defeated him. His counterpoint, Cândido Rondon, was a partially Indigenous frontiersman dedicated to acculturation and technological progress. Drawing on some of the same impulses for development and settlement as Rondon, Euclides da Cunha presents the Amazon as an area of conflict yet ripe with potential dependent on internal, Brazilian migration. In contrast, Mário de Andrade showcases the Amazon through his modernist photography and prose as an area central to Brazilian identity for the unique makeup of the individuals who live there. The fourth chapter examined one of Mário de Andrade's main sources of inspiration, the travel narratives of Theodor Koch-Grünberg in comparison with the ethnobotanical work of Richard Evans Schultes. These two explorers take new approaches to the discipline of anthropology and bring a more nuanced look to human and nature interactions through their fact finding and collecting missions. As director Ciro Guerra rereads travel narratives and natural histories to construct his own filmic travel narrative, *El abrazo de la serpiente*, this literature is told and retold, fitting the Amazon and its inhabitants into a global cultural frame, while unfairly tasking the Indigenous protagonist with speaking for the subaltern.

Each narrative examined in this book grappled with the place of the Amazon within a world geography and increasingly globalized culture. While Rondon, Euclides, and Mário attempt to situate the Amazon's place within Brazil, the narrative, mapping, collecting, and photographic projects of Roosevelt, Coudreau, Koch-Grünberg, and Schultes move the Amazon into an international discourse that operates on the "known." These justifications and projections serve to set the scene for the future of Amazonia, and therefore, the future of the planet.

The corpus examined here shows how a variety of outsiders to the Amazon, through travel to the region, put forward ideas about the future of the environment and Amazonian peoples. Those ideas, many of which came to fruition in varying ways, include the immigration of Europeans to manage the region, the establishment of small settlements by Brazilians, the integration of the region into a national cultural identity, the acculturation of Indigenous peoples, the reliance on Indigenous communities for their knowledge of plants, and overall pushes for increased economic and extractive development of Amazonia. Each explorer also engages with travel in different ways, some as commissioned geographers and anthropologists, others as writers or filmmakers intent on showing the nuances of the region and its peoples. In each case, the act of travel itself is commented on, conceptualized, and used to justify their thoughts and actions. The interactions these travelers experience within the social and biological contact zone of Amazonia reveal the ambiguities of knowledge creation.

At the heart of this study is modernity, characterized by the coming into being of modern nation states and citizens participating in global and national capitalist economies with all the gains and losses this implies. Modernity is built out of power and conflict and depends not only on economic and political processes, but also on ways of knowing, understanding, and being. Part of the project of modernity, nationalism, like imperialism, depends not just on economic expansion but on the erroneous idea that certain societies and places should be subjugated—that the savage, racialized Other *needs* subjugation and taming by Western societies.[1] These processes form the coloniality of power, where the legacy of European colonialism continues into the present through systems of hierarchies, knowledge, and culture. The Amazon is a space with competing national and international claims that provides a prism through which to recognize how raced and gendered subordinations across differing contexts produce modernity.

Narratives about the Amazon rely on the propagation and dissemination of representations of the Other through categorization, photography, and exotified voyeurism—geographer, explorer, and tourist's gazes. These diverse and complex documents, the knowledge they created about landscapes and people, and the way that they inscribe relations of power and ideas about economic, cultural, and national development worked to establish what we know as the contemporary Amazon. The writers and travelers examined in *Eyes on Amazonia* most often described a region in flux, one that could be developed for enterprising individuals or national interests. The Amazon, one of the most important global biomes for its climate benefits and wealth of biodiversity, has a history that is worth exploring to further understand the current rhetoric and developmental interests around the forest, and to better understand the cultural richness that also characterizes the region. Ultimately this book looks at issues of control, power, and dominance through the lens of various types of travel narratives. Within these narratives, most of the authors understood nature as separate from culture, repeating a Western discourse that does not actually fit an Amazonian reality.

The dynamic between humans and their environment reflects a key aspect of a decolonial approach: reimagining the nature-culture divide. Indigenous activist Ailton Krenak explains that the separation of nature and culture or the very concept of humanity has created a rift: "We have to abandon our anthropocentrism. There's a lot more to Earth than us, and biodiversity doesn't seem to be missing us at all. Quite the contrary."[2] As Krenak states, extractive practices, at least partially rooted in the Westernized separation of nature and culture, have created the current climate crisis, and thus it is with the utmost urgency that we must re-examine our worldview. Reflecting upon a human-ecological relationship is a means of an epistemic reconstitution that reimagines the natural environment and contributes to and interacts with different ways of looking at the world. Countries in the Global North used and continue to use their dominant position to industrialize their own economies, with colonies or former colonies as raw material exporters. Extractivism continues in many forms today, and across the world communities are struggling to defend their land, air, water, forests, and livelihoods from damaging projects and extractive activities with heavy environmental and social repercussions. The environmental impacts from extractive industries are externalized onto the most marginalized populations.

Indeed, Krenak rightly critiques the use of the word *resource* itself. If nature is characterized as a resource, it can therefore be expendable and understood as made for our own usage rather than a symbiotic relationship where nature is a sentient, feeling, and evolving being. As such, activists like Krenak conceptualize nature as much more than a site of potential resources. Instead, they actively campaign against the appropriation and exploitation of traditional knowledge for commercial gain and the inseparability of nature and culture, as well as the rights of Indigenous peoples as deeply linked to environmental rights.

As Mignolo explains, a decolonial politics is necessary to understand processes of modernity and expose the Eurocentric coloniality of power. However, to move from a decolonial politics that questions knowledge production into concrete actions requires applying decolonial politics to world-making. This means a "reconstitution, resurgence, reemergence, and re-existence to emancipate ourselves from mental slavery."[3] For Mignolo, decolonial analytics and decolonial enactment are two sides of the same coin. Part of a decolonial approach, as Joanne Rappaport argues, is *interculturalidad* ("the selective appropriation of concepts across cultures by the indigenous movement in the interest of building a pluralistic dialogue among equals and, ultimately, a more equal society"[4]). This presents a method of interaction between academics and activists for horizontal research with the goal of political change. Within a methodology of *interculturalidad*, Indigenous cosmovisions and Western academic approaches are merged to create new systems of knowledge production.[5] Some challenges to this model include bridging literacies and respecting differing epistemologies as well as languages. Ultimately, however, Rappaport argues that *interculturalidad* creates a greater malleability of ideas across contexts, richer overall experiences, and a shared research product.

The addendums of each chapter within *Eyes on Amazonia* attempted to show the legacy of these writers on the land they traveled through and alternative approaches to knowledge production—steps toward an *interculturalidad* and decolonial praxis. For example, we explored the important work of collectives like the PNCSA or Video nas Aldeias, as well as the practice of ethnomueseology. These projects redirect streams of knowledge by putting the power of representation directly into the hands of Indigenous and local peoples. Instead of extractive practices or collecting expeditions coming from the outside, this self-representation can lead to new ways of thinking the world that in the current context of climate change and the rise of far-right governments is ever more important.

And to end this book as it began, the 2019 Amazon fires created a sense of international outcry; however, subsequent years have seen fires and deforestation grow with much less attention. With Bolsonaro's 2022 loss to former president Lula da Silva, many of his damaging environmental actions are now in the process of being undone.[6] The destruction, anti-environmental rhetoric, opening of Indigenous lands to mining, and increased deforestation that Bolsonaro championed remain crucial problems, though, that require collaborative action. As climate issues have become increasingly mainstream, there is recognition that important biomes like the Amazon (perhaps the most important global biome of all) will play a role in the very survival of the planet. Rather than a new phenomenon of extraction and deforestation, we can see that the struggle to define the Amazon region has always held conflict and high stakes.

Not only are cultural representations of the utmost importance for actual political action, but because of the current reality of climate change, the fate of the environment is of even greater consequence. Cultural production that gives meaning and increased representation to the forest and its peoples can create a widespread impact that begins to halt, or at the very least calls attention to, practices of destruction. Issues of environmental protections in the current context of globalization and expanding access shape not only the advancement of knowledge in the field but also the role of educators and cultural heritage institutions in archiving and making information attainable. To critically approach international environmental issues, we need to look back at the developmental discourses and projects that created our current conceptions of nature and culture and forge a new way forward through multifaceted and interdisciplinary approaches that center the leadership of voices that have too often been dismissed and unheard. When addressing environmental issues, it is imperative to address structures of inequality and global disparities, topics that the environmental humanities are uniquely suited to address.

As Amazonian writer and journalist Márcio Souza states, "Amazonia will be free when we definitively recognize that this nature is our culture, where a felled tree is like a suppressed word and a polluted river is like a censured page."[7] The Amazon will be "free" when we can recognize the importance of the environment in making meaning. While correcting the errors of the past is impossible, a more equitable, just, inclusive, and sustainable way of being is achievable. Protecting the Amazon means understanding the historical precedent of the development of the region and the representation of its inhabitants. It means understanding the ways humans are dependent on nature and vice versa. It means collective action that supports and works with Indigenous and local peoples toward their right of territorial sovereignty. Ultimately, it means advocating for nature and culture as one and the same.

Notes

INTRODUCTION

1. McCoy, "Smoke Plunges São Paulo."
2. Coming on the heels of the fires, in September of the same year, the largest climate strikes in world history took place to protest a lack of action by leaders and lawmakers on climate issues. Started by Swedish activist Greta Thunberg, the Global Week for Future protests included over 4,500 locations in 150 countries where protesters, many of whom were young students, marched carrying signs (a popular refrain was "Our house is on fire") and demanding change. Between these two events, along with a myriad of other major climate catastrophes, 2019 solidified the state of climate emergency urgency and the importance of climate action on a global scale. The following year further revealed the connection between climate catastrophe and human networks. In 2020, the COVID-19 pandemic, classified as a zoonotic disease (transferred from vertebrate animals to humans), showed how increased deforestation could lead to greater interaction between humans and wildlife and ultimately the emergence of a disease that would also exacerbate deforestation in some areas.
3. In 2022, Bolsonaro narrowly lost re-election to the more environmentally friendly former president Luiz Inácio "Lula" da Silva.
4. Walker et al., "The Role of Forest Conversion."
5. Gatti et al., "Amazonia as a Carbon Source."
6. Klein, *Beyond Extractivism*, 169.
7. Klein, *Beyond Extractivism*, 170.
8. This book primarily focuses on the Brazilian Amazon, because of the percentage of the forest found within the country's borders and its rich history of cultural contact and representations of the region. I also touch on work done by explorers in the Colombian and Venezuelan Amazon.
9. Skidmore, *Brazil*, 3.
10. Carvalho, "Dreams Come Untrue," 67.
11. Leeds and Satyamurthy, "Country of the Future," 189.
12. Pratt, *Imperial Eyes*, 3.
13. Garland, "What Is a 'History of the Present,'" 373.
14. Nixon, *Slow Violence*.
15. Pratt, *Imperial Eyes*, 6.

16. Schiebinger, *Plants and Empire*, 83.
17. Martinez-Pinzón and Uriarte, *Intimate Frontiers*, 20.
18. Rogers, *Mourning El Dorado*, 7.
19. Rogers, *Mourning El Dorado*, 16. During the colonial period in Brazil, the Portuguese primarily exported brazilwood, sugar, and gold in a slave-based plantation system. Gold, coveted by the Portuguese, pushed colonists further inland from the coastal regions that they had initially settled in the sixteenth and seventeenth centuries. Gold was eventually found in the southeastern state of Minas Gerais, triggering widescale immigration and consolidating wealth in the southern regions of the country. In 1807 the Portuguese crown family, led by King João IV, were forced to flee Napoleon's invading forces in Portugal, ultimately packing up the court and residing in Rio de Janeiro. After the end of the Napoleonic wars, the monarchy remained in Brazil and founded a joint kingdom of Portugal, Brazil, and the Algarve in 1815. Brazil declared its independence from this union in 1822, and João IV's son, Dom Pedro, remained as leader over the empire of Brazil. Regional revolts began to break out as different initiatives from the crown meant to decentralize the government, such as an act that allowed each province to control taxation and expenditure, created discord throughout the country.
20. Although only fully available in the nineteenth century, Carvajal's chronicle was excerpted in the famous *Historia general de las Indias* which was published a year later, in 1542.
21. Fernández de Oviedo y Valdés, *About the Natural History*, 206.
22. Fernández de Oviedo y Valdés, *About the Natural History*, 214.
23. The Amazon name was commonly etymologized from the Greek a-mazdos, meaning "without a breast," referring to their practice of cutting off a breast so they could be better archers. This can tie in with the idea of Mother Earth as a land described as a "green breast" in various travelogues.
24. Like the former thirst for gold, the Amazon came to be reconceived of as a biological goldmine: "During this time, dreams of Amazonian gold yielded to fantasies about scientific treasures awaiting discovery. Botanists and naturalists like La Condamine, Humboldt, Rodrigues de Ferreira, Henry Bates, and Alfred Russell Wallace all debunk the concepts of El Dorado and Amazon maidens, yet at the same time they envision Amazonia as a scientific wonderland. In his study of Victorian scientific travelers, Peter Raby calls the South American tropics 'the naturalists' El Dorado' (77), thus indicating the extent to which the trope of El Dorado infuses even scientific discourse." Rogers, *Mourning El Dorado*, 34.
25. Gomes, "Ciclos econômicos."
26. Driver and Martins, *Tropical Visions*, 5.
27. Campbell and Grondona, *Indigenous Languages*, 179.
28. Wylie, "Colonial Tropes," 731.
29. Marcone, "De Retorno," 299.
30. Smith, *Mapping the Amazon*, 7.
31. Espelt-Bombin and Harris, "Changing Narratives," 151.
32. Quijano, "Coloniality and Modernity."
33. Slater, *Entangled Edens*, 96.
34. Marcone, "De retorno," 167.

35. Carvalho, "Dreams Come Untrue," 72.
36. Hecht and Cockburn, *Fate of the Forest*, 4.
37. And many tried; for example, one of the explorers examined in Chapter 1, Henri Coudreau, helped build a short-lived utopian project—the Republic of Counani (1892–1911).
38. Quijano, "Coloniality and Modernity," 171.
39. Quijano, "Coloniality and Modernity," 173.
40. Schiebinger, *Plants and Empire*, 11.
41. Massey, *For Space*, 56.
42. Stam and Shohat, *Race in Translation*, 6.
43. See Hecht and Cockburn, *Fate of the Forest*; Anderson, May, and Balick, *Subsidy from Nature*; Cleary, "After the Frontier"; Garfield, *Indigenous Struggle*; Caviglia-Harris, Sills, and Mullan, "Migration and Mobility."
44. These frontiers took on multiple conceptualizations, depending on the era: "These simplifying characterizations are enhanced by the tendency for Amazonia to be continuously nested within a recurrent, and often mythologized, notion of the frontier: the colonial frontier, the frontier of green hell, the frontier of Brazilian nation building, the advancing frontier of commercial agriculture, pastoralism, and extraction, conjuring up a pristine remoteness just out of reach that overwhelmed indigenous societies are seen to exemplify." Nugent, *Scoping the Amazon*, 222.
45. Nugent, *Scoping the Amazon*.
46. Conservationism works in hand with modernization. Where modernization encroached on frontiers, conservation was meant to preserve supposedly untouched areas. In conservation initiatives, local peoples have often been displaced.
47. As Lúcia Sá points out, writing about the Amazon owes much to the Indigenous peoples living there. As a response to this gap, Sá wrote *Rainforest Literatures* (2004), an important in-depth analysis of how narratives like *Macunaíma* and others were shaped by Indigenous folklore, much of which was recorded by naturalist/explorers.
48. De la Cadena, "Indigenous Cosmopolitics," 347.
49. quoted in Rivera Andía and Odegaard, "Introduction: Indigenous Peoples," 8.
50. Escobar describes development as a historically singular experience based on three axis: "the forms of knowledge that refer to it and through which it comes into being and is elaborated into objects, concepts, theories, and the like; the system of power that regulates its practice; and the forms of subjectivity fostered by this discourse, those through which people come to recognize themselves as developed or underdeveloped." Embedded in contemporary terminology such as first and third world, center and periphery, development occurs in relation to "differences, subjectivities, and social orders." Escobar, *Encountering Development*, 10, 9.
51. Mbembe, "Necropolitics," 25.
52. Mbembe, "Necropolitics," 26.
53. Mbembe, "Necropolitics," 24.
54. Mignolo, "Colonial Situations," 95.
55. E-International Relations, "Interview—Walter Mignolo."
56. Tuhiwai Smith, *Decolonizing Methodologies*, 10.

57. Blunt, *Travel, Gender, and Imperialism*, 97.
58. Poole, *Vision, Race*.
59. Mirzoeff, *Right to Look*, 483.
60. Rose, *Visual Methodologies*, 6.
61. hooks, "The Oppositional Gaze," 116.
62. Cleary, "Towards an Environmental History," 90.
63. As Susanne Oakdale explains about the Rondon Comission: "The contact missions of Rondon also featured 'modern' technology, much like the Roncador-Xingu Expedition. In addition to the telegraph, they also celebrated 'modern' photography and used the latest equipment from Germany to document the activities of bringing progress to native peoples or, later, to scientifically document both native ways of life that were the starting point of the state's actions and ways of life that would eventually be destroyed (Maciel 1997; Lima 1995:164; Tacca 2002). These photos were sent to newspapers and published widely (Diacon 2004; Tacca 2002), displaying the state's power to represent the hidden interior." Oakdale, "Brazil's March to the West," 58.
64. Driver and Martins, *Tropical Visions*, 4.
65. Ashcroft, *Post-Colonial Studies*, 187.
66. Sá Carvalho and Lissovsky, "Fotografia e representação."
67. Sá Carvalho and Lissovsky, "Fotografia e representação," 78.
68. Sá Carvalho, "How to See."
69. Rogers, *Mourning El Dorado*, 2.
70. The legacies of extractivism help explain current environmental issues in Latin America: "Extractivism epitomises the contemporary situation in many South American countries in several ways, raising issues of environmental degradation, sustainable development, resource sovereignty, and vulnerable (often indigenous) populations' position and options." Rivera Andía and Odegaard, "Introduction: Indigenous Peoples," 13.
71. Spruce, *Notes of a Botanist*.
72. Weinstein, *Amazon Rubber Boom*, 23.
73. Hecht, *Scramble for the Amazon*, 285.
74. Hecht, *Scramble for the Amazon*, 203.
75. This moment was also characterized by Joseph Conrad's seminal jungle and human rights narrative *Heart of Darkness* (1899). Raising questions about imperialism and racism, *Heart of Darkness* details the slavery and abuse of rubber workers in the African Congo. Roger Casement, an Anglo-Irish diplomat (who would later become an Irish nationalist), was also active in the human rights struggle in the African Congo in addition to being personal friends with Joseph Conrad. After his experience in Africa, Casement was commissioned to investigate rubber-era abuses in the Peruvian Amazon. His diaries created an international stir and increased attention to rubber boom atrocities, which resulted in some reforms.
76. Rogers, *Mourning El Dorado*, 30.
77. Escobar, "Thinking-Feeling," 28.
78. Sutthiphisal, "Learning by Producing," 995.
79. Tutino, *New Countries*, 380.

80. In the Brazilian Amazon, the Cabanagem revolt (1835–1840) took place in Belém, starting with initial fighting between monarchists and regionalists, and eventually transformed into a battle between the elites and the lower classes, primarily composed of Indigenous peoples. Regional fighting led to this empire's dissolution into an independent nation in 1889, one year after the abolition of slavery. Throughout these regime changes, the Brazilian Amazon often reported directly to Portugal, as it was closer to Lisbon than the Brazilian capital—at that time housed in Rio de Janeiro. By the early 1900s around 84 percent of the Brazilian population lived in two major coastal regions—those surrounding Rio de Janeiro and Salvador, Bahia, in the Northeast. This created the task of consolidating the Brazilian nation through systematically opening the interior regions—a feat that also attracted a large swath of foreign explorers enticed by the exotic promise of a lush, "virgin" forest.
81. Brooke, "Manaus Journal."
82. In Taussig's seminal study of violence during the rubber boom, he examines how the nature of the region has contributed to its history: "But of course it is not the jungle but the sentiments men project into it that is decisive in filling their hearts with savagery. And what the jungle can accomplish, so much more can its native inhabitants, the wild Indians, like those tortured into gathering rubber. It must not be overlooked that the colonially constructed image of the wild Indian here at stake was a powerfully ambiguous image, a seesawing, bifocalized, and hazy composite of the animal and human." Taussig, "Culture of Terror," 483.
83. Gomes, "Ciclos econômicos."
84. As Weinstein notes, "Rather than eroding existing relations of production, the Amazon rubber trade built upon them, reinforcing traditional modes of extraction and exchange." *Amazon Rubber Boom*, 15.
85. Musgrave, *Empire of Plants*, 173. There was a brief resurgence in the economic importance and international demand for rubber when Asian markets were shut off to Allied forces during WWII. Garfield, *In Search of the Amazon*, 2013. During this time, the United States actively sought economic exchange and a friendly, good-neighbor approach toward Latin America.
86. Zilly, "Sertão e nacionalidade," 3.
87. In Brazil, the abundant natural resources of the country are seen as key to realizing the potential of a nation that is just barely pulling out of an economic recession amid years of political turmoil. At the time, Brazil's ability to combat the 2019 fires and political will to do so was brought into question. Brazil has sovereignty over their part of the forest, and it is worthwhile to acknowledge the history of colonialism and US/European exploitation of Latin America and their history of intervention in the region. It is also important to note that deforestation is mostly fueled by multinational corporations feeding the needs of those in the global north.
88. "'Brasil é uma virgem que todo tarado de fora quer', diz Bolsonaro ao falar sobre Amazônia," Globo Política, July 6, 2019, https://g1.globo.com/politica/noticia/2019/07/06/brasil-e-uma-virgem-que-todo-tarado-de-fora-quer-diz-bolsonaro-ao-falar-sobre-amazonia.ghtml.
89. Viscidi and Ortiz, "How to Save."

CHAPTER 1

Portions of Chapter 1 were published in the journal *Gender, Place, and Culture* in June 2017. Carey-Webb, "Gendered Politics of Empire." All translations appearing in this chapter are my own, unless otherwise noted.

1. In some sources Octavie is referred to as Otille, in others simply as O. Coudreau.
2. In this chapter I use Octavie and Henri's first names rather than last to distinguish them.
3. Souza Filho, "Os retratos."
4. The "white man's burden," coined by English writer Rudyard Kipling, drew on social Darwinism to project a racially prejudiced idea that it was the white man's duty to take care of nonwhite subjects in the colonies.
5. Valente, "Madame Coudreau," 2.
6. See Domosh, *Towards a Feminist*; Rose, *Feminism and Geography*; Blunt, *Travel, Gender*; Kearns, "The Imperial Subject"; McEwan, "Cutting Power Lines"; Maddrell, *Complex Locations*.
7. Blunt, *Travel, Gender*, 26.
8. See Spruce, *Notes of a Botanist*; Bates, *The Naturalist*; da Cunha, *À margem*; Koch-Grünberg, *Do Roraima*; Roosevelt, *Through the Brazilian Wilderness*, among others.
9. Like the Coudreaus, Elizabeth and Louis Agassiz, a far more famous pair of Amazonian explorer-naturalists, documented their travels throughout Brazil during the 1860s. Their joint publication, *A Journey in Brazil* (1868), also includes highly racialized (overtly racist) depictions of Black and Indigenous people that they encounter, while demonstrating a pointed difference between Louis's more scientific observations and Elizabeth's molding of the narrative that gives nuance to the relationships between different races. Unlike the Coudreaus, the Agassizs were not directly involved in creating cartography; they were more concerned with observations of the natural world that Louis hoped could be used to refute Charles Darwin's theories of evolution. Bergmann, "A Troubled Marriage." Elizabeth Agassiz, like Octavie, continued publishing after her husband's death. Beyond Elizabeth Agassiz, female explorers from Europe and the US such as Flora Tristan (1838), Maria Graham (1823), Lady Florence Dixie (1878), and Marion McMurrough Murphy (1881) published some travel narratives about Latin America. However, in contrast to Octavie, these women were often in more urban centers, and did not travel to the Amazon during the rubber boom.
10. Coudreau and Coudreau, *Voyage au Trombetas*, 134.
11. Kearns, "Imperial Subject," 451.
12. McClintock, *Imperial Leather*, 3.
13. McClintock, *Imperial Leather*, 8.
14. McClintock, *Imperial Leather*, 7.
15. There are a few analyses of Octavie, including a historical analysis in the form of a PhD dissertation from the Brazilian academy (Souza Filho, "Os retratos dos Coudreau"), a two-page cultural news bulletin from a small town in Pará (Valente, "Madame Coudreau"), and a website sponsored by the French government (Leroy, "Sur les traces d'Henri Coudreau"). Octavie is also examined in a 2018 article by Federico Ferretti, "Imperial Ambivalences: Histories of Lady Travelers and the French Explorer Octavie Renard-Coudreau (1867–1938)."

There is a biography of Henri Coudreau by Sébastien Benoit, . *Henri Anatole Coudreau, 1859–1899: Dernier explorateur français en amazonie: Une première biographie*.

Henri Coudreau's travel narratives were translated in 1977 in a collection of other travel/adventure literature about Brazil, collectively called *Reconquista do Brasil*. The forward promotes the importance of Henri's narratives for learning about the Indigenous peoples and landscapes of the Brazilian state of Pará.

16. McClintock, *Imperial Leather*, 112.
17. Mirzoeff, "Right to Look," 483.
18. Poole, *Vision, Race*, 15.
19. de la Torre, *People of the River*.
20. Coudreau and Coudreau, *Voyage au Trombetas*, 130.
21. Coudreau and Coudreau, *Voyage au Trombetas*, 5.
22. Morgan, *Place Matters*, 17.
23. See Domosh, "Towards a Feminist History," 99.
24. Coudreau, *Voyage au Cuminá*, 5.
25. Kearns, "Imperial Subject," 455.
26. As McClintock notes, "Clothes are the visible signs of social identity but are also permanently subject to disarrangement and symbolic theft." McClintock, *Imperial Leather*, 67.
27. Souza Filho, "Os retratos," 162.
28. Kearns, "Imperial Subject," 451.
29. Coudreau, *Viagem ao Tapajós*, 45.
30. Ferretti, "Imperial Ambivalences," 238.
31. Benoit, *Henri Anatole*, 120.
32. Coudreau, *Viagem ao Tapajós*, 38.
33. As evidenced by other male travel narratives and romanticist ideology popular around this time, including José de Alencar's Indigenous romances such as *Iracema* (1865) and *O Guarani* (1857), the ideal of a beautiful, welcoming Indigenous woman unsullied by the drudgery of civilization formed part of the appeal of the "noble savage." Devine Guzman, *Native and National*, 67.
34. Coudreau, *Voyage au Cuminá*, 100.
35. McClintock, *Imperial Leather*, 126.
36. Kaplan, *Looking for the Other*, 20.
37. Coudreau, *Voyage au Cuminá*, 127.
38. Domosh, "Towards a Feminist," 99.
39. Figêna was considered a spiritual leader of her community; she thus has a sense of authority and importance within her *mocambo*.
40. Coudreau and Coudreau, *Voyage au Trombetas*, 20.
41. Coudreau, *Voyage au Cuminá*, 120.
42. Coudreau, *Voyage au Cuminá*, 27.
43. Coudreau, *Voyage au Cuminá*, 115.
44. Coudreau, *Voyage au Cuminá*, 74.
45. Coudreau, *Viagem ao Tapajós*, 112.
46. Coudreau, *Viagem ao Tapajós*, 100.
47. Hecht, *The Scramble*, 133.

48. Coudreau and Coudreau, *Voyage au Trombetas*, 86.
49. Pratt, *Imperial Eyes*, 64.
50. Following Certeau's definitions of space and place, where a place indicates a sense of stability in a defined location, and space consists of various mobile elements—a mobile act of the present, the Coudreaus' map and write a particular place in their material production. Certeau, *The Practice of Everyday Life*, 117. In speaking on the differences between representations—illustrations, tours, or other describers, the map ultimately asserts all-encompassing knowledge other forms leave out. "But the map gradually wins out over these figures; it colonizes space; it eliminates little by little the pictural figurations of the practices that produce it." Certeau, 121. Maps serve to exhibit the products of knowledge, taken and presented to the public as the absolute truth, where space is a practiced place.
51. As McClintock notes of the role of map-making in coloniality, "the map is a technology of knowledge that professes to capture the truth about a place in pure, scientific form, operating under the guise of scientific exactitude and promising to retrieve and reproduce nature exactly as it is." McClintock, *Imperial Leather*, 27.
52. Driver, *Geography Militant*, 22.
53. Coudreau and Coudreau, *Voyage au Trombetas*, 10.
54. Leroy, "Sur les traces."
55. Coudreau, *Viagem ao Trombetas*, 15.
56. The PNCSA also has initiatives throughout the rest of Brazil and in urban centers.
57. de la Torre, *People of the River*.
58. Phillips, "Their Forefathers."
59. The community itself presented their territorial limits using GPS and mapping techniques they learned from workshops with the PNCSA. There were some conflicts of territorial designation between Indigenous groups and the *quilombolas*. Several meetings between the two groups were organized by the public minister until they reached a collective land agreement.

CHAPTER 2

1. McClintock, *Imperial Leather*, 193.
2. Maligo, *Land of Metaphorical Desires*; Stepan, *Picturing Tropical Nature*; Slater, *Entangled Edens*; Nugent, *Scoping the Amazon*; Vieira, "Phytofables."
3. French, "Voices in the Wilderness," 158.
4. French, "Voices in the Wilderness," 159.
5. Diacon, *Stringing Together*, 158.
6. Diacon, *Stringing Together*, 185.
7. Pace, "The Amazon Caboclo," 82.
8. Borges, "Puffy, Ugly," 10.
9. Skidmore, *Black into White*, 103; Lima and Hochman, "Pouca saúde," 494.
10. Skidmore, *Black into White*, 120.
11. In Latin America broadly, positivism came in two varieties: Comtean, a social positivism, and Spencerian, an evolutionary positivism. The Spencerians viewed change as

continual, as societies moved from simple to complex. Darwin's theories of evolution and particularly his concept of "survival of the fittest" quickly became intertwined with positivistic ideals and were used to examine the racial and ethnic composition of Latin American populations. In Brazilian intellectual thought, Darwinism covered all processes of culture and social life. This meant that context was of the utmost importance—there could be no meaning outside of the culture that produced it.

12. "Theodore Roosevelt's Annual Message to Congress."
13. Roosevelt, *Through the Brazilian Wilderness*, 298.
14. Watts, *Rough Rider*, 20.
15. Roosevelt, *Through the Brazilian Wilderness*, 67.
16. The wilderness wanderer thus embodies a "blending of rationality and physicality . . . creating an ideal figure that was both the lone, romantic frontiersman whose rugged physical vigor enabled him to escape the stultifying feminine influences of civilization and to master (female) nature, and simultaneously the educated professional who mapped and civilized the wilderness." Cronon, "The Trouble," 336.
17. Cronon, "The Trouble," 70.
18. Slater, *Entangled Edens*, 26.
19. Poole, *Vision, Race*, 160.
20. As historian Todd Diacon has discussed, Rondon is a polarizing figure because of his work to incorporate Indigenous peoples that eliminated their ways of life. However, his policies of nonviolence were also quite ahead of his time. Diacon centers his study of Rondon on positivism, the ideology that propelled Rondon's exploratory work and life trajectory. Diacon, "Candido Mariano"; Diacon, *Stringing Together*.
21. Diacon, *Stringing Together*, 187.
22. Diacon, *Stringing Together*, 189.
23. As Luciana Martins argues in her article on Hamilton Rice's Amazonian expeditions in the 1920s, "such expeditions were not simply bringing modernity to the Amazon; they were re-locating modernity itself, offering the possibility of a new way of imagining both the region and the nation of which it was a part." Martins, "Illusions of Power," 287.
24. Quoted in Haag, "Science to Create a Nation," 77.
25. Following Quijano's definition of coloniality as the imposition of European epistemologies and Eurocentric values during the colonial period, that perceived difference was necessary to construct a power structure that racialized bodies to serve the labor needs of Europeans in the New World. Quijano, "Coloniality and Modernity," 170.
26. Roosevelt, *Through the Brazilian Wilderness*, 124.
27. Blunt, *Travel, Gender*, 28.
28. "E assim chegámos ambos a um acôrdo, concluindo o Sr. Roosevelt:

-- Conheci, em minha vida, dois grandes coronéis: o que resolveu o problema do canal de Panamá e . . . Rondon . . . Lembrando-me de que era êle *verista*, nada lhe respondi . . .

Prosseguia o levantamento topográfico, sem que a necessidade de andar depressa nos permitisse tirar todo o proveito de nossos recursos técnicos." Rondon and de Viveiros, *Rondon conta sua vida*, 411.

29. Roosevelt, *Through the Brazilian Wilderness*, 1.
30. As Diacon explains about the relationship between the two men, "Thus, while Rondon's on-going task was to display the authority of the central state and explain the power of his vision of the Brazilian nation to those in the interior, at this point he faced his own and his country's subservience to a more powerful nation, as well as to the powerful personality of Theodore Roosevelt." Diacon, *Stringing Together*, 44.
31. "O eminente chefe da Comissão Americana não mais voltou a gozar a saúde com que iniciara a expedição; seu filho Kermit estava também muito combalido pelos acessos de febre. Lira e Cherrie, com afecções gástricas; nossos homens, atacados de febres, esmagados de cansaço, enfraquecidos, estariam literalmente derrotados se não tivessem a têmpera de nossos admiráveis caboclos." Rondon and de Viveiros, *Rondon conta sua vida*, 421.
32. Pace, "The Amazon Caboclo," 85.
33. Diacon, "Candido Mariano," 175.
34. Roosevelt, *Through the Brazilian Wilderness*, 225.
35. Roosevelt, *Through the Brazilian Wilderness*, 245.
36. Roosevelt, *Through the Brazilian Wilderness*, 183.
37. Roosevelt, *Through the Brazilian Wilderness*, 184.
38. Roosevelt, *Through the Brazilian Wilderness*, 173.
39. Roosevelt, *Through the Brazilian Wilderness*, 241.
40. Roosevelt, *Through the Brazilian Wilderness*, 209.
41. Roosevelt, "Brazil and the Negro," 409.
42. Roosevelt, "Brazil and the Negro," 409.
43. Roosevelt, "Brazil and the Negro," 408.
44. Roosevelt, "Brazil and the Negro," 409.
45. "Morrer se for preciso . . . matar nunca!"
46. Roosevelt, *Through the Brazilian Wilderness*, 110.
47. Diacon, *Stringing Together*, 123.
48. "Era perfeito nosso entendimento. Compreendeu o Sr. Roosevelt qual fôra o meu incentivo, o que me empolgara acima de tudo—a obra político-social, a pacificação dos índios pela bondade, pela justiça e pela compreensão, o trazêlos á civilização gradualmente, com a orientação que me davam as luzes do Positivismo, preocupado em melhorar o material humano, em educar, no sentido lato da palavra." Rondon and de Viveiros, *Conta sua vida*, 385.
49. Machado Domingues, "A comissão," 13.
50. Martins, "Illusions of Power," 287.
51. "A incorporação dos índios, sílvicolas, aborígenes—nunca porém bugres, descabida injúria de origem francesa—assim como a das massas proletárias, ainda acampadas a margem da civilização, constituem casos particulares—de angustiante importância e urgência—do problema geral, problema religioso imposto com veemência cada vez maior." Rondon and de Viveiros, *Conta sua vida*, 328.
52. Roosevelt, a champion of secular education, believes "sympathetic understanding" toward Indigenous people is an essential tool of colonization. "The Indians must be treated with intelligent and sympathetic understanding, no less than with justice and firmness; and until they become citizens, absorbed into the general body politic, they

must be the wards of the nation, and not of any private association, lay or clerical, no matter how well-meaning." *Through the Brazilian Wilderness*, 128. Thus, according to Roosevelt, the absorption of Indigenous peoples into the Brazilian state is crucial in nation building, but the Indigenous population will need to remain "wards of the nation" that are not yet deserving of autonomy.

53. "Expluso da terra, de que era legítimo dono, pelo invasor que viera, com mostras de paz, trazer sangue, ruínas, destruição, é êle o mais digno de benemerência. Trata-se do resgate da mais sagrada dívida de honra, da reparação das mais dolorosas culpas e erros sociais de nossos antepassados." Rondon and de Viveiros, *Conta sua vida*, 326.
54. "Quebrando a tradição dos penetradores das selvas que, em caráter de aventuras industriais ou de estudos científicos, atropelavam sempre os íncolas da região, varou tal reconhecimento as terras dos parecis, nhambiquaras, quep-queri-uates, orumis, jarus, urupás, ariquêmes, caritianas e caripumos, sem lhes causar a menor pertubação ou violência" (Rondon and de Viveiros, *Conta sua vida*, 597).
55. Diacon, "Candido Mariano," 165.
56. Mies examines the reasons for man's desire of landscape as a reaction to society's industrialization, leading to the creation of a cult of nostalgia around Nature or the "wilderness." Mies and Shiva, *Ecofeminism*.
57. Roosevelt, *Through the Brazilian Wilderness*, 221.
58. Slater, *Entangled Edens*, 45.
59. Roosevelt, *Through the Brazilian Wilderness*, 52.
60. The imperial project depends upon the subjugation of land, people, and animals. As Madhudaya Sinha points out in her analysis of hunting scenes in the imperial novel *She*, "hunting and imperialism went hand in hand because both projects shared a belief: that wild lands, capable of being tamed and rendered economically productive, must be allowed to remain so [wild], even at the cost of violent confrontations." Sinha, "Triangular Erotics," 38.
61. Mignolo, *Darker Side*, 109.
62. McClintock, *Imperial Leather*, 27.
63. *River of Doubt*, 01:35–01:40.
64. "E que, por ordem do Govêrno Brasileiro, êsse rio, o maior afluente do rio Madeira, com suas nascentes a 13 grados e sua foz a 5 grados de latitude Sul, inteiramente desconhecido dos cartógrafos e até, em grande parte, das próprias tribos locais, tinha recibido o nome de rio Roosevelt. Modestamente, sugeriu êste que se chamasse rio Theodore." Rondon and de Viveiros, *Conta sua vida*, 421.
65. See Slater, *Entangled Edens*; Enright, *The Maximum of Wilderness*; Vieira, "Phytofables."
66. Diacon, *Stringing Together*, 204.
67. Roosevelt, *Through the Brazilian Wilderness*, 183.
68. "A ciência transforma o mundo, e o paraíso sonhado pela gente de outras idades começa a se delinear aos olhos da moderna geração, com possibilidades com que o passado não ousava sonhar. O aquecimento central e o ar condicionado resolveram o problema do 'espaço vital', porque é possível obter, por tôda parte, agradável ambiente, com a temperatura desejada." Rondon and de Viveiros, *Conta sua vida*, 327.
69. Arini, Mota, and Jarrah, "Roosevelt River."

70. Arini, Mota, and Jarrah, "Roosevelt River."
71. Despite some highways, the Guariba-Roosevelt reserve remains remote. In a territory so isolated, the lack of state attention and enforcement of existing protections is a massive issue. Even after almost thirty years the reserve has not been officially demarcated, and the government has yet to place signs or notices to identify the reserve as protected land.
72. Arini, Mota, and Jarrah, "Roosevelt River."
73. Unidades de Conservação no Brasil, "Reserva Extractivista."
74. Sadly, Chico Mendes was shot and killed by large landowners in December 1988.
75. Hochstetler and Keck, *Greening Brazil*; Hecht, "Factories, Forests."
76. Ehringhaus, "Analysis of Land-Use."
77. Watts and Rocha, "Brazil's 'Lost Report.'"
78. Unidades de Conservação no Brasil, "Reserva Extractivista."
79. Gomes, Carlos Valério, "Extractive Reserves," 93.

CHAPTER 3

1. "E o Amazonas, nesse construir o seu verdadeiro delta em zonas tão remotas do outro hemisfério, traduz, de fato, a viagem incógnita de um território em marcha, mudando-se pelos tempos adiante, sem parar um segundo, e tornando cada vez menores, num desgastamento ininterrupto, as largas superfícies que atravessa." da Cunha, *A margem*, 9.
2. "Aquele bote do jacaré me deixou num estado de religiosidade muito sério. Palavra de honra que senti Deus no bote do jacaré. Que presteza! Que eternidade incomensurável naquele gesto!" Andrade, *O turista*, 170.
3. In this chapter I used Euclides's and Mário's first names following Brazilian tradition and to distinguish Mário de Andrade from other famous Andrades of the modernist movement.
4. Gabara, *Errant Modernism*, 49.
5. Schelling, "Mário de Andrade," 110.
6. See Costa Lima, *Control of the Imaginary*; Levine, *Vale of Tears*; Abreu, "O livro"; Johnson, "Subalternizing Canudos."
7. In this chapter I reference excerpts from *À márgem da história* using my own translations (cross-referenced with the 2006 English translation, *The Amazon: Land without History*). I also refer to *Um paraíso perdido: Reunião dos ensaios amazônicos* (A lost paradise: Collection of Amazonian essays), which includes *À margem da história* with additional Amazonian essays by Euclides.
8. Hecht, *Scramble for the Amazon*, 238.
9. "Daí esta singularidade: é de toda a América a paragem mais perlustrada dos sábios e é a menos conhecida. De Humboldt a Emílio Goeldi—do alvorar do século passado aos nossos dias, perquirem-na, ansiosos, todos os eleitos." (da Cunha, *Paraíso perdido*, 101).
10. Hecht, *Scramble for the Amazon*, 25.
11. Gómez, *Darwinism*, 3.
12. Gómez, *Darwinism*, 17.
13. As Amory explains about Euclides' relationship with positivism: "Da Cunha nonetheless really outgrew both French and Brazilian Positivism in his maturity, through his

adherence to Darwinian principles of evolution and his empirical reliance on the social and the life sciences which Comte had relegated to the bottom of his hierarchy of sciences." Amory, "Euclides da Cunha," 89.
14. "A adaptação exercita-se pelo nomadismo. Daí, em grande parte, a paralisia completa das gentes que ali vagam, há três séculos, numa agitação tumultuária e estéril." da Cunha, *A margem*, 14.
15. Moreira, "Songs and Intellectuals," 223.
16. "Grito imperioso de brancura em mim" (Andrade, *Poesias Completas*, 19).
17. "Me sinto só branco agora, só branco em minha alma crivada de raças!" (Andrade, *Poesias Completas*, 19)
18. Schelling, *Mário de Andrade*, 110.
19. Gabara, *Errant Modernism*, 46.
20. "Aliás, força a notar que o número de sons que eles possuíam era muito maior que a nossa pobre escala crómatica." Andrade, *O turista*, 129.
21. Resende, "Brazilian Modernism."
22. Pratt, *Imperial Eyes*, 234.
23. In the introduction to the English translation of *The Amazon: Land without History*, Lúcia Sá traces Euclides's travels and ideas about the Amazon to an imperialist nostalgia (citing Renato Rosaldo), where in the process of modernization, or under imperialism, people "mourn for the passing of what they themselves have transformed." Sá, Introduction, xiii.
24. Sá, Introduction, xv.
25. Carvalho, "Dreams," 62.
26. Carvalho, "Dreams," 63.
27. Carvalho, "Dreams," 67.
28. "Escapa-se-nos, de todo a enormidade que só se pode medir, repartida: a amplitude, que se tem de diminuir, para avaliar-se; a grandeza, que só se deiza ver, apequenando-se, através dos microscópios: e um infinito que se dosa, a pouco e pouco, lento e lento, indefinidamente, torturantemente. . . . Mas ao mesmo passo, convém-se em que esta marcha sobremaneira analítica, e de longo discurso remorado, é fatal. A inteligência humana não suportaria, de improviso, o peso daquela realidade portentosa." da Cunha, *Paraíso perdido*, 287.
29. Hecht, *Scramble for the Amazon*, 234.
30. "Tal é o rio; tal, a sua história: revôlta, desordenada, incompleta." da Cunha, *A margem*, 11.
31. Anderson, "Treacherous Waters."
32. Hecht, *Scramble for the Amazon*, 30.
33. "Sente-se deslocado no espaço e no tempo; não já fora da pátria, senão arredio da cultura humana, extraviado num recanto da floresta e num desvão obscurecido da História." da Cunha, *A margem*, 32.
34. Nielson, "Amazonian El Dorados," 22.
35. "A impressão dominante que tive, e talvez correspondente a uma verdade positiva, é esta: o homem, ali, é ainda um intruso impertinente. Chegou sem ser esperado nem querido—quando a natureza ainda estava arrumando o seu mais vasto e luxuoso salão. E encontrou uma opulenta desordem . . ." da Cunha, *Paraíso perdido*, 101.

36. Hecht, *Scramble for the Amazon*, 236.
37. "Abra-se qualquer regulamento de higiene colonial. Ressaltam à mais breve leitura os esforços incomparáveis das modernas missões e o seu apostolado complexo que, ao revés das antigas, não visam arrebatar para a civilização a barbaria transfigurada, senão transplantar, integralmente, a própria civilização para o seio adverso e rude dos territórios bárbaros." da Cunha, *A margem*, 35.
38. "Naqueles lugares, o brasileiro salta: é estrangeiro, e está pisando em terras brasileiras. Antolha-se-lhe um contra- senso pasmoso: à ficção de direito estabelecendo por vêzes a extraterritorialidade, que é a pátria sem a terra, contrapõe-se uma outra, rudemente física: a terra sem a pátria." da Cunha, *A margem*, 9.
39. Madan, "Provincializing World Geography."
40. Zilly, "Sertão," 3.
41. Lesser, *Immigration, Ethnicity*, 6.
42. As Jeffery Lesser, scholar of immigration in Brazil, explains, "Immigration was one of the main components in the improvement and, thus, the experience of movement did not end with the physical arrival of foreigners. Immigration was, and is, about creating a future, superior Brazil." Lesser, *Immigration, Ethnicity*, 3.
43. Euclides sees the Amazon as a place where racial identity plays a fundamental role. In *Os sertões*, Euclides positions the *sertanejo* as the central figure of Brazilian nationality. The *sertanejos* of the Northeast demonstrated a clash between the coast and the interior. Similarly, in the Amazon, Euclides focuses on the rubber tapper, many of whom were *sertanejos* who had migrated to the region following years of drought in the Northeast and economic opportunities to rubber tap in the Amazon. Guimarães, "Euclides da Cunha," 715.
44. Greenfield, "The Great Drought."
45. "Policiou, saneou, moralizou. Elegeu e elege para a vida os mais dignos. Eliminou e elimina os incapazes, pela fuga ou pela morte. E é por certo um clima admirável o que prepara as paragens novas para os fortes, para os perseverantes e para os bons." da Cunha, *A margem*, 43.
46. "vieram apesar do ambiente. . . . eles foram vitoriosos em uma batalha até a morte." da Cunha, *A margem*, 42.
47. Leu, *Defiant Geographies*, 3.
48. Amory, "Historical Source," 669.
49. da Cunha, *A margem*, 3.
50. "O problema brasileiro, para Euclides da Cunha, era civilizar, assistir e desenvolver, antes de tudo, os sertanejos-seringueiros abandonados no interior do país e da Floresta." Guimarães, "Euclides da Cunha," 714.
51. As Maligo explains, "Euclides' evolving approach to social reality suggested that the struggle between individuals, or even the existential, internal conflict of the individual with the self, was less important than the result of that struggle for society since the replacement of individuals was perceived as a necessary step in the advancement of the group." Maligo, *Land of Metaphorical Desires*, 34.
52. Anderson, "Treacherous Waters," 212.
53. "Dela ressalta impressionadoramente a urgência de medidas que salvem a sociedade ob-

scura e abandonada: uma lei do trabalho que nobilite o esfôrço do homem; uma justiça austera que lhe cerceie os desmandos; e uma forma qualquer do homestead que o consorcie definitivamente à terra." da Cunha, *A margem*, 17.

54. "É um caso de mimetismo psíquico de homem que se finge bárbaro para vencer o bárbaro. É caballero e selvagem, consoante as circunstâncias." da Cunha, *A margem*, 52.

55. "Um brasileiro descobriu o caucho; ou, pelo menos, instituiu ali a indústria extrativa correspondente. No reconstruir êste trecho da nossa História, que versado mais tarde por um historiador merecerá o título de 'Expansão Brasileira na Amazônia', não vamos desacompanhados." da Cunha, *A margem*, 70.

56. Hecht explains the differences in rubber growth in the area: "The terrains of the upper Juruá and Purús were an untapped frontier and incarnated a loose economic boundary between the production systems associated with Hevea—rubber or seringa—and those of Castilla, or caucho. A simple dichotomy can be made from the forms of extraction of latex and labor. Caucho extraction required killing the tree, so exploiting it was a nomadic but highly profitable proposition. The latex of one caucho tree could equal the returns of a year of tapping rubber. Hevea trees, on the other hand, were tapped every few days by a sedentary population. Caucho was largely worked by native labor under varying forms of coercion. Hevea trees were tapped by migrants in more or less stable settlements under many forms of labor deployment, including debt peonage." Hecht, *Scramble for the Amazon*, 183.

57. "Um brasileiro descobriu o caucho; ou, pelo menos, instituiu ali a indústria extrativa correspondente. No reconstruir êste trecho da nossa História, que versado mais tarde por um historiador merecerá o título de 'Expansão Brasileira na Amazônia', não vamos desacompanhados." da Cunha, *A margem*, 71.

58. Da Cunha, *A margem*, 17.
59. Stepan, *Picturing Tropical Nature*, 82.
60. Gabara, *Errant Modernism*, 15.
61. Borges, "Puffy, Ugly," 235.
62. Resende, "Brazilian Modernism," 205.
63. Gabara, *Errant Modernism*, 5.
64. Resende, "Brazilian Modernism," 212.
65. Resende, "Brazilian Modernism," 213.
66. Kirshenblatt-Gimblett, "Theorizing Heritage," 150.
67. The images from this trip are housed at the IEB Archive in the University of São Paulo. The archive prohibits the reproduction of images that show Indigenous and riverine populations.
68. "Sei bem que esta viagem que vamos fazer não tem nada de aventura nem perigo, mas cada um de nós, além da consciência lógica possui uma consciência poética também. As reminiscências de leitura me impulsionaram mais que a verdade, tribos selvagens, jacarés e formigões. E a minha laminha santa imaginou: canhão, revólver, bengala, canivete." Andrade, *O turista*, 51.
69. Urry, *Tourist Gaze*, 41.
70. Sá Carvalho, "How to See a Scar," 372.
71. "Lá se goza mais que em New York ou Viena!

> Só cada olhar roxo de cada morena
> De tipo mexido, cocktail brasileiro,
> Alimenta mais que um açaizeiro,
> Nosso gosto doce de homem com mulher!
> No Pará se pára, nada mais se quer!
> Prova Tucupi! Prova tacacá!
> Que alegre porto,
> Belém de Pará." Andrade, O turista, 186.

72. "Sentada no chão, era uma blusa branca branca numa preta preta que levantando pra nós os dentes os olhos e as angelicas da trunfa, tudo branco, oferecia com o braço estendido preto uma cuia envernizada preta donde saía a fumaça branquinha do munguzá branco branco . . . Tenho gozado por demais. Belém foi feita pra mim e caibo nela que nem mão dentro de luva." Andrade, *O turista*, 67.
73. Gabara, *Errant Modernism*, 63.
74. Hecht and Rajão, "From 'Green Hell,' " 6.
75. Garfield, *In Search of the Amazon*, 2013.
76. Hecht and Rajão, "From 'Green Hell,' " 8.
77. Hecht and Rajão, "From 'Green Hell,' " 10.
78. Crist et al., "Contemporary Settlement Patterns."
79. Kimbrough, "Mongabay's Top Amazon Stories."
80. "Deforestation in the Amazon Rainforest Continues to Plunge," Mongabay, September 8, 2023, https://news.mongabay.com/2023/09/deforestation-in-the-amazon-rainforest-continues-to-plunge.

CHAPTER 4

1. "Os sonhos são realidade para o índio, ações indpendentes da sombra livre do corpo, a alma." Koch-Grünberg, *Do Roraima ao Orinoco*, 79.
2. Mário de Andrade used Koch-Grünberg's accounts about the Pemon people of Brazil as a primary source of Indigenous folktales for his novel *Macunaíma* (1928). Mário borrowed so heavily from Koch-Grünberg that he was accused of plagiarism (López, "O turista aprendiz na Amazonia," 30). In *Macunaima*, Mário creates one of the foundational fictions of a Brazilian nation attempting to define itself as different from its European influences, and in so doing constructs a "hero without a character" who racially transforms and travels throughout Brazil. Thus Koch-Grünberg leaves a lasting impact on Brazilian cultural identity.
3. Schultes and Reis, "Burning the Library," 24.
4. Along with his photography and narrative, Koch-Grünberg also became active in making Amazonian films. Sadly, many of those have not survived, as they were kept in Germany and were destroyed during WWII bombings.
5. Kandell, "Richard E. Schultes Dies."
6. Although Schules is considered the father of ethnobotany, the term was first used by the American botanist John William Hershberger in 1895. Initially, studies were made up of lists of plants with their associated preparations.

7. Rogers, *Mourning El Dorado*, 7.
8. Pratt, *Imperial Eyes*, 34.
9. Koch-Grünberg corresponded with several notable Brazilians (for example Capistrano de Abreu, a Brazilian historian, and subject of Chapter 2, Cândido Rondon), exchanging correspondence on Indigenous languages, daily issues, and the difficulties of exploration.
10. As Hempel notes, the German idea of *bildung*, or the idea of self-cultivation through personal and cultural harmony, was key to the German anthropological tradition, of which Koch-Grünberg forms part. The middle class in Germany advanced ideas of *bildungs* into academic practices and museums through scientific societies and private initiatives. This approach attempted to answer questions about the human condition through using inductive scientific methods. Hempel, "Theodor Koch-Grünberg," 247. German ethnology began to decline as a discipline due to the first World War, while at the same time American anthropology forged ahead, carving out prestigious positions for academics involved in the study of others.
11. North American museums and universities were better funded and gained a large advantage over their German counterparts as they published books and increased ethnographic collections, particularly by sending ethnographers into the field. Petschelies, "Theodor Koch-Grünberg," 211. Koch-Grünberg followed North American advances in anthropology and was once asked to comment on the Roosevelt-Rondon mission by the *New York World* newspaper, an offer which he (sadly) declined. Understandably, Koch-Grünberg was disappointed that the field was shifting so heavily toward North America, due to the resources of the Americans.
12. I reference the 2005 edition translated into Portuguese as *Do Roraima ao Orinoco*. English translations appearing in this chapter by the author.
13. Beebee, "Cultural Entanglements," 98.
14. As detailed in *Vom Roraima zum Orinoco*, his journey moves from the urban Amazon into peripheral regions, gradually becoming more remote. Upon arrival in Manaus in 1916, Koch-Grünberg describes how different the city looks from his last voyage; it has modernized and improved, a result of the influx of rubber money. It is but a brief interlude where he references the city, as his interest lies outside of more populated areas where he can live among various Indigenous peoples, cataloguing their lives and cultures.
15. Beebee, "Cultural Entanglements," 101.
16. "Agora estou novamente no genuíno ambiente doméstico indígena, com seu típico cheiro meio ácido de mandioca fermentada, de caxiri, pimenta e muitas outras coisas, com sua confusão de cestos, potes e instrumetnos variados, com seus numerosos xerimbabos (animais domésticos) que, a princípio, são tíimodos, mas logo se tornam tão íntimos quanto seus donos e donas, e tenho de admitir, sinto-me muito melhor neste ambiente selvage do que na caricatural civilização que deixei há pouco." Koch-Grünberg, *Do Roraima*, 49.
17. Poole, *Vision, Race*, 165.
18. For instance, Koch-Grünberg describes showing the Makuschí photographs from his previous journeys, objects that they examined with some interest. He notes that they looked at the photographs in the opposite way a Westerner would, placing portrait

photographs with people's heads facing down, or to the side. Koch-Grünberg, *Do Roraima*, 29.

19. Hempel explains the importance of photography within a nineteenth–century German context as part of a scientific practice: "In late nineteenth-century German anthropology, the appreciation of the photographic medium was based precisely on the unquestioned ability to not only depict but to define and mobilize facts. It is thereby not surprising that in contrast to drawings and sketches, which in the context of scientific practice have always been associated with observational techniques, photography was considered to have stronger affinities to modes of collection (e.g., Schlaginhaufen 1915)." Hempel, "Theodor Koch-Grünberg," 240.
20. For more on participant observation see Jorgensen, *Principles, Approaches*.
21. Poole, "An Excess," 167.
22. French, "Voices in the Wilderness," 162.
23. Cheng, *Ornamentalism*, 18.
24. Quoted in Cheng, *Ornamentalism*, 3.
25. Indigenous communities would trade with Koch-Grünberg because he had political connections, which they needed for aid and goods. Koch-Grünberg's gift giving is both large and small, and he expresses surprise when a group is uninterested in the gifts that he has to offer. In initially approaching tribes, he would offer a larger gift, and as he became more acquainted, he would give out small things to "make friends." He characterizes his relationship with the Indigenous people he lives among as "friend" or "protector," and while *protector* carries a patriarchal and imperial weight, *friend* moves toward a more reciprocal relationship, much as the tension within Figure 4.1.
26. Beebee, "Cultural Entanglements," 109.
27. Clifford, *Writing Culture*.
28. Sá Carvalho, "How to See a Scar," 389.
29. "Quando vencem a timidez inicial ante o estrangeiro, essas crianças são as criaturinhas mais confiantes e alegres que se possa imaginar. Aceitam cada brincadeira minha com alegria, mas nunca se comportam mal. São amáveis e educadas comigo e vivem em grande harmonia entre si. Se dou um pedaço de chocolate a um deles, imediatamente o divide com os demais. Nunca vi dois deles brigando, ou mesmo um batendo no outro." Koch-Grünberg, *Do Roraima*, 64.
30. "Agora já faz quase um mês que estou em Koimélemong e sou bom amigo de todos os moradores. Sou benquisto porque sempre tenho tempo para todos, cou simpatico com todo mundo, nunca fico bravo e recompense cada pequeno serviço com miçangas, tabaco e pequenos anzóis." Koch-Grünberg, *Do Roraima*, 81.
31. Hempel, "Theodor Koch-Grünberg," 252.
32. "Manda que os moradores se pintem festivamente, pois eu disse que queria tirar algumas fotos. Manda todo o seu povo se alinhar. Algumas moças vestiram saias européias de chita. Dou-lhes a entender que não acho isso nem um pouco bonito. Imediatamente, deixam as saias cair e mostram as bontinas tangas de miçangas que estavam usando por baixo da civilização" (Koch-Grünberg, *Do Roraima*, 59).
33. Tuhiwai Smith, *Decolonizing Methodologies*, 74.
34. Koch-Grünberg was said to be the first non-Indigenous person to visit the Taulipang,

or Pemon. The Pemon live throughout the inland mountain savannahs of Venezuela and northern Brazil, which are dotted with *tepuis*, or large sandstone plateaus, creating a rolling and dramatically changing topography. In the Pemon language, the day is divided into "dawning," morning, noontime, and afternoon, with no word for year. The Makunaima creation story comes from the Pemon people.

35. "Parece que a inocência feminine aqui vai tão mal quanto no Uaupés e em outras partes. Percebo isso pelas conversas do meu pessoal. Dois de meus heróis até deixaram suas redes de dormir novas como oferenda de amor! Mas que pessoa sensta pode levar essa moças a mal? É uma raça extraordinariamente robusta e fogosa, dotada de sadia sensualidade, e o excesso de mulheres é grande. Elas que se divirtam! (Koch-Grünberg, *Do Roraima*, 128).
36. "Elas amam o branco que veio de longe até sua terra, tão diferente dos brasileiros mestiços que, de tempos em tempos, visitam sua aldeia e levam consigo os rapazes para trabalhar para eles, os quais só voltam depois de alguns anos e não querem saber mais nada dos costumes antigos. Amam o branco porque não se julga melhor do que eles, porque vive com eles como um dos seus, caça com eles, bebe com eles, dança com eles." Koch-Grünberg, *Do Roraima*, 67.
37. D'Argenio, "Decolonial Encounters," 136.
38. Schiebinger, *Plants and Empire*, 83.
39. Schiebinger, *Plants and Empire*, 74.
40. Gagliano, Ryan, and Vieira, eds., *Language of Plants*, ix.
41. Mirzoeff traces the history of racialized visuality in plantation systems of surveillance and control. He explains how culture and cultivation were intertwined on French colonies in the Caribbean, and how these systems of cultivation became codified and globalized. Mirzoeff, *The Right to Look*, 52. Furthermore, he examines how the plantation system brutalized the environment quickly due to soil depletion and deforestation.
42. Mirzoeff, *Right to Look*, 52.
43. The movement and circulation of plants, particularly in Amazonia, has also been an impetus to development and migration in and to the region. See Weinstein, *Amazon Rubber Boom*; Maligo, *Land of Metaphorical Desires*; Diacon, *Stringing Together*; Hecht, *Scramble for the Amazon*; Garfield, *In Search of the Amazon*.
44. Petschelies, "From Berlin," 35.
45. From *Zwei Jabre unter den Indianern*, quoted in Schultes, "Domestication," 482.
46. From *Zwei Jabre unter den Indianern*, quoted in Schultes, "Domestication," 483.
47. Roger Casement, an Anglo-Irish diplomat (who would later become an Irish nationalist), was also active in the human rights struggle in the African Congo due to rubber extraction. After his experience in Africa, Casement was commissioned to investigate rubber abuses in the Peruvian Amazon. He wrote about the enslavement and abuse of Indigenous peoples, and his diaries created an international stir and increased attention to rubber boom atrocities, which resulted in some reforms.
48. As described by his former students and others who worked with him, Schultes was quite a character. He also claimed to be a royalist who did not believe in the American Revolution. Davis, *One River*, 23. However, according to his students (and one can see this readily in his own writing), there is a tongue and cheek nature to his old-school ways.

49. An American botanist, Spruce traveled to South America in 1849 and carried out an exploratory and botanical collecting mission of the northern part of the continent. Spruce collected many species from difficult to access areas, and he noted their medicinal properties. The book was later edited by Alfred Russel Wallace and was published with Spruce's illustrations in 1908.
50. Schultes' mission quickly changed with the United States' entry into WWII after the December 1941 bombing of Pearl Harbor. Schultes was commissioned by the US government to find high quality rubber.
51. Schultes worked most closely with the Cofán and Witoto peoples. The Cofán, who live in Ecuador and Colombia, have a long history of disastrous contact with outsiders, characterized by extractive industries such as oil drilling that have displaced them from their ancestral lands. According to Schultes, the Cofán possessed perhaps the most "extensive plant pharmacopoeias of all the tribes of the Colombian Amazon." Schultes and Reis, "Burning the Library," 3.
52. Davis, *One River*, 22.
53. More than eighty thousand plant species and around 25 percent of all drugs used today are derived from rainforest plants. In the Amazon region, more than forty thousand plant species have been scientifically classified. It's estimated that there is a novel species found in Amazonia every other day. Some of the most-used plant derivates from the Amazon include quinine, a muscle relaxant used to treat malaria, and tubocurarine, derived from curare (studied by Schultes) and now used in anesthesia. Other Amazonian extracted medicines include vincristine and vinblastine, both used to treat types of cancer, particularly leukemia. The untapped potential of the Amazon to heal is often heralded as the best reason to protect the forest. And with new technologies, there is continually more potential to uncover plant-based cures that were previously overlooked.
54. Schultes, "Domestication," 8.
55. Indeed, Schultes helped spur on increased environmental conservation: "Through Schultes's studies of nature and his applications of indigenous knowledge, conservation of cultural diversity became an integral component of environmental conservation." Enright, *Maximum of Wilderness*, 140.
56. Enright, *Maximum of Wilderness*, 137.
57. Schultes and Reis, "Burning the Library," 2.
58. In describing bioprospecting, Hecht and Rajão explain that "specialists in bioprospecting like Richard Schultes . . . use modern science to pivot from an extractive "wild forest past" into modern rubber plantations informed by empirical evidence, social science models and economic rationalization that inhered in the translocation of the natural resource ideas of the US progressive movement as it engaged 'frontier' areas." Hecht and Rajão, "From 'Green Hell,'" 5.
59. Schultes was an ethnobotanist with an activist agenda: "ethnobotanists' studies might feed into bioprospecting enterprises—a form of extractive colonialism—by which 'indigenous knowledge' might be transformed into Western pharmaceutical capital and intellectual property. In other situations, ethnobotanists with an activist agenda might use their studies as 'staging grounds' to prove the truth of 'indigenous knowledge' within their own scientific and cultural frameworks and argue for the remuneration of

the sources of knowledge, whether countries or communities. Both approaches are loaded with epistemological charge." Sheldrake, "The Enigma," 348.

60. Shamans are particularly important in many Amazonian cultures: "Shamans are 'species androgynous', and able to cross boundaries, and take on the perspectives of others. Indeed, it is by taking on the point of view of others, by occupying different subjectivities, that knowledge is acquired in the first place. For example, self-consciousness is achieved by occupying the perspective of another and seeing oneself from there (Viveiros de Castro, 2004). Ayahuasca is one of the means by which such shifts in perspective are made possible. Amazonian cosmologies are thus directly reinforced by ayahuasca's ritual ingestion." Scheldrake, "The Enigma," 359.

61. He even became the first person to academically examine the now increasingly popular drug ayahuasca.

62. Practices of participant observation have changed over time: "For many years participant observers were warned against crossing over the artificial boundary separating active participation as a researcher to participating fully as a societal member in some setting. Anthropologists traditionally refer to breeching this taboo against the most active form of participation as 'going native.' For many early anthropologists, going native signified abandoning the objectivity of a Western scientific worldview for the subjective vantage point of indigenous peoples. By the late 1970s, however, anthropologists deliberatively were going native for its strategic research advantages and sociologists were 'becoming the phenomenon' for similar reasons." Jorgensen, *Principles, Approaches*, 3.

63. Schultes advocated for other researchers to take on his approach of fully interacting with Indigenous communities: "Schultes urged researchers to conserve culture and nature, telling them to stop exploratory expeditions with the singular goal of finding new medicines and instead become part of indigenous communities." Enright, *Maximum of Wilderness*, 144.

64. Schultes' travels in the Sibundoy Valley, an area between the Andes and Amazon in Colombia, yielded a wide variety of findings. The groups that he worked with most closely included the Inga and the Kamentsá. It was here that Schultes encountered his guide and teacher Salvador Chindoy, a Kamentsá shaman who was skilled in traditional plant usages from both tribes. Chindoy appears throughout Schultes' photography in traditional garb such as a jaguar teeth necklace, a crown of macaw feathers, and a fan of palm fronds. Chindoy was a well-known healer who traveled to public markets from Bogotá to Quito sharing his knowledge about medicinal plants and selling barks, roots, and herbs that he had grown or collected. He learned how to use plants for medicinal purposes from the plants themselves. He would consume yagé or another hallucinogen plant concoction, *borrachero*, and have a young apprentice record his vision-induced insights throughout the night, which the apprentice would share with the shaman the next morning. Hettler, Plotkin, and and Amazon Conservation Team, "Amazonian Travels."

65. Schultes and Reis, "Burning the Library," 205.
66. Weinstein, "Filming Modernity," 204.
67. Weinstein, "Filming Modernity," 205.
68. Schultes, "The Domestication," 43.

69. Hettler and Plotkin, "Amazonian Travels," 3.
70. "US Searches Americas for Rubber Source: Good-Neighbor Policy." *Christian Science Monitor*, Oct. 12, 1940; ProQuest Historical Newspapers.
71. Correa, "A borracha," 65.
72. Schultes meticulously documented rubber production throughout his travels: "After leaving the Chiribiquete highlands, Schultes descended the full length of the Apaporis, observing and recording a high quantity of rubber trees on its banks. He later returned in the early 1950s to establish rubber stations at Soratama, near the mouth of the Pacoa River, and Jinogoje, near the mouth of the Pira Paraná River. During this time, Schultes meticulously charted the course of the Apaporis and made detailed counts of *Hevea* on its banks." Hettler and Plotkin, "Amazonian Travels," 8.
73. Garfield, *In Search of the Amazon*, 174.
74. Tuhiwai Smith, *Decolonizing Methodologies*, 63.
75. Sá, *Rainforest Literatures*, 129.
76. Petschelies, "From Berlin," 35.
77. Petschelies, "From Berlin," 38.
78. Shepard et al., "Objeto, sujeito," 3.
79. Shepard et al., "Objeto, sujeito," 4.
80. Shepard et al., "Objeto, sujeito," 6.
81. Shepard et al., "Objeito, sujeito," 11.
82. Shepard et al., "Objeito, sujeito," 19.
83. Shepard et al., "Objeitos, sujeitos," 23.
84. Shepard et al., "Objeitos, sujeitos," 34.

CHAPTER 5

1. [ch5] Whitfield, "Communicating beyond," 178.
2. Castrillón, "La sensatez"; D'Argenio, "Decolonial Encounters."
3. Beyer, *Singing to the Plants*, 28.
4. Gleghorn, "Filmic Disciples," 33.
5. Sadly, Antonio Bolívar, a respected elder who lived in Leticia, Colombia, died due to complications from COVID-19 during the pandemic.
6. Guerra, *El abrazo*; Kearney, "Is This the Greatest"; Páramo, "Un débil abrazo"; Rueda "El abrazo"; Cubides and Garay, "Entre lo salvaje."
7. Llano, "El espacio audiovisual."
8. For more on the ethical debates around informants in anthropology and the imperial baggage of the term see Bourdieu, "Participant Observation"; Jorgensen, *Principles, Approaches*; Medina, *Negotiating Economic Development*; Metcalf, *They Life, We Life*; Rosaldo, *Culture and Truth*.
9. "Es ficción, pero los eventos están inspirados en hechos reales. Los personajes de Koch-Grünberg y Schultes tampoco son ellos exactamente; están inspirados en ellos pero son una construcción que parte también de otros antropólogos. Es una obra de ficción. . . . A través de la ficción uno crea para poder hablar. No es un documental, es una historia inspirada en eventos y también un modo de acercar a quien no entiende de esto." Llano, "El espacio audiovisual."

10. Mutis, "El abrazo," 161.
11. Shepard et al., "Trouble in Paradise."
12. Mutis "El abrazo"; Muredda, "Embrace of the Serpent."
13. Krenak, Ideas to Postpone, 5.
14. Krenak, Ideas to Postpone, 24.
15. Descola, Beyond Nature, 11.
16. In her article "Ch'ixinakax utxiwa: A Reflection on the Practices and Discourses of Decolonization," Silvia Rivera Cusicanqui takes theorists located in the Global North such as Walter Mignolo to task for the dilution of ideas originally formulated by Indigenous communities and using them within academic arenas of exclusion under the guise of inclusivity. "Through the game of who cites whom, hierarchies are structured, and we end up having to consume, in a regurgitated form, the very ideas regarding decolonization that we indigenous people and intellectuals of Bolivia, Peru, and Ecuador have produced independently." Cusicanqui, "Ch'ixinakax utxiwa," 103. This valid critique of Mignolo's take on decoloniality again begs the question of the generation and circulation of knowledge.
17. de la Cadena, "Indigenous Cosmopolitics," 341.
18. de la Cadena, "Indigenous Cosmopolitics," 341.
19. de la Cadena, "Indigenous Cosmopolitics," 349.
20. Cusicanqui, "Ch'ixinakax utxiwa," 105.
21. Cusicanqui, "Ch'ixinakax utxiwa," 100.
22. Gleghorn, "Filmic Disciples," 34.
23. D'Argenio, "Decolonial Encounters," 145.
24. As Eduardo Viveiros de Castro pointed out soon after the film's release, "living completely alone is part of this fiction, because the indigenous logic is completely different from ours, and it would be very difficult for someone to maintain traditional customs in isolation from others." Quoted in Shepard, "Fifty Shades."
25. D'Argenio, "Decolonial Encounters," 138.
26. Viveiros de Castro, The Relative Native, 471.
27. Viveiros de Castro, The Relative Native, 473.
28. Guerra, El abrazo, 00:10:40–00:11:00.
29. This may be an homage to the Pemon people who Koch-Grünberg describe in his travel narratives. As Lúcia Sá explains, "The pre-Cambrian rocks from the Guiana and Brazilian shield, some hundred million years old, are among the oldest geological formations in the planet. The Pemon know stories that explain the strange shapes of many of these rocks, and their sense of history is intimately linked to them." Sá, Rainforest Literatures, 12.
30. Mutis, "El abrazo," 35.
31. Guerra, El abrazo, 00:11:55–00:12:07.
32. Guerra, El abrazo, 00:31:03–00:32:00.
33. Gleghorn, "Filmic Disciples," 140.
34. This could also be seen an instance of imperial nostalgia where the narrative of progress laments the loss of traditional societies while actively destroying them. As Rosaldo explains, "Mourning the passing of traditional society and imperialist nostalgia cannot neatly be separated from one another. Both attempt to use a mask of innocence to cover their involvement with processes of domination." Rosaldo, Culture and Truth, 86.

35. Mutis, "*El abrazo*," 34.
36. Guerra, *El abrazo*, 00:38:16–00:39:30.
37. As Vieira notes, "Life in the forest is hellish due to the exploitative labor conditions that reduce workers, many of them migrants from other regions to de-facto slaves, who give their lives for the enrichment of rubber lords." Vieira, *Phytographia*, 227.
38. Guerra, *El abrazo*, 00:39:19–00:40:02.
39. Guerra, *El abrazo*, 00:1:00–00:1:05.
40. D'Argenio, "Decolonial Encounters," 140.
41. Guerra, *El abrazo*, 1:01:00–1:02:10.
42. While missionaries were sent to evangelize cannibals, Christian tradition revolves around the Eucharist, symbolically eating Christ's body and drinking his blood.
43. Guerra, *El abrazo*, 1:45:00–1:46:02.
44. Gleghorn, "Filmic Disciples," 40.
45. Classical music in the jungle pays homage to previous films about the Amazon as well as nods to the well-known obsession of implanting Western "high" culture onto the space of the rainforest (nowhere better encapsulated than the famous Amazon Theatre—the Manaus opera house built during the first rubber boom). Films such as *Fitzcarraldo* (1982) also work with themes of imperial designs on the Amazon and the implantation of high culture into the otherwise savage space of the jungle. In an iconic scene that *El abrazo de la serpiente* quite obviously pays homage to, Fitzcarraldo, a foppish Irish rubber baron commissions a ship to survey the jungle to later build an opera house. As the ship forays deeper into Indigenous territory and the crew begins to hear the distant cries and beating drums of as yet invisible tribes, Fitzcarraldo puts Caruso on the gramophone, projecting opera into the jungle, partially drowning out the cries, while the drumbeat remains. A shot shows Fitzcarraldo behind the large gramophone, leaning back slightly with a face completely captivated by the sounds. Through the juxtaposition of the Indigenous cries with Caruso's booming voice, a remix of sounds portrays Fitzcarraldo's wish to dominate and subdue the howl of the wild with the sonic sphere of the opera. An attempt to dominate this green hell, the melodrama of the opera seems to reflect the unruly and passionate nature of the jungle itself. However, what is accomplished becomes a noise in between—neither sound drowns the other out—and the forest is a space where both the would-be rubber baron and Indigenous peoples exist in a type of remix. In some ways like Evan's relationship with Karakamate, Fitzcarraldo believes he will be bettering the lives of local peoples by bringing them opera. This is another form of domination and conquest that ignores the Indigenous population's existing culture and, in the case of Fitzcarraldo, employs them as a workforce to accumulate Western capital. Music seems to signal a soft violence, or the assumption that in hearing the high cultural artifacts of the West, the forest and its peoples will fall into harmony, or obedience. The sonic dominance of *Fitzcarraldo* is rewritten as a peaceful, bonding process in *El abrazo de la serpiente*.
46. Guerra, *El abrazo*, 1:27:00–1:28:10.
47. Tuhiwai Smith, *Decolonizing Methodologies*, 146.
48. Guerra, *El abrazo*, 1:38:00–1:39:25.
49. Viveiros de Castro, *The Relative Native*, 481.

50. As DiNovelli-Lang notes on modernity and indigeneity, "The hallmark of modernity's destructiveness is its treatment of other nature-cultures, who must become modern or perish." DiNovelli-Lang, "The Return of the Animal," 10.
51. Gleghorn, "Filmic Disciples," 42.
52. Gleghorn, "Filmic Disciples," 43.
53. Deforestation and environmental destruction are directly linked to the spread of disease and pandemics. With increasing encroachment, humans encounter pathogens from other species. Human actions such as land-use change, intensive livestock production, wildlife trade, and climate change created the conditions for the initial transfer of COVID-19, a zoonotic pathogen.
54. Mathiesen, "Embrace of the Serpent Star."
55. Osorio, "The Death of Antonio."
56. Pugley and Salazar, "Were Indigenous Peoples."
57. Graham, "Three Decades," 86.
58. Aufderheide, "You See the World."
59. *Awotsi Yorenkatsi Tasori*, 00:22:00.
60. Bessire, "From the Ground," 10.

CONCLUSION

1. Said, *Orientalism*, 9.
2. Krenak, *Ideas to Postpone*, 6.
3. E-International Relations, "Interview with Walter Mignolo."
4. Rappaport, *Intercultural Utopias*, 9.
5. Rappaport, *Intercultural Utopias*, 9.
6. Lula's administration has already made important strides as deforestation in the Brazilian Amazon fell by 22 percent in 2023. Butler, "Deforestation."
7. Souza, *Amazonia indígena*, 27.

Bibliography

Abreu, Regina. "O livro que abalou o Brasil: A consagração de *Os sertões* na virada do século." *História, Ciências, Saúde: Manguinhos*, no. 5 (1998): 93–115.

Almeida Farias, Emmanuel de. "Megaprojetos inconcludentes e territórios conquistados: Diferentes processos sociais de territorialização da comunidade quilombola de Cachoeira Porteira, Oriximiná, Pará." PhD diss., Universidade Federal do Amazonas, 2016.

Amory, Frederic. "Euclides da Cunha and Brazilian Positivism." *Luso-Brazilian Review* 36, no. 1 (Summer 1999): 87–94.

Amory, Frederic. "Historical Source and Biographical Context in the Interpretation of Euclides da Cunha's *Os Sertões*." In "Brazil: History and Society," special issue of *Journal of Latin American Studies* 28, no. 3 (1996).

Anderson, Anthony B., Peter H. May, and Michael Balick. *The Subsidy from Nature: Palm Forests, Peasantry, and Development on an Amazon Frontier*. New York: Columbia University Press, 1991.

Anderson, Mark D. "Treacherous Waters: Shipwrecked Landscapes and the Possibilities for Nationalistic Emplacement in Brazilian Representations of the Amazon." Hispanic Issues On Line, vol. 12 (Spring 2013), 111–26. University of Minnesota Digital Conservancy, https://hdl.handle.net/11299/184419.

Andrade, Mario de. *O turista aprendiz*. São Paulo: Livraria Duas Cidades, 1976.

Andrade, Mário. *Poesias completas*, vol. 1. Rio de Janeiro: Nova Fronteira, 2013.

Andrade, Mário de. *The Apprentice Tourist Travels along the Amazon to Peru, along the Madeira to Bolivia, and around Marajó before Saying Enough Already*. Translated by Flora Thomson-DeVeaux. New York: Penguin Books, 2023.

Arenas, Fernando. *Utopias of Otherness: Nationhood and Subjectivity in Portugal and Brazil*. Minneapolis: University of Minnesota Press, 2003. Ebook.

Arini, Juliana, Caio Mota, and Ahmad Jarrah. "Roosevelt River: Life in the Most Dangerous Region of the Amazon." Pulitzer Center, March 10, 2020, https://legacy.pulitzercenter.org/projects/roosevelt-river-life-most-dangerous-region-amazon.

Ashcroft, Bill, Gareth Griffiths, and Helen Tiffin. *Post-Colonial Studies: The Key Concepts*. New York: Routledge, 2000.

Aufderheide, Pat. "'You See the World of the Other and You Look at Your Own': The Evolution of the Video in the Villages Project." *Journal of Film and Video* 2, no. 60 (Summer 2008): 26–34.

Awotsi Yorenkatsi Tasori. YouTube, posted by Video nas Aldeias, Dec. 23, 2016. https://www.youtube.com/watch?v=wEjT755P5I0.

Bates, Henry Walter. *The Naturalist on the River Amazons*. London: Murray, 1864.

Beebee, Thomas O. "Cultural Entanglements and Ethnographic Refractions: Theodor Koch-Grünberg in Brazil." In *KulturConfusão – On German-Brazilian Interculturalities*, edited by Anke Finger, Gabi Kathöfer and Christopher Larkosh, 95–116. Berlin, München, Boston: De Gruyter, 2015. https://doi.org/10.1515/9783110408225-005.

Benoit, Sébastien. *Henri Anatole Coudreau, 1859–1899: Dernier explorateur français en amazonie: Une première biographie*. Paris: Harmattan, 2000.

Bergmann, Linda S. "A Troubled Marriage of Discourses: Science Writing and Travel Narrative in Louis and Elizabeth Agassiz's *A Journey in Brazil*." *Journal of American Culture* 18, no. 2 (1995), 83–88.

Bessire, Lucas. "From the Ground, Looking Up: Report on the Video nas Aldeias Tour," *American Anthropologist* 111, no. 1 (2009), 101–3.

Beyer, Stephen. *Singing to Plants: A Guide to Mestizo Shamanism in the Upper Amazon*. Albuquerque: University of New Mexico Press, 2009.

Blunt, Alison. *Travel, Gender, and Imperialism: Mary Kingsley in West Africa*. New York: Guilford Press, 1997.

Bourdieu, Pierre. "Participant Observation." Huxley Memorial Lecture, Royal Anthropological Institute, no. 9 (2003): 281–94.

Borges, Dain. "Puffy, Ugly, Slothful and Inert: Degeneration in Brazilian Social Thought, 1880–1940." *Journal of Latin American Studies* 25, no. 2 (1993).

Brooke, James A. "Manaus Journal: For the Rubber Soldiers of Brazil, Rubber Checks." *New York Times*, May 14, 1991, www.nytimes.com/1991/05/15/world/manaus-journal-for-the-rubber-soldiers-of-brazil-rubber-checks.html.

Butler, Rhett. "Deforestation in the Brazilian Amazon Falls 22% in 2023." Mongabay, November 11, 2023. https://news.mongabay.com/2023/11/deforestation-in-the-brazilian-amazon-falls-22-in-2023.

Campbell, Lyle, and Veronica Grondona. *The Indigenous Languages of South America: A Comprehensive Guide*. Berlin: De Gruyter Mouton, 2012.

Carey-Webb, Jessica. "Gendered Politics of Empire: The Female Explorateur and Natural Histories of the Amazon Basin 1899–1901." *Gender, Place, and Culture* 24, no. 4 (2017): 465–81.

Carvalho, José Murilo de. "Dreams Come Untrue." In "Brazil: The Burden of the Past; the Promise of the Future," special issue, *Daedalus* 129, no. 2 (2000): 57–82.

Castrillón, Camilo Jaramillo. "La sensatez del conocimiento." *Revista Canadiense de Estudios Hispánicos* 43, no. 3 (Spring 2019): 579–601. https://www.jstor.org/stable/10.2307/26956039.

Caviglia-Harris, Jill, Erin O. Sills, and Katrina Mullan. "Migration and Mobility on the Amazon Frontier." *Population and Environment* 34, no. 3 (2013).

Certeau, Michel de. *The Practice of Everyday Life*. Berkeley: University of California Press, 1980.

Cheng, Anne Anlin. *Ornamentalism*. Oxford: Oxford University Press, 2019.

Cleary, David. "After the Frontier: Problems with Political Economy in the Modern Brazilian Amazon." *Journal of Latin American Studies* 25, no. 2 (1993): 331–49.

Cleary, David. "Towards an Environmental History of the Amazon: From Prehistory to the Nineteenth Century." *Latin American Research Review* 36, no. 2 (2001): 64–96. http://www.jstor.org/stable/2692088.

Clifford, James. *Writing Culture: The Poetics and Politics of Ethnography*. Berkeley: University of California Press, 1986.

Crist, Raymond E., Alarich R. Schultz, James J. Parsons, and Editors of Encyclopaedia Britannica. "Amazon River: Contemporary Settlement Patterns." *Britannica*, last updated Oct. 31, 2023. https://www.britannica.com/place/Amazon-River/Contemporary-settlement-patterns.

Corrêa, Luiz de Miranda. *A borracha da Amazônia e a II Guerra Mundial*. Manaus: SCA/Edições Governo do Estado, 1967.

Costa Lima, Luiz. *Control of the Imaginary: Reason and Imagination in Modern Times*. Minneapolis: University of Minnesota Press, 1988.

Coudreau, Henri Anatole, and Octavie Coudreau. *Voyage au Trombetas, 7 Août 1899–25 Novembre 1899*. Paris: A. Lahure, 1900.

Coudreau, Henri Anatole. *Viagem ao Tapajós; 28 de Julho de 1895–7 de Janeiro de 1896*. São Paulo: Companhia Editora Nacional, 1897.

Coudreau, Henri Anatole. *Coleção reconquista do Brasil*, vol. 44. São Paulo: Itatiaia, 1977.

Coudreau, Octavie. *Voyage au Cuminá, 20 Avril 1900–7 Septembre 1900*. Paris: A. Lahure, 1901.

Cronon, William. "The Trouble with Wilderness: Or, Getting Back to the Wrong Nature." *Environmental History* 1, no. 1 (1996): 7–28.

Cubides, Edwin, and Luz Garay. "Entre lo salvaje y la inocencia: Lectura intertextual de *La vorágine* y *El abrazo de la serpiente*." *La Palabra*, no. 40 (2021).

Cusicanqui, Silvia Rivera. "Ch'ixinakax utxiwa: A Reflection on the Practices and Discourses of Decolonization." *South Atlantic Quarterly* 111, no. 1 (Winter 2012): 95–109.

da Cunha, Euclides. *À margem da história*. Biblioteca Virtual do Estudante Brasileiro, Escola do Futuro da Universidade de São Paulo, http://www.bibvirt.futuro.usp.br.

da Cunha, Euclides. *The Amazon: Land without History*. Translated by Ronald W. Sousa, edited by Lúcia Sá. Oxford: Oxford University Press, 2006.

da Cunha, Euclides. *Obra completa*. Edição organizada sob a direção de Afrânio Coutinho. J. Aguilar. Rio de Janeiro: Editora Nova Aguilar, 1995.

da Cunha, Euclides. *Um paraíso perdido: Reunião dos ensaios amazônicos*. Petrópolis: Dimensões do Brasil, Editora Vozes Limitadas, 1976.

Davis, Wade. *One River*. New York: Simon and Schuster, 1996.

D'Argenio, Maria Chiara. "Decolonial Encounters in Ciro Guerra's *El abrazo de la serpiente*: Indigeneity, Coevalness and Intercultural Dialogue." *Postcolonial Studies* 21, no. 2 (2018): 131–53. https://doi.org/10.1080/13688790.2018.1466426.

de la Cadena, Marisol. "Indigenous Cosmopolitics in the Andes: Conceptual Reflections beyond 'Politics.'" *Cultural Anthropology* 25, no. 2 (2010): 334–70.

de la Cadena, Marisol, and Orin Starn. "Introduction." *Indigenous Experience Today*. Oxford: Bloomsbury Publishing, 2007.

de la Torre, Oscar. *The People of the River*. Chapel Hill: University of North Carolina Press, 2018.

Descola, Phillipe. *Beyond Nature and Culture*. Chicago: University of Chicago Press, 2013.
Devine Guzman, Tracy. *Native and National in Brazil Indigeneity after Independence*. Chapel Hill: University of North Carolina Press, 2013.
Diacon, Todd A. "Candido Mariano da Silva Rondon and the Politics of Indian Protection in Brazil." *Past & Present* 177, no. 1 (2002): 157–94.
Diacon, Todd A. *Stringing Together a Nation: Candido Mariano da Silva Rondon and the Construction of a Modern Brazil, 1906–1930*. Durham, NC: Duke University Press, 2004.
DiNovelli-Lang, Danielle. "The Return of the Animal: Posthumanism, Indigeneity, and Anthropology." *Environment and Society* 4, no. 1 (2013): 137–56. http://dx.doi.org/10.3167/ares.2013.040109.
Domosh, Mona. "Towards a Feminist Historiography of Geography." *Transactions of the Institute of British Geographers* 16, no. 1 (1991): 95–104.
Driver, Felix. *Geography Militant: Cultures of Exploration and Empire*. Oxford: Blackwell Press, 2001.
Driver, Felix, and Luciana Martins. *Tropical Visions in an Age of Empire*. Chicago: University of Chicago Press, 2005.
E-International Relations. "Interview—Walter Mignolo / Part 2: Key Concepts." E-International Relations, January 21, 2017. https://www.e-ir.info/2017/01/21/interview-walter-mignolopart-2-key-concepts.
Enright, Kelly. *The Maximum of Wilderness: The Jungle in the American Imagination*. Charlottesville: University of Virginia Press, 2012.
Ehringhaus, Christiane. "Analysis of Land-Use Change in the Extractive Reserves of Amazonia, Brazil." Center for Earth Observation, September 2022. https://yceo.yale.edu/analysis-land-use-change-extractive-reserves-southwestern-amazonia-brazil.
Escobar, Arturo. *Encountering Development: The Making and Unmaking of the Third World*. Princeton, NJ: Princeton University Press, 1993.
Escobar, Arturo. "Thinking-Feeling with the Earth: Territorial Struggles and the Ontological Dimension of the Epistemologies of the South." *Revista de Antropología Iberoamericana* 11, no. 1 (January-April 2016): 11–32.
Espelt-Bombin, Silvia, and Mark Harris. "Changing Narratives of Race and Environment in the Nineteenth-Century and Early Twentieth-Century Brazilian Amazon." *Bulletin of Latin American Research* 38, no. 2 (2019): 150–63.
Emmet, Robert S. and David E. Nye. *The Environmental Humanities: A Critical Introduction*. Boston: MIT Press, 2017.
Fernández de Oviedo y Valdés, Gonzalo. *About the Natural History of the Indies*. Toledo: Ramon Petras, 1526. Pdf. https://www.loc.gov/item/2021666764.
Ferretti, Federico. "Imperial Ambivalences: Histories of Lady Travelers and the French Explorer Octavie Renard-Coudreau (1867–1938)." *Human Geography* 99, no. 3 (2017): 238–55.
Fiala, Anthony, and Theodore Roosevelt. *The River of Doubt, No. 2*. Edited by Caroline Gentry, Itor [United States: Roosevelt Film Library, ?, 1928]. Video. https://www.loc.gov/item/mp76000367.
French, Jennifer L. "Voices in the Wilderness: Environment, Colonialism, and Coloniality." *Review: Literature and Arts of the Americas* 45, no. 2 (2012): 157–66. https://doi.org/10.1080/08905762.2012.719766.

Gabara, Esther. *Errant Modernism: The Ethos of Photography in Mexico and Brazil*. Durham, NC: Duke University Press, 2008.

Gagliano, Monica, John C. Ryan, and Patrícia Vieira, eds. *The Language of Plants: Science, Philosophy, Literature*. Minneapolis: University of Minnesota Press, 2017.

Garfield, Seth. *Indigenous Struggle at the Heart of Brazil: State Policy, Frontier Expansion, and the Xavante Indians, 1937–1988*. Durham, NC: Duke University Press, 2001.

Garfield, Seth. *In Search of the Amazon: Brazil, the United States, and the Nature of a Region*. Durham, NC: Duke University Press, 2013.

Garland, David. "What Is a 'History of the Present'?: On Foucault's Genealogies and Their Critical Preconditions." *Punishment and Society* 16, no. 4 (2014): 365–84. https://doi.org/10.1177/1462474514541711.

Gatti, Luciana V., et al. "Amazonia as a Carbon Source Linked to Deforestation and Climate Change," *Nature*, no. 595 (July 14, 2021), https://www.nature.com/articles/s41586-021-03629-6.

Gleghorn, Charlotte. "Filmic Disciples and Indigenous Knowledges: The Pedagogical Imperative in El abrazo de la serpiente," *Diálogo* 23, no. 1 (Spring 2020): 31–45.

G1 – Política, "Brasil é uma virgem que todo tarado de fora quer,' diz Bolsonaro ao falar sobre Amazonia." Globo Comunicação, July 7, 2019. https://g1.globo.com/politica/noticia/2019/07/06/brasil-e-uma-virgem-que-todo-tarado-de-fora-quer-diz-bolsonaro-ao-falar-sobre-amazonia.ghtml.

Gomes, Carlos Valério. "Ciclos econômicos do extrativismo na Amazônia na visão dos viajantes naturalistas." *Boletin Museu Paraense Emílio Goeldi* 13, no. 1 (January 2018): 129–46.

Gomes, Carlos Valério. "Extractive Reserves in the Brazilian Amazon Thirty Years after Chico Mendes." *Desenvolvimento e Meio Ambiente* 48, no. 1 (November 2018): 74–98.

Gómez, Leila. *Darwinism in Argentina: Major Texts (1845–1909)*. Lewisburg, PA: Bucknell University Press, 2011.

Guerra, Ciro, director. *El abrazo de la serpiente*. Buffalo Films, 2015.

Guillén, Michael. "Embrace of the Serpent: An Interview with Ciro Guerra." *Cineaste* 41, no. 2 (Spring 2016). https://www.cineaste.com/spring2016/embrace-of-the-serpent-ciro-guerra.

Guimarães, Leandro Belinaso. "Euclides da Cunha na Amazônia: Descontinuidades históricas nos modos de ver e narrar a floresta." *História, Ciências, Saúde—Manguinhos* 17, no. 3 (July–Sept. 2010): 705–18.

Greenfield, Gerard M. "The Great Drought and Elite Discourse in Imperial Brazil." *Hispanic American Historical Review* 72, no. 3 (1992): 375–400.

Graham, Zoe. "Three Decades of Amazonian Filmmaking." *Anthropology Now* 6, no. 1 (April 2014): 86–91. https://doi.org/10.5816/anthropologynow.6.1.0086.

Haag, Carlos. "Science to Create a Nation." *Pesquisa FAPESP*, Special International Edition (October 2012): 70–77.

Hecht, Susanna. "Factories, Forests, Fields and Family: Gender and Neoliberalism in Extractive Reserves." *Journal of Agrarian Change* 7, no. 3 (July 2007): 316–47.

Hecht, Susanna. *The Scramble for the Amazon and the "Lost Paradise" of Euclides da Cunha*. Chicago: University of Chicago Press, 2013.

Hecht, Susanna, and Alexander Cockburn. *The Fate of the Forest: Developers, Destroyers, and Defenders of the Amazon*. Chicago: University of Chicago Press, 2010.

Hecht, Susanna, and Raoni Rajão. "From 'Green Hell' to 'Amazonia Legal': Land Use Models and the Re-imagination of the Rainforest—a New Development Frontier." *Land Use Policy*, no. 96 (2020).

Hempel, Paul. "Theodor Koch-Grünberg and Visual Anthropology in Early Twentieth Century German Anthropology." In *Photography, Anthropology and History: Expanding the Frame*, edited by Christopher Morton and Elizabeth Edwards, 193–219. Farnham, UK: Ashgate, 2009.

Hettler, Brian, Mark Plotkin, and the Amazon Conservation Team. "Amazonian Travels of Richard Evans Schultes." Banrepcultural, April 8, 2019. https://www.banrepcultural.org/schultes.

Herzog, Werner, dir. *Fitzcarraldo*. Werner Herzog Filmproduktion, 1982.

Hochstetler, Kathryn, and Margaret E. Keck. *Greening Brazil: Environmental Activism in State and Society*. Durham, NC: Duke University Press, 2007.

hooks, bell. "The Oppositional Gaze: Black Female Spectators." In *Black Looks: Race and Representation*. Boston: South End Press, 1992.

Johnson, Adriana M. C. "Subalternizing Canudos." *MLN* 120, no. 2 (March 2005): 335–82.

Jorgensen, Danny L. *Principles, Approaches and Issues in Participant Observation*. Oxfordshire: Routledge, 2020.

Kandell, Jonathan. "Richard E. Schultes, 86, Dies; Trailblazing Authority on Hallucinogenic Plants." *New York Times*, April 13, 2001. https://www.nytimes.com/2001/04/13/us/richard-e-schultes-86-dies-trailblazing-authority-on-hallucinogenic-plants.html.

Kaplan, E. Ann. *Looking for the Other: Feminism, Film and the Imperial Gaze*. Oxfordshire: Routledge, 1997.

Kearney, Ryan. "Is This the Greatest Film Ever Made about the Amazon?" *New Republic*, February 15, 2016. https://newrepublic.com/article/129673/greatest-film-ever-made-amazon.

Kearns, Gerry. "The Imperial Subject: Geography and Travel in the Work of Mary Kingsley and Halford Mackinder." *Royal Geographical Society with the Institute of British Geographers* 22, no. 4 (1997): 450–72.

Kimbrough, Liz. "Mongabay's Top Amazon Stories from 2021." Mongabay, Dec. 29, 2021. https://news.mongabay.com/2021/12/mongabays-top-amazon-stories-from-2021.

Kirshenblatt-Gimblett, Barbara. "Theorizing Heritage." *Ethnomusicology* 39, no. 3 (Autumn 1995): 367–80. https://doi.org/10.2307/924627.

Klein, Naomi. *Beyond Extractivism*. New York: Simon and Schuster, 2014.

Koch-Grünberg, Theodor. *Do Roraima ao Orinoco*. São Paulo: Fundação Editora da UNESP, 2005.

Kopenawa, Davi, and Bruce Albert. *The Falling Sky: Words of a Yanoami Shaman*. Cambridge: Harvard University Press, 2013.

Krenak, Ailton. *Ideas to Postpone the End of the World*. Toronto: Groundwood Books, 2020.

Leeds, Roger, and Nadiya Satyamurthy. "Brazil: The Country of the Future." In *Private Equity Investing in Emerging Markets*, edited by Roger Leeds and Nadiya Satyamurthy, 189–219. New York: Palgrave MacMillan, 2015.

Leroy, Michel. "Sur les traces d'Henri Coudreau . . . deux siècles d'exploration de la Guyane." Muséum d'Histoire Naturelle, October 2011. https://www.henricoudreau.fr.

Lesser, Jeff. *Immigration, Ethnicity, and National Identity in Brazil, 1808 to the Present.* Cambridge: Cambridge University Press, 2013.

Leu, Lorraine. *Defiant Geographies: Race, Space, and Modernity in 1920s Rio de Janeiro.* Pittsburg, PA: University of Pittsburg Press, 2020.

Levine, Robert M. *Vale of Tears: Revisting the Canudos Massacre in Northeastern Brazil, 1893–1897.* Berkeley: University of California Press, 1992.

Lima, Nísia Trinidade, and Gilberto Hochman. "Pouca saúde, muita saúva, os males do Brasil são: Discurso medico-sanitário e interpretação do país." *Ciência Saúde Coletiva* 5, no. 2 (2000). https://doi.org/10.1590/S1413-81232000000200007.

Llano, Sara Magalón. "El espacio audiovisual iberoamericano." Programa Ibermedia, Jan. 25, 2016. https://www.programaibermedia.com/nuestras-cronicas/el-abrazo-de-la-serpiente-el-corazon-del-amazonas.

López, Kimberle S. "Modernismo and the Ambivalence of the Postcolonial Experience: Cannibalism, Primitivism, and Exoticism in Mário de Andrade's 'Macunaíma.'" *Luso-Brazilian Review* 35, no. 1 (Summer 1998): 25–38.

Lopez, Telê Ancona. "*O turista aprendiz* na Amazônia: A invenção no texto e na imagem." *Anais do Museu Paulista: História e Cultura Material* 13, no. 2 (2005).

Machado Domingues, Cesar. "A commissão de linhas telegráficas do Mato Grosso ao Amazonas e a integração do Noroeste." *Associação Nacional de Historia* 14 (2010): 1–24.

Madan, Aarti S. "Provincializing World Geography: Land and Letters in Euclides da Cunha's *Os Sertões*." *Romance Notes* 52, no. 2 (2012): 113–21.

Maddrell, Avrill. *Complex Locations: Women's Geographical Work in the UK, 1850–1970.* Hoboken, NJ: Wiley-Blackwell, 2009.

Maligo, Pedro. *Land of Metaphorical Desires: The Representation of Amazonia in Brazilian Literature.* Bristol: Peter Lang Publications, 1998.

Marcone, Jorge. "De retorno a lo natural: La serpiente de oro, la 'novela de la selva' y la crítica ecológica." *Hispania* 81, no. 2 (1998): 299–308.

Martinez-Pinzón, Felipe, and Javier Uriarte. *Intimate Frontiers: A Literary Geography of the Amazon.* Liverpool: Liverpool University Press, 2019.

Martins, Luciana. "Illusions of Power: Vision, Technology and the Geographical Exploration of the Amazon, 1924–1925." *Journal of Latin American Cultural Studies* 16, no. 3 (2007): 285–307.

Massey, Doreen B. *For Space.* Thousand Oaks: Sage Publications, 2005.

Mathiesen, Karl. "Embrace of the Serpent Star: 'My Tribe Is Nearly Extinct,'" *Guardian*, June 8, 2016. https://www.theguardian.com/film/2016/jun/08/embrace-of-the-serpent-star-my-tribe-is-nearly-extinct.

Mbembe, Achille. "Necropolitics." *Public Culture* 15, no. 1 (2003): 11–40.

McClintock, Anne. *Imperial Leather: Race, Gender, and Sexuality in the Colonial Contest.* Oxfordshire: Routledge, 1995.

McCoy, Terrence. "Smoke Plunges São Paulo into Sudden Darkness, Baffling the Western Hemisphere's Largest City." *Washington Post*, August 20, 2019. https://www.washingtonpost.com/world/2019/08/20/sudden-darkness-befalls-sao-paulo-western-hemispheres-largest-city-baffling-thousands.

McEwan, Cheryl. "Cutting Power Lines within the Palace?: Countering Paternity and Eurocentrism in the 'Geographical Tradition.'" *Transactions of the Institute of British Geographers* 23, no. 3 (Sept. 1998): 371–84.

Medina, Laurie. *Negotiating Economic Development: Identity Formation and Collection Action in Belize*. Tucson: University of Arizon Press, 2004.

Metcalf, Peter. *They Life, We Life: Getting on with Anthropology*. New York: Routledge, 2002.

Mies, Maria, and Vandana Shiva. *Ecofeminism*. Nova Scotia: Fernwood Publications, 1993.

Mignolo, Walter. "Colonial Situations, Geographical Discourses and Territorial Representations: Toward a Diatopical Understanding of Colonial Semiosis." *Dispositio* 14, no. 36/38 (1989): 93–104.

Mignolo, Walter. *The Darker Side of the Renaissance: Literacy, Territoriality, and Colonization*, 2nd ed. Ann Arbor: University of Michigan Press, 2003.

Millard, Candice. *River of Doubt: Theodore Roosevelt's Darkest Journey*. New York: Doubleday, 2005.

Mirzoeff, Nicholas. *The Right to Look: A Counterhistory of Visuality*. Durham, NC: Duke University Press, 2011.

Moreira, Luiza Franco. "Songs and Intellectuals: The Musical Projects of Alain Locke, Alejo Carpentier and Mário de Andrade. "Comparative Perspectives on the Black Atlantic," special issue of *Comparative Literature Studies* 49, no. 2 (2012): 210–26.

Morgan, Susan. *Place Matters: Gendered Geography in Victorian Women's Travel Books about Southeast Asia*. Rutgers, NJ: Rutgers University Press, 1996.

Musgrave, Toby. *An Empire of Plants: People and Plants that Changed the World*. London: Cassell, 2007.

Mutis, Ana María. "*El abrazo de la serpiente* o la re-escritura del Amazonas dentro de una ética ecológica y poscolonial." *Hispanic Research Journal* 19, no. 1 (2018): 29–40.

Muredda, A. "Embrace of the Serpent." *Cinema Scope*, no. 66 (2016): 74–75.

Nielson, Rex P. "Amazonian El Dorados and the Nation: Euclides da Cunha's *A margem da historia* and José Eustasio Rivera's *La vorágine*." *Ometeca*, no. 16 (2011): 16–31.

Nixon, Rob. *Slow Violence and the Environmentalism of the Poor*. Cambridge: Harvard University Press, 2011.

Nugent, Stephen. *Scoping the Amazon*. New York: Taylor and Francis, 2016.

Oakdale, Suzanne. "Brazil's 'March to the West': Memories of an Indigenous Shaman and Other 'Moderns.'" *Journal of Anthropological Research* 74, no. 1 (Spring 2018): 54–73.

Osorio, Camila. "The Death of Antonio Bolívar, an Indigenous Elder in the Amazon Rainforest." *New Yorker*, May 27, 2020. https://www.newyorker.com/news/daily-comment/the-death-of-antonio-bolivar-an-indigenous-elder-in-the-amazon-rainforest.

Pace, Richard. "The Amazon Caboclo: What's in a Name?" *Luso-Brazilian Review* 34, no. 2 (1997): 81–89.

Páramo, Carlos. "Un débil abrazo." *El malpensante*, no. 163 (May 2015). https://elmalpensante.com/articulo/3563/un-debil-abrazo.

Petschelies, Erik. "From Berlin to Belém: Theodor Koch-Grünberg's Rio Negro Collections." *Museum History Journal* 12, no. 1 (2019): 29–51.

Petschelies, Erik. "Theodor Koch-Grünberg (1872–1924): A 'Field Ethnologist' and his Contacts with Brazilian Intellectuals." *Revista Atropológica* 62, no. 1 (2019): 196–216.

Phillips, Dom. "Their Forefathers Were Enslaved. Now, 400 Years Later, Their Children Will Be Landowners." *Guardian*, March 5, 2018. https://www.theguardian.com/world/2018/mar/05/descendants-of-slaves-celebrate-brazil-land-rights-victory.

Poole, Deborah. "An Excess of Description: Ethnography, Race and Visual Technologies." *Annual Review of Anthropology*, no. 34 (2005): 159–79. https://doi.org/10.1146/annurev.anthro.33.070203.144034.

Poole, Deborah. *Vision, Race, and Modernity: A Visual Economy of the Andean Image World*. Princeton, NJ: Princeton University Press, 1997.

Pratt, Mary Louise. *Imperial Eyes: Travel Writing and Transculturation*. Oxfordshire: Routledge, 1992.

Pugley, Deborah Delgado and Dámaris Herrera Salazar. "Were Indigenous Peoples Vulnerable or Resilient?: Strategies to Cope with COVID-19 in the Peruvian Amazon Basin." Items: Insights from the Social Sciences, August 2021. https://items.ssrc.org/covid-19-and-the-social-sciences/covid-19-fieldnotes/were-indigenous-peoples-vulnerable-or-resilient-strategies-to-cope-with-covid-19-in-the-peruvian-amazon-basin.

Quijano, Aníbal. "Coloniality and Modernity/Rationality." *Cultural Studies* 21, no. 2 (2007): 168–78.

Rappaport, Joanne. *Intercultural Utopias: Public Intellectuals, Cultural Experimentation, and Ethnic Pluralism in Colombia*. Durham, NC: Duke University Press, 2005.

Resende, Beatriz. "Brazilian Modernism: The Canonised Revolution." In *Through the Kaleidoscope: The Experience of Modernity in Latin America*, edited by Vivian Schelling, 199–216. New York: Verso, 2000.

Rivera Andía, Juan Javier, and Cecilie Vindal Odegaard. "Introduction: Indigenous Peoples, Extractivism and Turbulence in South America." In *Indigenous Life Projects and Extractivism: Approaches to Social Inequality and Difference*, edited by Juan Javier Rivera Andía and Cecilie Vindal Odegaard, 1–50. Cham: Palgrave Macmillan, 2019.

"Theodore Roosevelt – *The River of Doubt*, Part 1." Presented by the Roosevelt Film Library. 1928[?]. YouTube, uploaded by the Library of Congress, Theodore Roosevelt Association Collection, January 4, 2010. https://youtu.be/fKXOtJeaTEQ?si=GP23pp2rxAs84PdF.

"Theodore Roosevelt - *The River of Doubt*, Part 2." Presented by the Roosevelt Film Library. 1928[?]. YouTube, uploaded by the Library of Congress, Theodore Roosevelt Association Collection, January 4, 2010. https://youtu.be/ToqblXco5us.

Rogers, Charlotte. *Mourning El Dorado: Literature and Extractivism in the Contemporary American Tropics*. Charlottesville: University of Virginia Press, 2019.

Rondon, Cândido Mariano a Silva, and Esther de Viveiros. *Rondon conta sua vida*. São Paulo: Livraria São José, 1958.

Roosevelt, Theodore. "Brazil and the Negro." Sagamore Hill National Historic Site. Theodore Roosevelt Digital Library, Dickinson State University. https://www.theodorerooseveltcenter.org/Research/Digital-Library/Record?libID=o279297.

Roosevelt, Theodore. *Through the Brazilian Wilderness*. New York: C. Scribner's, 1914.

Rosaldo, Renato. *Culture and Truth: Renewing the Anthropologist's Search for Meaning*. Boston, MA: Beacon Press, 1993.

Rose, Gillian. *Feminism and Geography: The Limits of Geographical Knowledge.* Cambridge: Cambridge University Press, 1993.

Rose, Gillian. *Visual Methodologies: An Introduction to Researching with Visual Materials.* New York: Sage Publications, 2012.

Rueda, Mario. "El abrazo de la serpiente." *LaFuga,* no. 19 (2017). https://web.archive.org/web/20200925192953/http://2016.lafuga.cl/el-abrazo-de-la-serpiente/820.

Sá, Lúcia. *Rainforest Literatures.* Minneapolis: University of Minnesota Press, 2004.

Sá, Lúcia. Introduction to *The Amazon: Land without History,* by Euclides da Cunha. Translated by Ronald W. Sousa, edited by Lúcia Sá. Oxford: Oxford University Press, 2006.

Sá Carvalho, Carolina, and Mauricio Lissovsky. "Fotografia e representação do sofrimento." *Revista Galáxia,* no. 15 (June 2008): 77–90.

Sá Carvalho, Carolina. "How to See a Scar: Humanitarian and Colonial Iconography in the Putumayo Rubber Boom." *Journal of Latin American Cultural Studies* 27, no. 3 (2018): 371–97.

Said, Edward W. *Culture and Imperialism.* New York: Knopf, 1993.

Said, Edward W. *Orientalism.* New York: Vintage, 1979.

Schelling, Vivian. "Mário de Andrade and Paulo Freire: Two Primitive Intellectuals." *Portuguese Studies* 3 (1987): 106–25.

Schelling, Vivian. *Mário de Andrade: A Primitive Intellectual.* Liverpool: Bulletin of Hispanic Studies, 1988.

Schiebinger, Londa L. *Plants and Empire: Colonial Bioprospecting in the Atlantic World.* Cambridge, MA: Harvard University Press, 2004.

Schultes, Richard Evans, and Von Reis. "Burning the Library of Amazonia." *Sciences* 34, no. 2 (March 1994): 24–33.

Schultes, Richard Evans, Albert Hofmann, and Christian Rätsch. *Plants of the Gods: Their Sacred, Healing and Hallucinogenic Powers.* New York: Healing Arts Press, 1992.

Schultes, Richard Evans. "The Domestication of the Rubber Tree: Economic and Sociological Implications." *American Journal of Economics and Sociology,* 52, no. 4 (Oct. 1993): 479–85.

Sheldrake, Merlin. "The 'Enigma' of Richard Schultes, Amazonian Hallucingenic Plants, and the Limits of Ethnobotany." *Social Studies of Science* 50, no. 3 (2020): 345–76. https://doi.org/10.1177/0306312720920362.

Shepard, Glenn H., Jr. "Fifty Shades of Green." Chacruna.net, May 2020. https://chacruna.net/fifty-shades-of-green.

Shepard, Glenn H., Jr., Claudia Leonor López Garcés, Pascale de Robert, and Carlos Eduardo Chaves. "Objeto, sujeito, inimigo, vovô: Um estudo em etnomuseologia comparada entre os Mebêngôkre-Kayapó e Baniwa do Brasil." *Boletim do Museu Paraense Emílio Goeldi: Ciências Humanas* 12, no. 3 (2017): 765–87.

Shepard, Glenn H., Jr., Klaus Rummenhoeller, Julia Ohl-Schacherer, and Douglas W. Yu. "Trouble in Paradise: Indigenous Populations, Anthropological Policies, and Biodiversity Conservation in Manu National Park, Peru." *Journal of Sustainable Forestry,* no. 29 (2010): 252–301.

Sinha, Madhudaya. "Triangular Erotics: The Politics of Masculinity, Imperialism and Big-Game Hunting in Rider Haggard's *She*." *Critical Survey* 20, no. 3 (2008): 29–43.

Skidmore, Thomas E. *Black into White: Race and Nationality in Brazilian Thought*. Durham, NC: Duke University Press, 2005.

Skidmore, Thomas E. *Brazil: Five Centuries of Change*. Oxford: Oxford University Press, 2021.

Slater, Candace. "Visions of the Amazon: What Has Shifted, What Persists, and Why This Matters." *Latin American Research Review* 50, no. 3 (2015): 3–23.

Slater, Candace. *Entangled Edens: Visions of the Amazon*. Berkeley: University of California Press, 2002.

Smith, Amanda M. *Mapping the Amazon: Literary Geography after the Rubber Boom*. Oxford: Oxford University Press, 2021.

Souza, Márcio. *Amazônia indígena*. Rio de Janeiro: Editora Record, 2015.

Souza Filho, Durval. "Os retratos dos Coudreau: Índios, civilização e miscigenação através das lentes dum casal de visionários que percorreu a Amazonia em busca do 'bom selvagem.'" PhD diss., Universidade Federal Do Pará, 2008.

Sommer, Doris. *Foundational Fictions: The National Romances of Latin America*. Berkeley: University of California Press, 1991.

Spruce, Richard. *Notes of a Botanist on the Amazon and Andes*. London: Macmillan, 1908.

Stam, Robert, and Ella Shohat. *Race in Translation: Culture Wars around the Postcolonial Atlantic*. New York: New York University Press, 2012.

Stepan, Nancy. *Picturing Tropical Nature*. Ithaca, NY: Cornell University Press, 2001.

Stoler, Ann Laura. *Along the Archival Grain: Epistemic Anxieties and Colonial Common*. Princeton, NJ: Princeton University Press, 2009.

Sutthiphisal, Dhanoos. "Learning by Producing and the Geographic Links between Invention and Production: Experience from the Second Industrial Revolution." *Journal of Economic History* 66, no. 4 (December 2006).

Taussig, Michael. "Culture of Terror—Space of Death. Roger Casement's Putumayo Report and the Explanation of Torture." *Comparative Studies in Society and History* 26, no. 3 (1984).

"Sonia Guajajara: 'Não dá para falar de direitos indígenas sem falar de direitos ambientais.'" Terras Indígenas no Brasil, May 5, 2020. https://terrasindigenas.org.br/es/noticia/208213.

"Theodore Roosevelt's Annual Message to Congress for 1904." House Records HR 58A-K2, Records of the US House of Representatives. Record Group 233. Center for Legislative Archives, National Archives.

Tuhiwai Smith, Linda. *Decolonizing Methodologies: Research and Indigenous Peoples*. London: Bloomsbury Publishing, 1999.

Tutino, John. *New Countries: Capitalism, Revolutions, and Nations in the Americas, 1750–1870*. Durham, NC: Duke University Press, 2016.

"Reserva Extractivista Guariba-Roosevelt." Unidades de Conservação no Brasil, accessed November 14, 2023. https://uc.socioambiental.org/en/arp/1141.

Urry, John. *The Tourist Gaze: Leisure and Travel in Contemporary Societies*. London: Sage Publications, 1990.

Valente, Luiz Ismaelino, ed. "Madame Coudreau—a francesa que desvendou o Curuá." *Boletim cultural digital: O Marimbiré* 1, no. 11 (Nov. 10, 2011): 1–2. http://sites.siteturbo.com.br/_gerador/upload/1287/Boletim_Cultural_Digital_-_O_MARAMBIRE_-_Ano_I_-_Numero_11.pdf.

Vieira, Patrícia. "Phytofables: Tales of the Amazon." *Journal of Lusophone Studies* 1, no. 2 (2016): 116–34.

Vieira, Patricia. "Phytographia: Literature as Plant Writing." In *The Language of Plants*, edited by Monica Gagliano, John C. Ryan, and Patrícia Vieira, 215–33. Minneapolis: University of Minnesota Press, 2017.

Viscidi, Lisa, and Enrique Ortiz. "How to Save the Amazon Rainforest." *New York Times*, July 19, 2019. https://www.nytimes.com/2019/07/19/opinion/amazon-rainforest-deforestation.html.

Viveiros de Castro, Eduardo. *The Relative Native: Essays on Indigenous Conceptual Worlds*. Chicago: University of Chicago Press, 2016.

Walker, Wayne S., et al. "The Role of Forest Conversion, Degradation, and Disturbance in the Carbon Dynamics of Amazon Indigenous Territories and Protected Areas," *PNAS* 117, no. 6 (Jan. 2020): 3015–25. https://doi.org/10.1073/pnas.1913321117.

Watts, Jonathan, and Jan Rocha. "Brazil's 'Lost Report' into Genocide Surfaces after 40 Years." *Guardian*, May 29, 2013. https://www.theguardian.com/world/2013/may/29/brazil-figueiredo-genocide-report.

Watts, Sarah. *Rough Rider in the White House*. Chicago: University of Chicago Press, 2003.

Weinstein, Barbara. *The Amazon Rubber Boom: 1850–1920*. Redwood City, CA: Stanford University Press, 1983.

Weinstein, Barbara. "Filming Modernity in the Tropics: The Amazon, Walt Disney, and the Antecedents of Modernization Theory." In *Intimate Frontiers: A Literary Geography of the Amazon*, edited by Felipe Martínez-Pinzón and Javier Uriarte, 193–207. Liverpool: Liverpool University Press, 2019.

Whitfield, Joey. "Communicating beyond the Human: Posthumanism, Neo-Shamanism, and Ciro Guerra's *El abrazo de la serpiente*." In *Latin American Culture and the Limits of the Human*, edited by Lucy Bollington and Paul Merchant. Online edition. Gainesville, FL: Florida Scholarship Online, 2020. https://doi.org/10.5744/florida/9781683401490.003.0008.

Wylie, Lesley. "Colonial Tropes and Postcolonial Tricks: Rewriting the Tropics in the 'Novela de la selva.'" *Modern Language Review* 103, no. 3 (2006): 728–42.

Zilly, Berthold. "Sertão e nacionalidade: Formação étnica e civilizatória do Brasil segundo Euclides da Cunha." *Estudos sociedade e agricultura* 7, no. 1 (April 1999): 5–45.

Index

À margem da história (*The Amazon: Land without History*) (Cunha), 6, 94–95, 96–97, 103–10
abrazo de la serpiente, El (*The Embrace of the Serpent*) (Guerra, 2015)
   chullachaqui (spirit wandering the forest) in, 164–65, 167, 173–74, 175
   Koch-Grünberg and Schultes's works and, 6, 128, 136–37, 161–62, *162*, 166–67, 171–75, 176–85
   nature-culture divide in, 161, 164–65, 168–78
   production and distribution of, 165–66
   rubber industry in, 161–62, 175–78
   yakruna (fictional plant) in, 161–65, 172–75, 180–83, *182–83*
African people, 22–23, 77. *See also* Black women; *mocambos* (escaped-slave communities); race and racial order
Agassiz, Elizabeth and Louis, 202n9
Aguirre, the Wrath of God (Herzog, 1972), 166
Alencar, José de, 203n33
Amazon, cultural representations of
   as Eden, 13–14, 61, 101
   as El Dorado, 9–10, 16, 130
   feminization of land and, 15, 59–60, 78, 118–20
   grandeza (greatness) and, 4, 101–2, 106–7, 110
   photography and, 18–21
   travel narratives and, 4–18, 190–95

See also imperialism and imperial gaze; wilderness; *specific authors and narratives*
Amazon Rainforest wildfires (2019), 1–2, *2*, 8, 28, 127, 194–95
Amazonian perspectivism, 164–65, 169, 172, 175
Amory, Frederic, 97, 106, 208n13
anarchism, 31, 42, 51–52
Anderson, Mark D., 107
Andrade, Mário de
   Brazilian nation building and, 6, 12, 94–96, 99–100, 110–18, 123–24, 191–93
   Cunha and, 117–18, 123–24
   Indigenous peoples and, 110–11, 112–13, 118–23, *120–21*
   Koch-Grünberg and, 128
   life and career of, 95–96, 98–100
   photographs of, 113–15, *114*
   photography and, 98, 99–100, 110–11, 112–21, *117*
   racial identity of, 98–99
   Schultes and, 128
   women and, 118–20, 122–23
   See also O turista aprendiz (*The Apprentice Tourist*) (Andrade)
anti-historicism, 41
Arara Indians, 43
Ashininka people, 188–89
Awotsi Yorenkatsi Tasori (2016 short film), 188–89
ayahuasca (*yagé*), 152, 164, 217n64

235

Baniwa people, 159
Bates, Henry Walter, 23
Beebee, Thomas, 132, 138
Berlin Conference (1884–1885), 24
bicycle, 62
biocontact zones
   concept of, 8–9, 15
   in *El abrazo de la serpiente*, 168, 171–72, 175–78
   plant-based knowledge and, 146, 151–52, 156
Black women
   Andrade and, 122–23
   O. Coudreau and, 47–50, *48*, 55–56
Blunt, Alison, 33
Bolívar, Antonio, 165, 186–87
Bolsonaro, Jair, 1–2, 3, 28, 126–27, 194–95
Borges, Dain, 112
Bororo people, 62
borrachero, 217n64
Botelho, André, 117
Brazil and Brazilian nation building
   Andrade and, 6, 12, 94–96, 99–100, 110–18, 123–24, 191–93
   H. Coudreau and, 51–52
   Cunha and, 6, 28, 94–97, 100–110, 123–24, 132, 191–93
   migration and, 105–10
   photography and, 19–20, *20*
   racial order and, 62–64, 68–73, 75, 80–82
   settlement in Amazon and, 124–27
   See also Expedição Scientífica Roosevelt-Rondon
Brazilian Institute of Environment and Renewable Natural Resources (IBAMA), 126
Brazilian Satellite Forest Monitoring Service (PRODES), 91
brazilwood (pau-brasil), 22
Burroughs, William, 129

Cabanagem revolt (1835–1840), 201n80
caboclos, 62–64, 74–76
Cachoeira Porteira, 55–58
camaradas, 74–76
Carpentier, Alejo, 129
cartography and map-making
   Brazil–Peru border and, 97, 100–101
   H. Coudreau and, 6, 30–31, 35–36, 51–52
   O. Coudreau and, 30–31, 35–36, 50–51, 52–54, *53*
   coloniality of power and, 16
   Cunha and, 100–101
   Expedição Scientífica Roosevelt-Rondon and, 60, 61, 65, 73–74, 84–87, *85–86*, 88–89
   first rubber boom and, 23
   nation building and, 101
   politics of naming and, 84–87
   Projeto Nova Cartografia Social da Amazônia (PNCSA) and, 55–58, 187
   Rondon Commission and, 62, 88
   travel narratives and, 7–8
   women and, 31, 33 (*see also* Coudreau, Octavie)
Carvajal, Gaspar de, 9–10
Carvalho, José Murilo de, 4, 13, 101
Casement, Roger, 21, 119, 200n75, 215n47
Castrillón, Camilo Jaramillo, 163
caucheros, 97–98, 108–10
Certeau, Michel de, 204n50
Cheng, Anne, 137–38, 142
Cherrie, George Kruck, 68, 74, 84
Chindoy, Salvador, 152–53
Christian Science Monitor (newspaper), 154
chullachaqui (spirit wandering the forest), 164–65, 167, 173–74, 175
Cinta Larga people, 93
Clifford, James, 138
climate change, 1, 8, 28–29, 194–95. *See also* Amazon Rainforest wildfires (2019)
Cofán people, 216n51
Colombia, 29, 129, 149, 154–55
colonial productivity, 15

colonialism. *See* imperialism and imperial gaze
coloniality of power
   concept of, 12–17, 192, 194
   O. Coudreau and, 31–34
   Koch-Grünberg and, 148
   Rondon and, 60, 74
Comte, Auguste, 64
Conrad, Joseph, 200n75
contact zones, 8–9, 146. *See also* biocontact zones
Coudreau, Henri
   anarchist colony of Counani and, 31, 42, 52
   on O. Coudreau, 32
   life and career of, 30–31, 37–38, 41–42
   map-making and, 6, 30–31, 35–36, 51–52
   on *mocambos* (escaped-slave communities), 49
   photographs of, 36, *37*
Coudreau, Octavie
   gender and racial identity of, 30–34, 36–41, *37*, *40*, 55–56, 191–93
   Indigenous peoples and, 30, 31–34, 40, 42–45, *44–45*, 47–50, 132
   Koch-Grünberg and, 147
   map-making and, 6, 30–31, 35–36, 50–51, 52–54, *53*
   photographs of, 36–37, *37*, 39–41, *40*, 134
   photography as tool of imperial gaze and, 6, 32, 35–36, 43–50, *44–46*, *48*, 54, 79
   racial order and, 31–34, 72
Counani (anarchist colony), 31, 42, 52
COVID-19 pandemic, 186–87, 197n2
Cronon, William, 61, 67
cultural anthropophagy, 115
Cunha, Euclides da
   Andrade and, 117–18, 123–24
   Brazilian nation building and, 6, 28, 94–97, 100–110, 123–24, 132, 191–93
   Brazil–Peru border and, 97, 100–101
   life and career of, 95–98
   nature-culture divide and, 94–95, 108
   wilderness and, 61–62
Cusicanqui, Silvia Rivera, 169, 170

D'Argenio, Maria Chiara, 168, 177
Darwin, Charles, 11, 202n9, 204n11
Darwinism, 97. *See also* social Darwinism
Davis, Wade, 130
de la Cadena, Marisol, 16, 169–70
DeBeers, 93
decoloniality, 17–18, 156–60, 169–70, 193–95
deforestation
   in *El abrazo de la serpiente*, 164
   Amazon Rainforest wildfires (2019) and, 1–2, 127
   Andrade and, 120
   H. Coudreau and, 51
   Guariba-Roosevelt Extractive Reserve and, 91–93
   national policies and, 28–29, 126–27, 194–95
   Rondon Commission and, 79
   Schultes and, 129, 151
degeneration, 106, 112. *See also* race and racial order
Descola, Phillipe, 168–69
Diacon, Todd, 62, 70, 205n20, 205n30
diamonds, 93
diário nacional, O (newspaper), 98
DiNovelli-Lang, Danielle, 221n50
Dixie, Florence, 202n9
dominio coletivo (collective domain), 57
Domosh, Mona, 33, 47
Driver, Felix, 20, 54
drogas do sertão (backcountry/wilderness drugs), 22

El Dorado, 9–10, 16, 130
Enright, Kelly, 151
environmental determinism, 98
environmental humanities, 3
environmental possibilism, 98, 106–10

Escobar, Arturo, 199n50
Espelt-Bombin, Silvia, 12
ethnobotany, 6, 128, 129–30, 149–53, 166, 191–93
ethnography, 134, 138–40
ethnomuseology, 156–60
evolutionary positivism, 204n11
Expedição Scientífica Roosevelt-Rondon
   coloniality of power and, 60
   documentation of, 6, 60–61, 66, 75
   Indigenous peoples and, 61, 65, 66, 71–73, *71*, 74–82, *79*
   Indigenous people's memories of, 90–91
   Koch-Grünberg and, 213n11
   map-making and, 60, 61, 65, 73–74, 84–87, *85–86*, 88–89
   masculinity and, 59–60, 61, 65, 66–69
   photography and, 59–60, 61, *63*, 68, *71*, 78–80
   racial order and, 59–60, 65, 74–82, *79*
   wilderness and, 59–60, 61–62, 66–69, 73–74, 82–90
extractivism, 4, 21–26, 28, 156, 167–68, 193

first rubber boom (ca. 1879–1912)
   overview of, 3–4, 21–26, 62–64
   in *El abrazo de la serpiente*, 161–62, 175–78
   Koch-Grünberg and, 130, 131, 147–48
Fitzcarraldo (Herzog, 1982), 166, 220n37
Ford Model T, 62
Foucault, Michel, 5
France Équinoxiale, La (H. Coudreau), 52
French, Jennifer, 61, 136
French Geographical Society, 31
Futurism, 99

Gabara, Esther, 99, 111–12, 124
gender. *See* masculinity; women
gift-giving, 71, *71*, 80, 133, 140–41
Gleghorn, Charlotte, 167, 174, 179, 184, 185
global capitalism, 6–7, 28, 34
Global Week for Future protests, 197n2

Goeldi, Emílio, 157
going native, 152
gold, 9, 42
Good Neighbor Policy, 128, 153, 201n85
Goodyear, Charles, 23
Graham, Maria, 202n9
Graham, Zoe, 188
grandeza (greatness), 4, 101–2, 106–7, 110
Great Drought (1877–78), 105
Guaicuruan languages, 131
Guarani, O (Alencar), 203n33
Guariba-Roosevelt Extractive Reserve, 91–94
Guerra, Ciro. See *abrazo de la serpiente, El* (*The Embrace of the Serpent*) (Guerra, 2015)
Guimarães, Leandro, 106–7

Harris, Mark, 12
Heart of Darkness (Conrad), 200n75
Hecht, Susanna, 35, 52, 125, 211n56, 216n58
Hempel, Paul, 134
Hershberger, John William, 212n6
Herzog, Werner, 166, 220n37
hevea trees, 154–55
Humboldt, Alexander von, 10–11
Huxley, Aldous, 129
hygienization, 112

imperialism and imperial gaze
   O. Coudreau and, 6, 32, 35–39, 43–50, *44–46*, *48*, 54, 79
   coloniality of power and, 12–17
   Cunha and, 100–105
   first rubber boom and, 23, 24–25
   Koch-Grünberg and, 141
   photography and, 35–36
   Roosevelt and, 60, 64, 67–68, 191–93
   travel narratives and, 6–8
   women and, 35
"Improviso do mal da América" (Improvisation on America's ills) (Andrade), 98–99
Indigenous children, 132, 139–41, *140*

Indigenous knowledge
  biocontact zones and, 146
  ethnomuseology and, 156–60
  Koch-Grünberg and, 155–56
  Schultes and, 128–31, 149–56
  scientific knowledge and, 150–53
  See also *abrazo de la serpiente, El* (*The Embrace of the Serpent*) (Guerra, 2015)
Indigenous languages
  in *El abrazo de la serpiente*, 165, 167, 170, 172, 176, 177–78, 185–86
  H. Coudreau and, 42
  Koch-Grünberg and, 131, 132–33
Indigenous peoples
  Amazon as carbon sink and, 2
  Andrade and, 110–11, 112–13, 118–23, *120–21*
  Bolsonaro and, 126–27
  Brazilian nation building and, 19–20
  H. Coudreau and, 30, 42–43, 52
  O. Coudreau and, 30, 31–34, 40, 42–45, *44–45*, 47–50, 132
  coloniality of power and, 16
  ethnomuseology and, 156–60
  Expedição Scientífica Roosevelt-Rondon and, 61, 65, 66, 71–73, *71*, 74–82, *79*
  Koch-Grünberg and, 128–29, 130–38, *135*, *137*, 147–48
  as Other, 8, 19
  positivism and, 62
  Rondon Commission and, 69–73, *71*, 76–77, 80, 82
  rubber industry and, 22–23, 25, 146–48
  Schultes and, 149–53
  self-representation and, 186–89
  See also *abrazo de la serpiente, El* (*The Embrace of the Serpent*) (Guerra, 2015)
Indigenous women
  Andrade and, 118–20
  H. Coudreau and, 41, 42–43
  Koch-Grünberg and, 132, 139, 141–45, *142–43*
  Rondon and, 71–73, *71*
  Roosevelt and, 77–78

Interamerican Development Bank (IDB), 91
interculturalidad, 194
Iracema (Alencar), 203n33

João IV, King of Portugal, 198n19
Jorgensen, Danny, 152
Journey in Brazil, A (Agassiz and Agassiz), 202n9

Kaplan, E. Anne, 47
Kearns, Gerry, 41
Kipling, Rudyard, 202n4
Kirshenblatt-Gimblett, Barbara, 113
Klein, Naomi, 4
knowledge
  coloniality of power and, 14–15
  decoloniality and, 17–18
  ethnomuseology and, 156–60
  Koch-Grünberg and, 155–56
  mocambos (escaped-slave communities) and, 37
  Schultes and, 153–56
  scientific colonialism and, 146
  travel narratives and, 7–8
  See also Indigenous knowledge; science and scientific knowledge
Koch-Grünberg, Theodor
  anthropological approach of, 6, 128–29, 130–38, *135*, *137*, 139–40, 157–58, 191–93
  life and career of, 129, 131–32
  photographs of, 134–38, *135*, *137*
  photographs of Indigenous women and children by, 139–45, *140*, *142–43*
  Schultes and, 147–49, 150–51, 153
  Theo in *El abrazo de la serpiente* and, 136–37, 161–62, 166–67, 171–75, 176–85
Kopenawa, Davi, 169
Krenak, Ailton, 168, 193

La Condamine, Charles Marie de, 10
Lesser, Jeffery, 210n42

Lula da Silva, Luiz Inácio, 29, 126, 194–95, 197n3

Macunaíma (Andrade), 12, 95–96, 212n2
Maddrell, Avril, 31, 33
Mahdist War (1881–1899), 47
Makuschí people, 213n18
Maligo, Pedro, 61, 210n51
Manifest Destiny, 64
map-making. *See* cartography and map-making
"March to the West" campaign (1938), 125
Marcone, Jorge, 11, 13
Martínez-Pinzón, Felipe, 9
Martins, Luciana, 20, 205n23
masculinity, 15, 59–60, 61, 64–65, 66–69, 82–84, 89–90
Mbembe, Achille, 17, 138
McClintock, Anne, 35, 46, 71–72, 86, 203n26, 204n51
Mebêngôkre-Kayapó people, 158–59
Medici, Lorenzo de,' 101
"Meditação sobre o Tietê" (Meditation on the Tietê) (Andrade), 98
Mendes, Chico, 91–92, 126
metamorphosis, 183
Mignolo, Walter, 17, 85, 194, 219n16
migration, 25, 105–10, 125, 126, 146–47
Mirzoeff, Nicholas, 36, 72, 215n41
miscegenation, 106. *See also* race and racial order
mocambos (escaped-slave communities)
  Coudreaus and, 30, 32, 45–50, *46*, *48*
  first rubber boom and, 23
  knowledge and, 37
  Projeto Nova Cartografia Social da Amazônia (PNCSA) and, 55–58, 187
modernismo, 12, 98–100, 111–15, 122
modernity and modernization
  O. Coudreau and, 34–35
  coloniality of power and, 12–17
  Good Neighbor Policy and, 153
  photography and, 35–36
  travel narratives and, 7–8
  See also cartography and map-making; Rondon Commission
Monroe Doctrine (1823), 64
More, Thomas, 14
Morgan, Susan, 38
Mundus Novus (Vespucci), 101
Murphy, Marion McMurrough, 202n9
Museu Paraense Emílio Goeldi (Belém), 133, 157, 158–60
Mutis, Ana María, 166–67, 173

National Geographic (magazine), 90
National Museum (Rio de Janeiro), 157
National Research Council, 149
nationalism. *See* Brazil and Brazilian nation building
Nature (journal), 2
nature-culture divide
  in *El abrazo de la serpiente*, 161, 164–65, 168–78
  Andrade and, 94–95, 118–23
  coloniality of power and, 14–15
  Cunha and, 94–95, 108
  decoloniality and, 193–95
  Koch-Grünberg and, 141–42, 155–56
  Schultes and, 155–56
necropolitics, 176
new imperialism, 24–25
New York World (newspaper), 213n11
Nhambiquara people, 77–80, *79*, 93
Nielson, Rex, 103
Nixon, Rob, 8
nomadism, 97–98, 107–10
Notes of a Botanist on the Amazon and the Andes (Spruce), 149
novela de la selva (jungle novel), 11
Nugent, Stephan, 61, 199n44

Oakdale, Susanne, 200n63
objectivity, 41
Ocaina people, 186–87
Odegaard, Cecilie Vindal, 200n70
Orellana, Francisco de, 9–10
Orientalism, 14

ornamentalism, 137–38, 142
Otherness and the Other, 8, 14, 19. See also African people; imperialism and imperial gaze; Indigenous peoples; race and racial order
Outlook, The (magazine), 78

Pace, Richard, 75
palenques, 23. See also *mocambos* (escaped-slave communities)
Paraguayan War (1864–1870), 49
Paresi people, 71–73, *71*, 75, 76–77
participant observation, 129, 136–37, 145
pau-brasil (brazilwood), 22
Pedro I of Brazil, 198n19
Pemon people (Taulipáng people), 129, 144–45, 219n29
Pereira dos Santos, Ailton, 92–93
Peru
  Brazil–Peru border and, 97, 100–101
  caucheros in, 97–98, 108–10
  COVID-19 pandemic in, 187
  genocide of Indigenous peoples in, 139
  rubber industry in, 97–98, 108–10
Peruvian Amazon Company, 139
peyote, 149
photography
  in *El abrazo de la serpiente*, 184–85
  Andrade and, 98, 99–100, 110–11, 112–21, *117*
  Brazilian nation building and, 19–20, *20*
  O. Coudreau's imperial gaze and, 6, 32, 35–39, 43–50, *44–46*, *48*, 54, 79
  O. Coudreau's self-representation and, 36–37, *37*, 39–41, *40*, 134
  cultural representations of Amazon and, 18–21
  ethnography and, 134, 139
  Expedição Scientífica Roosevelt-Rondon and, 59–60, 61, *63*, 68, *71*, 78–80
  Koch-Grünberg's self representation and, 134–38, *135*, *137*
  political change and, 20–21

Schultes and, 166–67, 184–85
  as tool of imperial gaze, 18–21, 35–36, 70–73, 80–81
photography of Indigenous peoples
  Andrade and, 110–11, 112–13, 118–21, *120–21*
  O. Coudreau and, 44–45, *44–45*, 47–50
  cultural representations of Amazon and, 18–21
  Expedição Scientífica Roosevelt-Rondon and, 61, 71–73, *71*, 78–80
  Koch-Grünberg and, 128, 131, 134–45, *135*, *137*, *140*, *142–43*, 166–67, 184–85
  Rondon and, *71*
  Schultes and, 128
Pianocotô people, 44–45, *44–45*
Plants of the Gods (Schultes), 129, 149
Plotkin, Mark, 130
Poole, Deborah, 18, 48, 68–69, 134, 136
positivism, 62–64, 70–73, 80–82, 89, 97–98, 104
Pratt, Mary Louise, 8, 130, 146, 173
primitivism, 115
Projeto Nova Cartografia Social da Amazônia (PNCSA), 55–58, 187
public health, 62

Questão do Amapá (Contesté Franco-Brasilien), 42
Quijano, Aníbal, 12–13, 205n25
quilombos, 23. See also *mocambos* (escaped-slave communities)

race and racial order
  Andrade and, 98–99, 110–13, 122–23
  Brazilian nation building and, 22–23, 62–64, 68–73, 75, 80–82
  coloniality of power and, 15
  O. Coudreau and, 30–34, 72
  Cunha and, 105–10
  ethnography and, 134
  Expedição Scientífica Roosevelt-Rondon and, 59–60, 65, 74–82, *79*

race and racial order (cont'd.)
  extractivism and, 22–23
  Rondon and, 62–64, 68–73
  rubber booms and, 146–48
  scientific racism and, 24, 112
  travel narratives and, 7–8
Rajão, Raoni, 125, 216n58
Rappaport, Joanne, 194
resource, use of term, 193
Rice, Hamilton, 148
River of Doubt: Roosevelt/Rondon Expedition (Roosevelt, 1928?), 66, 75, 86–87, *86*
Rivera, José Eustacio, 11, 13, 166
Rivera Andía, Juan Javier, 200n70
Rodrigues da Silva, Raimunda, 90
Rogers, Charlotte, 9, 130
Roncador-Xingu Expedition, 200n63
Rondon, Cândido
  Cunha and, 97, 104, 109
  Indigenous heritage and ideology of, 62–64, 68–73, 74–75, 78–82, *79*, 89, 191–93
  life and career of, 59, 89
  photographs of, *63*, 68, *69*, 71–73, *71*, 78–80, *79*, 85–86, *85*
  Roosevelt and, 73–74
  See also Expedição Scientífica Roosevelt-Rondon
Rondon Commission
  overview of, 59, 62
  deforestation and, 79
  Indigenous peoples and, 69–73, *71*, 76–77, 80, 82
  map-making and, 62, 88
  photography and, 19–20, *20*
Rondon conta sua vida (Rondon), 60–61
Roosevelt, Franklin D., 154–55
Roosevelt, Kermit, 59, 84
Roosevelt, Theodore
  imperialism and, 60, 64, 67–68, 191–93
  Indigenous peoples and, 74–80
  life and career of, 59, 89
  masculinity and, 59–60, 61, 64–65, 66–69
  photographs of, *63*, 68, *69*, 78–80, *79*, 83–84, *84–85*, 85–86
  Rondon and, 73–74
  See also Expedição Scientífica Roosevelt-Rondon
Roosevelt Corollary (1904), 64
Rosaldo, Renato, 219n34
Rousseff, Dilma, 126
Royal Museum of Ethnology (Berlin), 157
rubber industry
  caucheros and, 97–98, 108–10
  coloniality of power and, 14–15
  first rubber boom and, 3–4, 21–26, 62–64, 130, 131, 147–48, 161–62, 175–78
  synthetic rubber and, 155
  World War II secondary rubber boom and, 125–26, 130, 154–55, 161–62, 175–78
Rubber Reserve Company (RRC), 154–55
ruralistas (ruralists), 126–27

Sá, Lúcia, 100–101, 156, 199n47, 219n29
Sá Carvalho, Carolina, 21, 119, 139
Said, Edward, 14
salvage anthropology, 139–40, 144, 157–58
sanitation, 62
Santos, Silvino, 148
Sarmiento, Domingo Faustino, 61–62
Schelling, Vivian, 96, 99
Schiebinger, Londa, 8–9, 15, 146
Schultes, Richard Evans
  ethnobotany and, 6, 129–30, 149–53, 191–93
  Evan in *El abrazo de la serpiente* and, 162, 166–67, 171–75, 177–85
  Indigenous knowledge and, 128–31, 149–56
  Koch-Grünberg and, 147–49, 150–51, 153
  life and career of, 129, 149, 155
  World War II secondary rubber boom and, 130, 154–55

science and scientific knowledge
   O. Coudreau and, 34–35
   coloniality of power and, 14–15
   Eurocentric approach of, 155–56
   first rubber boom and, 23
   Indigenous knowledge and, 150–53
   photography and, 35–36, 134
   positivism and, 64
   See also cartography and map-making
scientific colonialism, 146
scientific racism, 24, 112. *See also* race and racial order
Scribner's (magazine), 60
Second Industrial Revolution (1870–1914), 23
self-representation
   Andrade and, 113–16, *114*
   O. Coudreau and, 50–51
   O. Coudreau and, 36–41, *37*, *40*, 134
   Indigenous peoples and, 186–89
   Koch-Grünberg and, 134–38, *135*, *137*
   Rondon and, *63*, 68, *69*, 71–73, *71*, 78–80, *79*, 85–86, *85*, 89
   Roosevelt and, *63*, 64–65, 66–69, *69*, 78–80, *79*, 83–84, *84–85*, 85–86, 89, 136–37
sentimentalism, 41
seringueiros, 97–98, 106–10
sertões, Os (Cunha), 95–96, 102, 106–7
Serviço de Proteção ao Índio (SPI, later FUNAI), 62, 127
Serviço do Patrimonio Histórico e Artístico Nacional, 113
sexualization of Indigenous women, 71–73, 77–78, 144–45
shamans, 149–50, 152
Shepard, Glenn, 158–60
Shohat, Ella, 15
Silva, Marina, 126
Sinha, Madhudaya, 207n60
Slater, Candace, 13, 61, 68
slavery, 22–23
Smith, Amanda M., 11
social Darwinism, 97–98, 202n4

social mapping, 56
social positivism, 204n11
Société de Géographie de Paris, 34
Sopemi, 93
Souza, Márcio, 16, 195
Spanish-American War (1898), 24, 64
Spencer, Herbert, 97
Spruce, Richard, 23, 149
Stam, Robert, 15
Stepan, Nancy, 61, 111
Sudan, 47
synthetic rubber, 130, 155

Tacca, Fernando de, 70
Taulipáng people (Pemon people), 129, 144–45, 219n29
Taussig, Michael, 25, 201n83
telegraph. *See* Expedição Scientífica Roosevelt-Rondon
Terne people, 62
Through the Brazilian Wilderness (Roosevelt), 60–61, *63*, 66–69, *69*, 73–74, 87–88, 90, 93
Thunberg, Greta, 197n2
Torres, Nílbio, 165
Trans-Amazonian highway, 125–26
transculturation, 8
transformation, 156
travel literature
   El abrazo de la serpiente and, 162–65
   cultural representations of Amazon and, 4–18, 190–95
   first rubber boom and, 23
   women and, 38–39
   See also specific authors and narratives
Tristan, Flora, 202n9
Tuhiwai Smith, Linda, 17–18, 144, 169, 180
Tukano people, 158
O turista aprendiz (The Apprentice Tourist) (Andrade)
   Brazilian nation building and, 6, 94–96, 110–18
   Indigenous peoples in, 118–23

Uriarte, Javier, 9
Utopia (More), 14

Vargas, Gétulio, 125
Venezuela, 129
Vespucci, Amerigo, 14, 101
Video nas Aldeias (Video in the Villages, VNA), 187–89
Vieira, Patrícia, 61, 220n37
Viveiros, Esther de, 60
Viveiros de Castro, Eduardo, 164–65, 169, 172, 183, 219n24
Vom Roraima zum Orinoco (From Roraima to the Orinoco) (Koch-Grünberg), 129, 132, 141
vorágine, La (*The Vortex*) (Rivera), 11, 13, 166
Voyage au Cuminá (O. Coudreau), 35, 38–39, 44–51, *44–46*, *53*, 54
Voyage au Rio Curuá (O. Coudreau), 55
Voyage au Trombetas (Coudreau and Coudreau), 31, 32, 35–38, 49–50, 54
vulcanization of rubber, 23

Wallace, Alfred Russell, 23
Wapischána people, 129, 133–34

Weinstein, Barbara, 153, 201n84
Whitfield, Joey, 163
Wickham, Henry, 26
wilderness
　Andrade and, 115–18
　Expedição Scientífica Roosevelt-Rondon and, 66–69, 73–74, 82–90
　feminization of, 15, 59–60, 78, 118–20
　United States vs. Latin American perspective on, 61–62, 67, 87–88
Witoto people, 216n51
women
　geography and, 31, 33, 38–39 (*see also* Coudreau, Octavie)
　imperialism and, 35
　See also Black women; Indigenous women
World War II secondary rubber boom
　in *El abrazo de la serpiente*, 161–62, 175–78
　migration and, 125–26
　Schultes and, 130, 154–55

yagé (ayahuasca), 152, 164, 217n64
Yekuná people, 129

www.ingramcontent.com/pod-product-compliance
Lightning Source LLC
Chambersburg PA
CBHW030538230426
43665CB00010B/936